TRIALS OF THE CENTURY

TRIALS OF THE CENTURY

*A Decade-by-Decade Look at
Ten of America's Most Sensational Crimes*

Mark J. Phillips and Aryn Z. Phillips

Prometheus Books

59 John Glenn Drive
Amherst, New York 14228

Published 2016 by Prometheus Books

Cover design by Jacqueline Nasso Cooke
Cover design © Prometheus Books
Cover image (Leo Frank) from the Library of Congress
Cover image (Bruno Hauptmann) from the Library of Congress
Cover image (Roscoe "Fatty" Arbuckle) from the Library of Congress
Cover image (O. J. Simpson) from Los Angeles Police Department
Cover image (Charles Manson) © Everett Collection Inc./Alamy
Cover image (Jean Harris)© ZUMA Press, Inc./Alamy
Cover image (Harry Thaw) from the Library of Congress
Cover image (Wayne Lonergan) © Bettmann /Getty Images

Inquiries should be addressed to
Prometheus Books
59 John Glenn Drive
Amherst, New York 14228
VOICE: 716–691–0133 • FAX: 716–691–0137
WWW.PROMETHEUSBOOKS.COM

20 19 18 17 16   5 4 3 2 1

Library of Congress Cataloging-in-Publication Data

Names: Phillips, Mark J., 1954- author. | Phillips, Aryn Z., 1990- author.
Title: Trials of the century : a decade-by-decade look at ten of America's most
    sensational crimes / by Mark J. Phillips and Aryn Z. Phillips.
Description: Amherst, New York : Prometheus Books, 2016. | Includes index.
Identifiers: LCCN 2016008067 (print) | LCCN 2016008477 (ebook) |
    ISBN 9781633881952 (paperback) | ISBN 9781633881969 (ebook)
Subjects: LCSH: Trials (Murder)–United States. | BISAC: TRUE CRIME / Murder
    / General. | SOCIAL SCIENCE / Criminology. | SOCIAL SCIENCE / Media
    Studies.
Classification: LCC KF221.M8 .P48 2016 (print) | LCC KF221.M8 (ebook) |
    DDC 345.73/070904–dc23
LC record available at http://lccn.loc.gov/2016008067

Printed in the United States of America

For Sandy, Michael, and Jake

CONTENTS

INTRODUCTION

Americans are addicted to violent crime. Not to committing it, particularly, notwithstanding a history of nineteenth-century gunslingers, twentieth-century gangsters, and the wide prevalence of handguns, which outnumber citizens. Rather, Americans love to talk about crime, to read about it, relive it, and revel in it.

In some respects, Americans, like citizens of all ages and nations, are simply drawn to bloodshed by their nature. It is in the human DNA. When Vespasian constructed the Coliseum in Imperial Rome nearly two thousand years ago, an arena intended purposely for the staging of blood sports, he built a structure designed for as many as 50,000 spectators. The Coliseum hosted gladiatorial contests of warrior pairs, even entire groups of warriors. Residents of Rome came to witness the slaughter of armed combatants, unarmed prisoners, wild animals of every stripe and feature, even elaborately staged executions of prisoners killed in various gruesome but mythologically authentic ways, such as being mauled by beasts or burned to death. On occasion, the exits were stopped up and the Coliseum flooded for naval battles.[1]

Over time, gladiatorial exhibitions have given way to medieval jousts, to public burnings at the stake, to stocks and pillories, and to the guillotine. Between 1792 and 1794, thousands of Frenchmen went to their public deaths at the Place de la Revolution in Paris, now the Place de la Concorde, victims of a revolution gone mad. Dangerous as Paris was in those years, the Place overflowed with spectators. Vendors sold programs listing the daily victims, women sat knitting, and children variously cried and cheered.[2]

While it is increasingly evident that the modern fascination for violent crime in American culture is slaked by the media, that influence itself is not modern. Sensationalized stories of crime in print date back at least to the eighteenth century with England's *Newgate Calendar*. Subtitled the *Malefactors' Bloody Register*, it was a monthly collection of executions at London's Newgate Prison, complete with lurid and highly inaccurate descriptions of the criminals and their murderous acts, illustrated with pen-and-ink drawings of stabbings, shootings, and poisonings. By 1774, the *Calendar* was published in bound volumes and commonly found in English homes for at least the next century.[3]

The *Calendar* crossed the Atlantic as the *American Bloody Register*, which collected and published accounts of America's misdeeds until the 1860s, when such tales were picked up and published in novel form by brothers Erastus and Erwin Beadle. These were sold for ten cents and became known, of course, as "dime novels," instantly popular and avidly consumed by young, working-class readers, reflecting a boom in literacy following the Civil War. Scandalous and excessive, the Beadles' dime novels and similar outpourings by numerous competitors became a mainstay of American literature and culture for the second half of the nineteenth century. By 1900, advances in printing and cheap pulp paper, coupled with increased demand for these stories, caused the novels to evolve into serialized magazines, beginning in 1896 with Frank Munsey's *Argosy*, followed by Street & Smith's *Popular Magazine* in 1903.[4] As the pulps transitioned to fiction, reporting of true crime was picked up by the nation's newspapers.

In 1880 there were 850 newspapers published in America with a total daily newspaper circulation of 3,100,00. By 1900, the number of newspapers had increased to 1,967 and circulation to 15,100,000. And by 1910, the number of newspapers had increased to 2,200 and circulation to 22,400,000. Over a span of only thirty years, circulation had increased seven-fold.[5]

Much of that explosive growth in newspaper readership can be traced to the sensational "yellow journalism" of ambitious publishers such as William Randolph Hearst and Joseph Pulitzer. In 1887, Hearst, the Harvard-educated son of wealthy mining magnate and US senator George Hearst, took over his father's *San Francisco Examiner*. Hiring the most-talented writers of the age, and showing little regard for truth or balance in reporting, he built an empire of newspapers across the country that informed, shaped, influenced, and entertained the public.

Pulitzer, by contrast, was an impoverished Hungarian immigrant, who through hard work and a flair for reporting turned the failing *New York World* of the 1880s into the spokesperson for the working-class readers in the East. The *World* was filled with advertising, illustrations, and entertaining news, and was soon in a circulation war with Hearst's *New York Journal*.

And newspaper circulation required grist for the mill. Sales depended upon lurid headlines and articles that caught the reader's eye and caused him or her to reach into a pocket or purse for change. As any watcher of nightly news knows, local violent crime and attendant trials lead the newscast, followed only distantly by sports, traffic, weather, and the political events of a wide world forever teetering on the edge of famine, war, and mutually assured destruction. For additional evidence, look no further than your television listings, where just a superficial glance will reveal programs like *Cold Case, Criminal Minds, NCIS, Bones,* and countless iterations of *Law and Order* and *CSI* on at seemingly every hour of the day and night. But real trials bring these dramas to greater life, and Americans revel in them when they contain additional intrigue or a twist: love, money, celebrity, sex, race, betrayal, or scandal. Each trial becomes theatre, with the courtroom as stage, the participants as actors, and enraptured Americans as audience.

Of course the Founding Fathers understood the necessity of a free press, and the First Amendment assures Americans among other rights the presence of independent inquiry into the operation of the government and its component parts. Without a curious press free of influence, courts cannot be relied upon to operate in a fair and even-handed manner. Thus, the public press is essential in keeping the judicial branch open and honest. The Fathers had experience with dependent courts of an autocratic government and knew that democracy would not thrive in the vacuum of a society without a public press.

But an unrestrained press driven to sell newspapers and radio and television ads will inevitably intrude on courts not equipped to insulate themselves from excess. Unrestrained, the press will threaten and cajole investigators, influence the courtroom behavior and tactics of lawyers and judges, and frighten jurors. Unrestrained, the press will so inflame a community that the environment becomes toxic, inhospitable to a fair judicial process.

At the 1906 trial of Harry Thaw for the murder of New York architect and socialite Stanford White, news reporters swamped the courtroom and crowds of spectators daily impeded access to the courthouse. At the 1925 trial of John Scopes for teaching evolution in a Tennessee school, proceedings had to be moved outdoors because the sheer number of those attending threatened the actual physical stability of the courthouse. Thereafter, five thousand observers watched from makeshift bleachers, and partisan banners hung in full view of the jurors.[6] Conviction unsurprisingly followed in an environment of a Bible revival meeting. In the 1934 trial of Bruno Hauptmann for the Lindbergh baby kidnapping, the reporters numbered 350, and the world came to witness what H. L. Mencken called "the greatest story since the Resurrection." In the 1954 trial of Sam Sheppard for the murder of his wife, Marilyn, reporters inundated the trial, occupying every inch of the courtroom, sitting mere feet from the jury, listening in on the private conversations of lawyers, and handling the evidence. And in 1992, when news reports hit the Los Angeles streets of the acquittal of four police officers on state charges for the beating of Rodney King, so did protestors. In the subsequent riots fifty-three people died and more than three thousand buildings were torched, assuring the officers' conviction in their subsequent federal trial.[7] The result of unrestrained media coverage is a justice system trajectory pushed from its necessary arc of fairness.

When the Hearst and Pulitzer newspapers reported the murder of Stanford White in New York City in 1906 and the trial that followed, the twentieth century was only six years old. No one could have predicted the coming media frenzy that would surround the trial of Roscoe "Fatty" Arbuckle, the kidnapping of the Lindbergh baby, the Tate/LaBianca killings, or the murders of Nicole Brown Simpson and Ron Goldman. And yet the trial of Harry K. Thaw for White's murder was promptly and confidently pronounced in newspapers to be the trial of the century.

Such is the origin of the "trial of the century," an overblown bit of media hype so frequently used to label high-profile murder trials, the frequency and selection of which are limited only by the prurient taste of Americans and the imagination of editors. In this country we have a trial of the century regularly once a decade, and in the chapters that follow we present ten trials, one from each decade, each different in character and context, but alike in telling ways.

CHAPTER 1

1900–1910:
"HE DESERVED IT"—
THE CASE OF HARRY KENDALL THAW

T he turn of the twentieth century represented the crest of what has become known as the "Gilded Age" in America. The country was rapidly industrializing and the economy rising faster than ever before. It was the era of railroads, oil, and high finance, of Andrew Carnegie, John Rockefeller, J. P. Morgan, and Cornelius Vanderbilt. There seemed to be no limit to the amount of money a person could acquire, or to what he could spend it on. The Gilded Age elite lived lives of conspicuous consumption and extravagance, full of high culture, sumptuous parties, easy leisure pursuits, and overindulgence. New York was the center of this world. Leonard Jerome, a financier, once threw a party at Delmonico's at which every woman in attendance was gifted a gold bracelet. Mrs. Stuyvesant Fish, whose husband was the president of the Illinois Central Railroad, once threw a dinner party for her dog, which attended wearing a $15,000 diamond collar.[1]

But "gilded" literally means to be covered only with a thin layer of gold. Not everyone had such massive personal fortunes and such sparkling leisurely lives. The majority of families in America lived on less than $1,200 a year, and sweatshops and tenements were sprouting up in every city in the country.[2] Most people simply could not relate to the lifestyles of the elite, and they were partially enchanted, partially disgusted, but always fascinated with them.

On June 25, 1906, Harry Kendall Thaw, the millionaire of Pittsburgh, and his young, breathtakingly beautiful wife, Evelyn Nesbit, attended a performance of *Mamzelle Champagne* at the Roof Garden Theatre of Madison Square Garden. Also in attendance was the much-acclaimed architect Stanford White, seated at a table in the front row. In the middle of the chorus's rendition of "I Could Love a Million Girls," Thaw calmly approached White's table, pulled a revolver from an overcoat pocket, and fired three shots into his head, killing him instantly. "He deserved it," Thaw explained, "he ruined my wife and then deserted the girl."[3]

With these three gunshots, Harry Thaw launched not only a lengthy murder trial but also a media spectacle and nationwide obsession, the pop culture legacies of which have lasted for decades. His public prosecution, coinciding with the explosion of newspaper readership, was the beginning of a century of American fascination with media-driven murder trials, sex, celebrity, and publicity.

The complicated story of this crime began five years earlier in the summer of 1901, when young Evelyn Nesbit, a bit player in the popular Broadway show *Florodora*, first met the famed Stanford White. Evelyn was then sixteen and White forty-eight. Evelyn was born in 1884 in Tarentum, Pennsylvania. Her father died when she was eight years old, and her mother, tasked with the care of two children, struggled to make ends meet. She shuttled Evelyn and her younger brother, Howard, around Pittsburgh and Philadelphia, opening and closing a sequence of unsuccessful boarding houses and trying other odd jobs, including dressmaking. At age fourteen, Evelyn quit school and worked as a stock girl to help support the family.[4]

Harry K. Thaw (center, bow tie) with unidentified gentleman.
From the Library of Congress.

About this time, Evelyn met John Storm, a well-known artist in Philadelphia. He was immediately taken with her beauty, for even as a young girl Evelyn was admired for her stunning good looks. She had smooth olive skin, large, heavy-lidded dark eyes, and her thick copper-colored hair fell in long curls. Storm began using her as a model for his work. He introduced her to a variety of industry professionals, and she began appearing in books, magazines, and newspaper advertisements. Hoping to capitalize on that modest success, the Nesbits moved to New York City in 1901, where Evelyn continued to model for artists and photographers, including Charles Dana Gibson, creator of the Gibson Girl. Evelyn gained substantial publicity and was finally cast as a "Spanish dancer" in *Florodora*. Since she was only sixteen, the other cast members called her "the baby" or "the kid."[5]

As for Stanford White, he was even then one of America's

visionary architects. A partner in the architectural firm McKim, Mead & White in New York City, alone he is responsible for the arch on Washington Square, the Player's Club, the Madison Square Presbyterian Church, said by some to be the most beautiful church in America, and, somewhat ironically, Madison Square Garden, where he would later die at the hands of Thaw. White designed university buildings throughout the country, residences for the Astors, the Vanderbilts, and other Gilded Age elite, and even Pullman cars and yachts. He has been called New York City's "leading designer, decorator, stylist and chief arbiter of taste."[6] White was born in 1853 and, despite an early desire to be a painter, entered into an architecture apprenticeship in 1870. He married Bessie Smith in 1884 and had one son. The family lived in Long Island, but Stanford spent much of his time in the city, where he lived an alternate life with an infamous reputation for living extravagantly, throwing lavish parties, and having tumultuous affairs, particularly with young girls in show business. He kept an opulently decorated apartment on Twenty-Fourth Street that housed in one room a silk-sheeted mirrored canopy bed, and in another a plush red velvet swing that hung from the ceiling. He was tall in stature and had red hair and a distinctively large mustache. He has been described as a libertine and a bon vivant, having drawn crowds to him with his passionate and exuberant disposition.[7]

In the summer of 1901, Emma Goodrich, a fellow chorus girl in *Florodora*, brought Evelyn to an intimate lunch party at White's apartment. Clearly smitten with her, White spent the next few months inviting Evelyn to lunches at his apartment and sending her expensive gifts. He met Mrs. Nesbit, who seemed to approve of him despite his reputation and allowed young Evelyn to spend a considerable amount of time with him. White fawned over the beautiful, young Evelyn. He paid for her dental work, arranged for her brother, Howard, to be admitted to Chester Military Academy in Philadelphia, and, when Mrs. Nesbit expressed a desire to visit Howard, offered to look after Evelyn while she was away.[8]

One night while Mrs. Nesbit was in Philadelphia, White invited Evelyn to a dinner at his apartment. Assuming it would be a small party, Evelyn was surprised to find that she was the only guest. They ate and drank champagne. White showed her around his lavish apartment, and, before the night was over, he seduced her. In the trial that was to follow, Evelyn would claim that he had gotten her drunk on champagne and taken advantage of her, that she only knew what transpired when she awoke naked in his bed. However, in her memoir, she claims to have been "head over heels in love with him" and remembers on this night feeling that "this, then, was what love meant."[9]

This tryst set off what would become an extended and not-so-secretive affair between White and Evelyn. After nearly every *Florodora* show, Evelyn would meet White and his friends for supper and stay late at his apartment, where he showered her with expensive jewelry and pushed her on the red velvet swing, Evelyn often wearing nothing but his jewelry. She accompanied him to parties at his studio in the tower above Madison Square Garden and often spent the night there, curled up on fur rugs while he worked on his designs. White moved Evelyn and her mother from their boarding house to an opulently decorated apartment in the Wellington Hotel, opened accounts for them at the New Amsterdam Bank and the Mercantile Trust Company, paid their bills, and gave them a twenty-five-dollar weekly allowance.[10]

However, by 1902, Evelyn had rocketed to stardom and become a widely recognized celebrity. She had the lead role in a new musical called *The Wild Rose*, for which avid fans reportedly threw at her feet flowers with fifty-dollar bills wrapped around the stems.[11] She was said to be one of the most beautiful women of the day, and she had countless male admirers.

One of these admirers was Harry Kendall Thaw. Dark-haired and of average build with wide, saucer-like eyes and a youthful face, Thaw, born in Pittsburgh in 1871, was the son of a wealthy railroad family. Even in the context of New York society he was rich beyond imagination. He purportedly lit his cigars with one-hundred-dollar bills.[12] However, he had a reputation for being eccentric, even unstable. He was known not only for his gambling, drinking, and bar fighting, but also for wild and often violent outbursts. He was rumored to have beaten women with riding crops and burned them with scalding water. He once drove his car through the front window of a shop because a saleswoman had been rude to him.[13]

In January 1902, Thaw began sending flowers to Evelyn backstage under the pseudonym "Mr. Monroe." He bribed a chorus girl in the show to persuade Evelyn to meet him for tea, and it was only at this meeting that she learned of Thaw's true identity.[14] Unimpressed, she claimed that she "like[d] him even less than [she did] his reputation."[15] But Thaw was smitten. He continued to call on her at her hotel and send flowers and gifts.

In late 1902, Evelyn, still only seventeen, left the stage and went away to the DeMille School in New Jersey. White paid for her tuition. She had been carrying on with another man, John Barrymore, a twenty-two-year-old cartoonist and the brother of acclaimed actress Ethel Barrymore, and both White and Mrs. Thaw thought she could benefit from some time outside New York. Although White had been the one to introduce Barrymore and Evelyn, both he and Mrs. Nesbit disapproved of the relationship. It is also possible that Evelyn was pregnant and that she was sent away to hide this fact from New York society and the show business industry.

While she was away, Thaw made an effort to befriend Mrs. Nesbit. Accordingly, when Evelyn was hospitalized in April of 1903 with appendicitis, or what may have been pregnancy complications, Mrs. Nesbit phoned both White and Thaw, and it was Thaw who drove her out to New Jersey to be with her daughter. White, however, arranged for Evelyn to be moved to a sanatorium in New York, and he and Thaw, although never at the same time, visited her throughout her recovery. Thaw was so compassionate and generous during Evelyn's convalescence that she tempered her earlier distaste of him, and when her doctor suggested a relaxing trip out of the city and Thaw offered to take Evelyn and her mother to Europe, she accepted.[16]

The trio set sail for Paris and spent months traveling around Europe. Thaw's behavior during this trip was, at best, eccentric and, at worst, violent and dangerous. He pampered Evelyn and Mrs. Nesbit with the best food and clothes and entertainment but exhibited unpredictable fits of rage and jealousy, often in public places.[17]

While the party was in London, Mrs. Nesbit decided she was ready to return to New York. She begged her daughter to come with her, but she refused. As Evelyn and Thaw continued their travels, she experienced an even darker side of his personality. The terrible rumors about him, she realized, were indeed true. He rented an isolated castle in Austria called the Schloss Katzenstein for the two of them and, while there, repeatedly choked her and beat her with a rattan cane and a dog whip until she was unable to get out of bed. She also became privy to his cocaine addiction.[18]

Thaw asked Evelyn to marry him several times during their travels, and each time she refused, giving a variety of reasons and excuses. On one such occasion, she told him that she previously had an affair, and could not marry him and bring the accompanying shame to him and his family. He begged her for the details, and one evening she finally relented and told him of her relationship with White. Thaw was distraught and called White "a filthy beast" for defiling a sixteen-year-old girl.[19]

Thaw had long despised White. His hatred had begun years before, when he had been engaged to another *Florodora* girl, Frances Belmont. He had planned a party for Frances and her friends, but happened upon her in a restaurant the day before and pretended not to recognize her. Insulted, Frances stood Thaw up the night of the party and instead took her friends to dinner at White's apartment. When an article about the party was published in the papers the next day, Thaw was humiliated. He had passionately hated White ever since.[20]

Evelyn's confession to Thaw was a turning point in their relationship. So when the two finally returned to New York, Evelyn broke off the relationship and ran to White, telling him everything. Although he expressed a concern for her and made arrangements for her to speak with an attorney for a lawsuit against Thaw (which was never filed), White was clearly no longer romantically interested in her.[21] She received occasional invitations to lunches and dinners, but their love affair was over.[22]

Meanwhile, Thaw launched an apology campaign, sending notes, telegrams, flowers, and begging Evelyn to see him.[23] She refused for months, but when she failed to receive an invitation to White's 1904 Christmas party, she accepted one from Thaw, and the two met for dinner at Rector's, the same place where a year before he had revealed himself as the mysterious "Mr. Monroe."[24]

Their relationship was rekindled. Thaw and Evelyn began seeing each other regularly again, and, after some coaxing from Thaw's mother, they were married in Pittsburgh on April 5, 1905. But Thaw was still prone to erratic behavior. He continued to have episodes of wild anger. He was consumed by jealousy and had Evelyn followed by private detectives.[25]

Thaw also now openly expressed his hatred for White. His marriage to Evelyn did nothing to ease the intensity of his anger toward the architect. In fact, it took on a new ferocity. His private detectives now followed White in the hopes of catching him in affairs with other young women. Thaw took to carrying a revolver with him and threatened to kill White on multiple occasions.[26] One day, he pointed the gun at Evelyn and told her that if she ever called White by name again he would kill her, and that she must from that moment on only refer to him as "the Beast."[27]

Thaw's uncontrollable obsession with White crested on June 25, 1906. Although they lived in Pittsburgh, Thaw and Evelyn spent a considerable amount of time in New York City. They were in the city in June 1906 and were planning on spending an evening at the Roof Garden Theatre of Madison Square Garden, where the new show *Mamzelle Champagne* was playing. Before the final number was over, Thaw approached White at his front row table and fired three shots into his head. He then emptied the rest of the chamber into the air.[28]

Amid the panicked and scrambling patrons, Thaw remained calm and did not resist arrest. Fireman Paul Brundi took his revolver, and Officer Debes of the Tenderloin District Command placed him under arrest, to which Thaw's only response was "Alright." When Evelyn later asked why he had done it, he simply replied, "It's all right, dear. It's all right. I have probably saved your life."[29] He later wrote in his autobiography that killing Stanford White "made New York safer for other girls" and brought Evelyn, for the first time, "a hope for . . . a cheerfulness [she] had never known."[30]

Denied bail, Thaw was taken to cell 220, Murderers' Row,

at the Tombs prison, the notorious detention complex at 125 White Street in lower Manhattan, to await his trial. Imprisonment for Thaw, however, did not mean a significant decrease in his standard of living; it was common knowledge that he sent out for pork chops, ice cream, and other delicacies for dinner.[31] In the meantime, trial preparations began. Thaw's mother, recently returned from Europe, organized his defense. She hired a team of five lawyers led by Delphin Michael Delmas. The son of a French escargot importer, sixty-three-year-old Delmas studied law at Yale University and served as the district attorney of Santa Clara County in California, where he was often called "the Napoleon of the Western Bar" before going into private practice.[32] Since thousands had witnessed the crime, there was no denying Thaw's complicity. Instead, Delmas set out to prove that Thaw was not guilty by reason of insanity. He claimed that, although sane now, Thaw was not responsible for the murder because he had been driven to a temporary form of dementia by White's behavior. New York district attorney William Travers Jerome, the prosecuting attorney and a cousin of Winston Churchill, maintained that Thaw was perfectly sane and that the murder was premeditated.[33]

The trial began on January 23, 1907, and lasted several months. It featured testimony from Stanford's son, witnesses present at Madison Square Garden on the night of June 25, Fireman Brundi and Officer Debes, mental specialists and physicians, and more, but the star witness was Evelyn. Although most testimony about White's behavior was ruled inadmissible, testimony about Evelyn's relationship with White was allowed as long as it was information she had told Thaw and, thus, pertained to his mental state. By eliciting this testimony from Evelyn, Delmas effectively put White on trial rather than Thaw. Evelyn told the entire story of her teenage love affair with the architect complete with every lewd detail: the parties in the tower studio, the gifts he gave her, the first night at his apartment, the red velvet swing, etc. Dressed demurely as possible to look even younger than her twenty-two years, she asked that only male stenographers be present, as what she had to say would be too scarring for women to hear.[34] She collapsed in the middle of her testimony and proclaimed, "I can't go on!"[35] The resulting impression, that White had predatorily drugged and seduced her against her will, proved insurmountable for the prosecution.

Delmas concluded the trial with a brilliant summation that would later become famous. He explained that Thaw's particular form of insanity was "that species of insanity which makes every American man believe . . . the honor of his wife is sacred" and that "whosoever invades his home, that whosoever stains the virtue of his threshold, has violated the highest of human laws and must appeal to the mercy of God, if mercy there be for him anywhere in the universe." He termed this brand of insanity "dementia Americana" and asked the jury members to "judge your fellow-man as ye would be judged" and "place yourselves as far as in your power lies in the place he stood."[36]

The jury deliberated for several days and re-emerged on April 12 with no verdict. Not all jurors were convinced of Thaw's guilt.[37] The hung jury was dismissed, and a new trial was ordered. The second trial began on January 6, 1908, and lasted through February 1. It contained similar testimony, and this time, the jury unanimously found Thaw not guilty by reason of insanity. He was sentenced to the Asylum for the Criminal Insane in Matteawan, New York, and made the journey to the institution that day in his own private railroad car, celebrating the verdict over champagne with friends.[38]

When White's son first heard of his father's murder by Harry

Thaw and his relationship with Evelyn Nesbit, he admitted that he had never heard of either of them.[39] However, his unfamiliarity with the couple was short-lived. The murder of Stanford White and the following trial became media sensations. White, Thaw, and Nesbit were the perfect representatives of the Gilded Age elite, and this case put their way of life on trial. If that were not enough, their narrative was interlaid with love, passion, and betrayal, and all three of the major participants were celebrities. The entire nation became completely enraptured. The *New York Times* put it aptly when it cited as reasons for interest in the case the "eminence of the victim, the wealth of the prisoner, the dramatic circumstance of the crime, and the light it sheds not only on Broadway life, but on the doings of the fast set in every capital."[40]

The publicity began immediately. On the night of the murder, reporters came calling at the apartment of May Mackenzie, a fellow chorus girl and friend, asking for Evelyn's whereabouts. Evelyn coincidentally was staying with Mackenzie that night, but she did not speak to them.[41] Reporters were already waiting for White's wife and son at his apartment in Gramercy Park when they arrived from Long Island the next day.[42]

The story of White's murder was front-page news the following day, and readers took notice. Daily newspaper circulation rocketed, and extra editions were printed and rushed to the streets. The *New York World*, which listed its circulation as 537,734 copies on June 25, reportedly gained 100,000 readers each day of the week following the murder.[43] The Hearst Corporation, the purveyor of countless newspapers over the years and known today for publications like *Harper's Bazaar, Cosmopolitan*, and *Esquire*, is said to have built its coming success on its reporting of White's murder.[44] Newspapers and magazines overflowed with not only the facts and rumors surrounding the crime, but also the intimate details of White, Thaw, and Nesbit's private lives. Pictures of Evelyn from her modeling days were found and printed. Reporters published statements from friends and family of the victim and the accused, and anyone else who claimed to know anything, from a random taxi driver who proclaimed he "knew that fellow [White] would be killed sooner or later"[45] to Anthony Comstock of the Society for the Suppression of Vice, who claimed to have been investigating White at Thaw's request and had evidence of the "revolting orgies" he held in his tower studio.[46] People were so voraciously hungry for information about the murder and those involved that White's funeral, scheduled to take place at St. Bartholomew's in New York, had to be canceled to prevent it from being overrun by sensation seekers.[47]

This publicity was not limited to New York City. On June 26, the front page of the *Washington Post* read "Harry Thaw, in Jealous Frenzy, Shoots Stanford White to Death,"[48] and the *Chicago Daily Tribune* ran a piece titled "Harry K. Thaw Murders Enemy in Gotham Show."[49] The *Atlanta Constitution* published an article crying, "Murder: Harry Thaw For a Woman Kills White,"[50] and the *Los Angeles Times* ran a similar article entitled "For a Woman, Thaw Kills Most Noted Architect."[51] One article claimed that the case was "being reported to the ends of the civilized globe."[52]

The media frenzy continued for months. The public simply could not get enough of White, Thaw, and Evelyn. Even when there were no new legal developments, daily circulations were filled with articles containing personal details and stories, from White's many affairs and Thaw's privileged upbringing to Evelyn's relationship with her mother and her first trip to Europe with Thaw. Other articles focused on the murder but from alternative, if not irrelevant, angles. One article boasted "Thaw

Fulfilled a Law as Old as the World Said Dr. Gregory: Writer and Clergyman Strongly Defends the Deed of Young Husband who Took Life of Stanford White."[53] Another was headlined "When Little Harry Thaw was Terror: Kindergarten Teacher Thinks Prisoner Showed Irrational Taint at 6 Years of Age."[54]

Finding an impartial jury for the trial proved to be extremely difficult, as so many people had already read the newspaper coverage and had formed their own opinions about the case.[55] The trial itself, in the words of one historian, "pour[ed] kerosene on a newspaper story that had never died."[56] More than one hundred reporters covered the trial, sending their stories of its progress and developments from a special telegraph office set up in the main hall of the Criminal Courts building.[57] Thousands of spectators waited outside the courthouse each day to see the principal characters as they came and went and to hear any news.

Despite his well-known "eccentricities," popular opinion seemed to favor Thaw. At the turn of the century, most Americans still behaved in accordance with and believed in the Victorian moral order, which championed family values and did not condone the kind of sexual promiscuity that had preceded White's murder. This commonly held conviction was mined by Mrs. Thaw's relentless publicity machine, which she unleashed on New York to drum up support for her son and portray him as a member of a well-bred, philanthropic family. Capitalizing on the widespread commercial interest in the case, she planted sympathetic newspaper articles and arranged for three plays and a book to be written about the incident, all of which portrayed Harry as a protector of female virtue and Stanford as a depraved villain.[58] Consequently, when Harry was acquitted and left for Matteawan, he was met at the train station by adoring fans.[59]

However, the real star of the case and trial was Evelyn, with whom America fell head over heels in love. Police officers had to clear a path for her through an impassioned crowd the first time she visited Harry at Tombs,[60] and a throng of nearly ten thousand people gathered outside the courthouse the day that Evelyn gave her testimony. It was common to read in newspapers not only about her "determination to hesitate at nothing that will in any way assist the man for whom she has already braved so much" or how she was "so earnest . . . in her effort to tell, no matter at what cost to herself" but also about how she behaved, dressed, and wore her hair.[61] She wore a blue suit and the same violet-trimmed velvet hat every day of the trial, and, even before jury selection was completed, the ensemble became New York's hottest fashion trend. Every store in the city that could get its hands on them sold similar black velvet hats.[62]

The murder trial was only the beginning of Thaw's legal troubles. He spent years at Matteawan, during which he made several attempts at habeas corpus, jury trials, and even bribes in order to be declared sane and released. In 1913, when all attempts had failed, he managed to escape from Matteawan and drove over the border into Canada, where he faced a long extradition battle before being brought back to New York and Tombs prison in December 1914. While in Canada, he was followed by starstruck crowds clamoring to shake his hand everywhere he went and was likewise met by adoring mobs as he made his way back to New York during his extradition.[63]

In the summer of 1915, Thaw was declared sane in a trial and set free, but his freedom was short-lived. He was arrested again in 1917 for kidnapping and beating a nineteen-year-old schoolboy from Kansas City. In order to avoid another criminal trial, Thaw went before a commission on lunacy, which judged him, once again, insane and committed him to the Pennsylvania State Hospital. He resided there until 1924, when a new trial deemed him sane. A free man once again, he continued to lead the extravagant lifestyle he had always led and had minor skirmishes with the law (there were reports of bar fights and him beating women) before he died of a heart attack in 1947.[64] He maintained an aura of celebrity for the rest of his life.

Although infamous for the scandal she caused, enduring fame, ironically, eluded Evelyn. Mrs. Thaw had promised her a divorce settlement of one million dollars if she cooperated and testified during the trial, but she learned afterward that Thaw could not divorce her because he had been deemed insane. Instead, she was given $25,000 (which she reportedly gave to the anarchist Emma Goldman to spite the wealthy Thaw family[65]) and a very modest living stipend in exchange for her promise to help in Thaw's future sanity proceedings. But this small retainer was not enough to support the lifestyle to which she had become accustomed. She moved out of her lavish house and into much smaller lodgings, and she sold her jewelry to make ends meet. She had trouble finding stage work for several years but made a glamorous comeback in 1912 when she starred in a new show called *Hello Ragtime* at the London Hippodrome. The show was an immediate success and subsequently came to New York and toured the United States.[66]

When Thaw was declared sane in 1915, he immediately divorced Evelyn. She later married her *Hello Ragtime* costar Jack Clifford, although that marriage was similarly short-lived.[67] After *Hello Ragtime*, she succumbed to drug and alcohol addiction. She appeared in a few movies and performed in a variety of cabaret acts and burlesque houses around the county but could never achieve the level of fame she had during her younger years. She lived out the rest of her days in Los Angeles in a more bohemian lifestyle, teaching ceramics and sculpting and trying to stay out of the public eye. She died in 1967 in Santa Monica.[68]

Despite Evelyn's declining personal celebrity, the murder of Stanford White and the trial of Harry Thaw did not fade into obscurity. The case became a cultural landmark, referenced in movies, books, and other venues throughout the century, both as an interesting case study and as a symbol of the Gilded Age. A movie called *The Girl in the Red Velvet Swing* premiered in 1955 and starred Joan Collins as Evelyn Nesbit, Ray Milland as Stanford White, and Farley Granger as Harry Thaw. Evelyn, still alive at the time, was paid $10,000 to work as a consultant on the film, although she claimed its portrayal of the events was not entirely accurate.[69] E. L. Doctorow's novel *Ragtime*, published in 1975 and set in New York after the turn of the century, features Evelyn Nesbit as a supporting character.[70] In the novel, she is admired by one of the wealthy main characters and becomes close to an immigrant family living on the Lower East Side and tries to help them escape poverty. The book was adapted into a film in 1981 and featured Robert Joy as Harry Thaw and Elizabeth McGovern as Evelyn.[71] In 1996, it was made into a smash Broadway musical that still runs today. The show features a musical number in which the character of Evelyn testifies at what is clearly her husband's trial. Instead of a witness stand, she sits on a red velvet swing and sings about jealous Thaw shooting "Stan."[72]

Photos of Evelyn taken by Rudolf Eickemeyer Jr., many commissioned by White, are currently on display at the Smithsonian,[73] and the popular HBO series *Boardwalk Empire*, which premiered in 2010, features a character said to have been loosely based on Evelyn.[74]

The trial of Harry K. Thaw for the murder of Stanford White played out like a perfectly crafted piece of drama, scripted by newspaper coverage, with the world's audience watching in fascination. One reporter explained that "it had in it wealth, degeneracy, rich old wasters, delectable young chorus girls and adolescent artists' models" and that in the "cast of [this] motley show were Bowery toughs, Harlem gangsters, Tenderloin panderers, Broadway leading men, Fifth Avenue clubmen, Wall Street manipulators, uptown voluptuaries and downtown thugs."[75] The plot was packed with love, passion, sex, betrayal, intrigue, and murder, not to mention smashing musical numbers, and left in its wake countless unanswered questions. The story captured the imagination of millions in 1906 and continues to do so today. The world, it seems, is still not ready to forget Stanford, Harry, and Evelyn and the first of what would be many trials of the century.

CHAPTER 2

1910–1920:
THE DEATH OF MARY PHAGAN—
THE TRIAL OF LEO MAX FRANK

The second decade of the twentieth century was one of sobering change in the lives of Americans. World War I brought an end to the nation's isolation in the world. With astonishing suddenness, Marconi's telegraph and the advent of programmed radio did the same for the country's most homebound citizen. The end of the Gilded Age of privilege, symbolized by the sinking of the Titanic in 1912, proved permanent with the imposition of both income and estate taxes during the decade. The explosive sales of Henry Ford's Model T, coupled with rapidly expanding public transportation, meant new mobility for Americans, shrinking the country and bringing people into contact with those beyond an afternoon's walk: people of different ethnicity, social status, race, and culture. Millions moved to the cities, where the friction of overcrowding, poverty, child labor, and dire workplace conditions produced riots, political agitation, and anarchists. It was the end of an age of innocence.

It was in that roiling decade of change that Leo M. Frank was tried for the murder of Mary Phagan, and perhaps no twentieth-century trial had more far-reaching effects on American society. Now largely forgotten, in its day the case was on everyone's lips, from Maine to Mobile, from street car to the Oval Office.

On a humid and overcast Saturday, April 26, 1913, thirteen-year-old Mary Phagan left her Atlanta home headed to the annual Confederate Memorial Day Parade. That day she was dressed in a lavender frock trimmed in lace, a blue hat adorned with flowers, and she carried a pink parasol along with a silver mesh bag.[1] Photographs show her looking older than her age, with dark hair and eyes, a clear white complexion, and full lips.

Mary had been born in Florence, Alabama, into a family of poor tenant farmers. Her father died when she was an infant, and her mother moved the family to East Point, Alabama, where she opened a boarding house. Phagan left school at the age of ten to work part-time in a textile mill, not unusual for girls at the turn of the twentieth century. In 1912 her mother, Frances Phagan, married John William Coleman, and she and the children moved with him to Atlanta. In the spring of 1912, Phagan took a job with the National Pencil Company at 37 South Forsythe Street where she ran a knurling machine, inserting rubber erasers into the metal bands at the end of pencils.[2] She earned $4.05 per week, or approximately seven and a half cents an hour for fifty-five hours.[3]

Confederate Memorial Day was a highlight of turn-of-the-century Atlanta. The city had suffered harshly at the hands of the Union Army and, after fifty years, was still populated by veterans and civilians for whom the loss to the North remained a raw memory. The parade that year featured bands and displays, and crowds lined Peachtree Street to watch and mourn, the celebration one of heritage, culture, and loss.

Mary Phagan never got there. Shortly after noon on that Saturday, she stopped at the factory to pick up her wages for the week. The pay was normally distributed on Fridays, but Mary had been laid off from her job the previous Monday due to a lack of materials, and so was not at work to collect the amount due her, the sum of $1.20 for a single day's work. Her body was found at three o'clock the next morning in the cluttered and filthy factory basement by Newt Lee, a tall, slender, and elderly black man who served as the night watchman. Frightened to be found with the body of a white girl, he immediately called the police.[4]

Leo Frank. From the Library of Congress.

Mary Phagan had been strangled with a length of cord used to tie up pencil boxes. Her face, hair, and clothing were covered with dirt, blood, and urine. Her face was bruised and scratched from having been dragged facedown across the floor. So dirty was she that the police had to turn down the edges of her stockings to see the color of her skin. Her skirt was thrown up above her hips, and a strip of cloth torn from her undergarments was wrapped around her throat. One shoe and the pink parasol were lying by the body, but the silver mesh bag had disappeared. A fresh pile of human excrement was found at the bottom of the nearby elevator shaft.

Two handwritten notes were found by Mary Phagan's head. Written in the first person as if she had written them as she was being assaulted, one said,

> He said he wood love me land down play like the night witch did it but that long tall black negro did boy his slef.[5]

The other note said,

> Mam that negro hire down here did this i went to make water and he push me down that hole a long tall negro black that hoo it wase long sleam tall negro i write while play with me.[6]

As was probably intended, the initial effect of the notes was to cast suspicion on the night watchman Newt Lee, and he was immediately arrested. When he read the note, Lee said, "Boss, that's me."[7]

But the notes were so fraught with problems that he couldn't be held on their strength alone. Reference to "night witch" was assumed to mean *night watchman*, but it was clear from the beginning that the notes were forgeries. Even supposing that Phagan could have written them as she struggled for her life, her spelling and grammar were known to be excellent, and the notes appeared to be the work of a semi-illiterate.[8]

Compared to modern standards, policing in the early decades of the twentieth century was a harsh and unscientific business. The crime scene was not secured, and even obvious clues such as blood and hair samples were not harvested. Harold Ross, the twenty-year-old reporter for the *Atlanta Journal* who would go on to create the *New Yorker*, one of the great periodicals of the twentieth century, had absconded with the murder notes. Instead, the police simply rounded up and browbeat anyone who had any connection with the location, crime, or victim. Over 200 people were questioned in connection with Phagan's murder, often held for long periods of time, shackled, and beaten. The police had no hesitation about intimidating witnesses.

Several people were arrested in connection with the crime. Along with Newt Lee, police arrested Arthur Mullinax, a streetcar conductor who had frequently driven Phagan to and from work and who knew her from church. Both Lee and Mullinax proclaimed their innocence and were soon released. On Monday, April 28, police arrested James Milton Gantt, a discharged bookkeeper at the National Pencil Company who had openly admired Phagan. Gantt had appeared at the factory on Saturday afternoon on the pretense of recovering lost shoes, and police considered him an excellent suspect. When he was arrested in nearby Marietta, Gantt was waiting with a suitcase to board a train.[9] Other suspects were similarly arrested and released.[10]

The Atlanta police were under the immediate and intense public scrutiny of the city's three daily newspapers. By Monday morning, the staffs of the *Journal, Constitution*, and *Georgian* were fully dedicated to the creation of front-page stories on

Mary Phagan's death. All three papers reported what they knew of the circumstances of the crime, but were spiced with uncorroborated theory and supposition.

The *Atlanta Constitution* had been the pre-eminent newspaper in Atlanta since the Civil War, and it broke the story on Sunday morning. At the time of Mary Phagan's murder, it was engaged in a heated battle for readers with the *Atlanta Georgian*, purchased just the year before by William Randolph Hearst. He had transformed the *Georgian* into an organ of yellow journalism, making it much more successful, if less respected. In April of 1913, the bombastic *Georgian* was in the hands of editor Foster Coates, who had crafted the headline "Remember the Maine" for Pulitzer's *World* in 1898. As many as forty extra editions were published by the three dailies that Monday morning. Sensational and eye-catching, some coverage was accidentally or intentionally slipshod. The *Georgian* dedicated five full pages to the crime, including a doctored morgue photo of Mary Phagan in which her head was shown on the body of another girl. The *Journal* reported that the authorities were following leads that Phagan was the victim of white slavers.[11]

But the harshest condemnation was saved for the police themselves. In articles reporting the heartbreaking details of Phagan's funeral on Tuesday, the newspapers demanded action. Their early suspects released, and smarting from editorial comments on Tuesday, police now focused their suspicion on Leo Max Frank, the twenty-nine-year-old Jewish superintendent of the National Pencil Company and the last person known to have seen Mary Phagan alive. Slight and fair, with a nervous personality, Frank was a highly educated and well-traveled factory manager from the industrial North. Although he was born in Texas, his parents had moved the family to Brooklyn, New York, when he was only three months old. Educated at

Cornell University in mechanical engineering, he dabbled in photography and played chess and tennis. He was thoroughly a Yankee in upbringing, looks, and disposition.

At the invitation of his uncle Moses Frank, Leo had traveled to Atlanta in 1907, where Moses offered him a job working for the National Pencil Company, of which the elder Frank was an owner. After a nine-month apprenticeship at Eberhard Faber in Germany, Frank settled in Atlanta in August of 1908 and began work as superintendent. He was known to be conscientious and hardworking. In November of 1910 he married Lucille Selig, the daughter of a prominent and wealthy Jewish Atlanta family. He was active in Atlanta Jewish life, serving as president of the local chapter of the B'nai B'rith. Numbering several thousand, the Jewish community in Atlanta was "the largest in the South, and the Franks moved in a cultured and philanthropic milieu whose leisure pursuits included opera and bridge."[12]

Evidence against Frank on that Tuesday morning was circumstantial at best, and manufactured at worst. Blond hairs and suspected blood spots were found at the second-floor workstation Phagan had used, but not analyzed. Officers Boots Rogers and John Black, who had picked Frank up from his home early Sunday morning and escorted him to the mortuary and factory, reported that he seemed nervous. Under police pressure, several fellow employees of the factory, including young George Epps, whom Phagan had planned to meet at the parade that afternoon, were induced to state that Frank had flirted with Phagan and frightened her.[13] Local brothel-keeper Nina Formby was questioned, and after being plied with alcohol told police that Frank had phoned her continuously through Saturday afternoon and evening seeking a room for himself and "an unconscious girl." Formby told police that she had turned him away, but she told reporters that Frank was a regular customer and "a pervert." She later recanted her statement, but her description of Frank as a pervert was indelible. Minola McKnight, the African American cook for Frank's family, was held overnight and questioned severely, eventually signing a statement saying that Frank was nervous and drinking heavily the night after the murder. She said she overheard Lucille say that Frank kept asking for a pistol so that he could shoot himself.[14] McKnight also later recanted her statement as having been forced from her by the police, but her original story was repeated by her husband. Factory worker Monteen Stover told investigators that Frank was absent from his office at the time of the presumed attack on Phagan, contradicting Frank's statement that he had never left his desk. She had come for her pay packet, but left when she found the offices empty. "The whole place was awfully quiet," she said, "and kind of scary."[15]

At 11:30 a.m. Tuesday morning, April 29, Atlanta police arrested Leo Frank. The *Georgian* extra ran the headline "Police Have the Strangler" with a photo of Frank.

The police desperately needed hard evidence on which he could be prosecuted, and they found that evidence on May 1. That afternoon, Jim Conley, an African American sweeper at the factory, was discovered rinsing out a bloodstained shirt in a factory watercooler and was taken into custody. Twenty-nine years old, short, and powerfully built, the native Atlantan had worked at the National Pencil Company for two years, his lack of promotion partially the result of heavy drinking. He had a long arrest record for drunkenness and disorderly conduct.[16]

Over the next four weeks in custody, he gave several conflicting accounts of the events of April 26. He at first denied being able to write, but when it became clear that he had lied about his illiteracy and examples of his handwriting matched the two murder notes, Conley told police on May 24 that he had written the notes, but claimed to have been forced to do so by Leo Frank on the day before the murder. His sworn affidavit stated:

> He asked me could I write and I told him yes I could write a little bit, and he gave me a scratch pad and. . . . He told me to put on there "dear mother, a long, tall, black negro did this by himself," and he told me to write it two or three times on there. I wrote it on a white scratch pad, single ruled. He went to his desk and pulled out another scratch pad, a brownish looking scratch pad, and looked at my writing and wrote on that himself.[17]

Inconsistencies troubled investigators. After four more days of intense questioning, Conley contradicted his prior statements and now told how he had met Frank on the street on Saturday and was instructed to follow him to his office at the factory. He said that Frank dictated the murder notes for him to write, gave him cigarettes, and told him to leave the factory. He said he did not learn of the murder until he went to work on Monday. Both the *Journal* and the *Georgian* gave Conley's new story front-page coverage.[18]

But Conley's revised testimony still did not satisfy the Atlanta police. They accepted that he had written the murder notes, but his absence from the factory during the afternoon of April 26 while Phagan met her death left too many questions unanswered. After another day of relentless examination, Conley gave yet another affidavit, and in this version he admitted to being at the factory the entire time. He now told police that Frank had summoned him up to the second floor, where the Jewish superintendent allegedly admitted to having accidentally killed Phagan and instructed him to dispose of her body in the basement. In this new account, Conley described how he and Frank

had carried the young girl to the elevator, rode down to the basement, and left her body on the refuse pile, then returned to the
second floor where Frank dictated the notes for Conley to write.
He purportedly told Conley, "Why should I hang?" The next
morning, May 30, the headline of the *Constitution* reported to an
excited population, "Conley Says He Helped Frank Carry Body
of Mary Phagan to Pencil Factory Cellar."[19]

The trial of Leo Frank commenced before Judge Leonard
Roan two months later on the blisteringly hot Atlanta morning
of July 28, 1913. During the course of the trial, the courtroom
windows had to be left open, and in addition to the hundreds
of spectators inside, a large and impassioned crowd collected
outside to watch and listen. The trial pitted two well-known
lawyers against each other. Thirty-two years old and a native
Georgian, prosecutor Hugh Dorsey was an ambitious lawyer
from a family of lawyers. Since 1911 he had been the solic-
itor-general of the Fulton County Superior Court, and thus
responsible for the prosecution of Mary Phagan's accused
killer. Bespectacled and intelligent, he had suffered a series of
embarrassing trial losses, which placed him in a position where
a win was necessary to salvage his reputation. Dorsey's oppo-
nent, fifty-three-year-old Luther Z. Rosser, was at the peak of his
career. Portly and old-fashioned, famous for never wearing a tie
in the courtroom, he had the deceptive air of a country lawyer,
but was considered then the best advocate in Georgia.[20]

The defense strategy was simple: in an era of endemic racial
prejudice, no white man had ever been convicted of murder in
the state of Georgia solely on the testimony of a black witness.
Rosser intended to pick apart the testimony of the prosecution's witnesses and present a parade of character witnesses on
Frank's behalf who would testify to his upstanding reputation
and paint a picture of a man incapable of this kind of crime.

The prosecution strategy was less clear. Dorsey did not publicly denounce Frank's Jewish faith or tie that faith to the commission of a crime, but chose to prosecute Frank first on the testimony of Conley, delaying any indictment of the latter until after Frank's trial, notwithstanding serious doubts about the credibility of his primary witness.

The trial was held in the old Atlanta City Hall, in the room formerly used for city council meetings. While accommodating hundreds of spectators on three sides, the courtroom was crowded for the parties, attorneys, and numerous reporters attending to write down every word of testimony and verbal exchanges between the lawyers. The room was also stifling. Photographs of the first day of trial show the many men present having removed their coats, which hung on their chair backs, although the principal lawyers and Frank kept theirs on.

Jury selection occupied the morning of that first Monday, and after lunch the prosecution commenced with the testimony of Phagan's weeping mother, followed by young George Epps, and finally the factory's night watchman, Newt Lee. His testimony was elicited to provide the jury with the physical layout of the factory, the timeline of the murder, and the discovery of Phagan's body. Over the following days, Dorsey called as witnesses the investigating police detectives, sixteen-year-old fellow worker Grace Hicks, the discharged bookkeeper and initial suspect James Gantt, other factory workers, and the physicians who had exhumed and examined Phagan's body. Every word of testimony was transcribed by the reporters present and reprinted for an enraptured public. When the week was finished, the prosecution had demonstrated that Frank had the opportunity to commit the murder of young Phagan, but not that he had done so.

On Monday morning, August 4, Dorsey called his star witness, Jim Conley, now washed, shaved, and resplendent in new clothes. Spectators had lined up for hours to get a seat in the courtroom, and they were not disappointed by the coming performance.

Dorsey began by asking how he had come to be at the factory on that Saturday. He was there to keep watch for Leo Frank, as he had on prior Saturdays. "For what purpose?" asked Dorsey. "While he was upstairs with young ladies," came the response.[21]

Conley then held the courtroom enthralled while he recounted his version of the events of April 26—the arrival of young Mary Phagan, misidentified as "Mary Perkins," who disappeared upstairs, then waiting for Frank's summoning whistle and, when it came, Leo Frank's appearance:

Conley: He was standing at the head of the stairs shivering.
   He was rubbing his hands together and acting funny.
Dorsey: What did he say?
Conley: He says, "Well, that one you say didn't come back down, she came into my office a while ago and wanted to know something about her work and I went back there to see if the little girl's work had come, and I wanted to be with the little girl, and she refused me, and I struck her and I guess I struck her too hard and she fell and hit her head against something, and I don't know how bad she got hurt. Of course, you know I ain't built like other men." The reason he said that was, I had seen him in a position I haven't seen any other man that has got children. I have seen him in the office two or three times before Thanksgiving and a lady was in his office, and she was sitting down in a chair and she had her clothes up to here, and he was down on his knees, and she had her hands on Mr. Frank. I have seen him another time there in the packing room with a young lady lying on the table, she was on the edge of the table. . . .[22]

This testimony was new and damning. It was unlike anything in Conley's prior sworn statements, offered a rapacious motive for the killing, implied a deviant sexual character for the superintendent, and described perverse acts that were crimes under Georgia law. Eventually the rest of the story emerged under the prosecutor's deft questioning. Conley claimed to have found Phagan lying dead on the factory's second floor, bundled up the body, and carried it with Frank's help by elevator to the basement, then returned upstairs to write the murder notes. Dorsey was done with him in four hours, and the court adjourned.[23]

When it reconvened, Judge Roan cleared the courtroom of women and children, deeming the testimony too sensational for gentle ears. What followed over the next three days was thirteen hours of cross-examination by Rosser, variously cajoling, quiet, angry, or sarcastic. Frank's lawyer took Conley through the day's alleged activities, compared his testimony with the contradictions of his three prior affidavits, all to no avail. When the object of the questioning was new, Conley was brilliantly retentive, adding fresh and startling details, and by turns apologetic, charming, shuffling, and clever. When Rosser challenged him with the inconsistent statements in his prior affidavits, he claimed not to remember, or simply admitted to lying to officers on the earlier occasions. In his book, *And the Dead Shall Rise*, author Steve Oney recounts in riveting detail how Rosser tried time and again to corner the clever Conley, only to have him dance away. "Within an hour, Conley had admitted to a multitude of falsehoods and dozen times claimed lapses in recall—none of which tarnished his major allegations."[24] Rosser gave up attempting to trap the sweeper, and by the last day of his testimony the defense attorney simply read the prior affidavits aloud, allowing the jury "to ponder the glaring discrepancies among the various statements."[25]

All three Atlanta papers reported the testimony of Conley nearly word for word to the impassioned citizens of the city.

When the court reconvened the next day, Judge Roan denied the motion of Frank's lawyers to strike the sexually explicit parts of Conley's testimony, and the hundreds of spectators in the courtroom burst into applause, hooting and clapping, some shouting the news out the windows to the throngs of onlookers assembled in the streets outside. There was no mistaking the sympathies of the citizens of Atlanta.[26] One more witness was called to testify, completing Dorsey's presentation of Frank's guilt, and the prosecution rested.

As damning as Conley's testimony had been, over the next two weeks Frank's lawyers orchestrated a thorough and painstaking defense. Rosser and his associates called an astonishing 169 witnesses, presenting testimony on every aspect of the crime, the science, and Frank's character. The one living person that Conley had identified as an illicit paramour of Frank was called to testify that she didn't know Frank and had never been in the factory with him. Medical experts challenged the conclusions of the prosecution's experts as to the time of death and the likelihood of sexual assault. Factory workers present that Saturday testified they witnessed neither Phagan nor evidence of an assault upon her. They also verified they had never seen Frank entertain women in the office on Saturdays. Accounting experts reconstructed Frank's work that day and opined that it was so time-consuming to complete that he could not have had time to commit the murder in the hours he was there. Minola McKnight, the Franks' cook, took the stand to repudiate the affidavit coerced from her by the Atlanta police. Local witnesses discredited every element of the prosecution's timeline, contradicting Conley's testimony of where Frank was and when. Scores of witnesses from Atlanta and New York swore to the excellent character of the defendant, including friends, family, factory workers, former Cornell schoolmates and instructors, his rabbi, president of the Chamber of Commerce, heads of charities, even one of prosecutor Dorsey's law partners. Others swore to the disreputable character of the prosecution's witnesses. Conley in particular was pilloried by fellow factory employees, both white and black. Physicians were even called to opine that they had examined Frank's genitals and that he was, indeed, like normal men, contradicting Conley's most sensational revelation. "I have examined the private parts of Leo M. Frank," testified Dr. Thomas Hancock, a graduate of Columbia University and chief of medicine for the Georgia Railway and Power Company, "and found nothing abnormal."[27]

On Monday, August 18, 1913, the nineteenth day of trial, Leo Frank took the stand in his own defense. Under Georgia court rules, he was allowed to read a statement without being subject to cross-examination. Throngs lined up to get seats, and hundreds were turned away. Unemotional and cool, Frank spoke for four hours, giving what at times was mind-numbingly tedious details of the accounting work that he performed in general and on that Saturday that Phagan was murdered. He exhibited little passion, devoting only a few moments in his recitation to the arrival and departure of Mary Phagan as she came for her pay that April afternoon. Coming at the close of the defense's case, Frank's statement moved no one, impressed no one, convinced no one. Rosser had apparently not read the superintendent's remarks in advance.[28]

In closing arguments, the unexpressed prejudice on both sides that had lurked for weeks just below the surface of the trial boiled over. Frank's attorney recounted the unlikely nature of the circumstantial evidence, summarized the testimony in favor of the defendant, and told the jury, "I tell everybody, all within the hearing of my voice, that if Frank hadn't been a Jew he never would have been prosecuted. I am asking my kind of people to give this man fair play. Before I do a Jew injustice, I want my throat cut from ear to ear." Then he publicly accused Conley of the murder of Mary Phagan, describing him in condemnation and derision: "Conley is a plain, beastly, drunken, filthy, lying nigger with a spreading nose through which probably tons of cocaine have been sniffed. But you weren't allowed to see him as he is."[29]

Prosecutor Dorsey was in his turn ferociously elegant. He explained away the character witnesses the defense had offered by characterizing Frank as a Jekyll and Hyde. "Dr. Marx, Dr. Sonn, all those other people who . . . run with the Dr. Jekyll of the Jewish Orphan's Home, don't know the Mr. Hyde of the factory."[30] Of Frank's religion he said, "This great people rise to heights sublime, but they sink to the depths of degradation, too, and they are amenable to the same laws as you or I and the black race." Pointing at Frank, his voice rising in power and volume, he intoned:

> You assaulted her and she resisted. She wouldn't yield. You struck her and you ravished her when she was unconscious. You gagged her, and then quickly you tipped up to the front, where you knew there was a cord, and got the cord and in order to save your reputation which you had among the members of the B'nai B'rith, in order to save, not your character because you never had it, but in order to save the reputation of the Haases and Montags and the members of Dr. Marx's church and your kinfolks in Brooklyn, rich and poor, and in Athens, then it was that you got the cord and fixed the little girl whom you'd assaulted, who wouldn't yield to your proposals, to save your reputation, because dead people tell no tales.[31]

It was now Saturday afternoon, August 23, and with a huge crowd outside and the state militia on call, Judge Roan halted proceedings until Monday morning. The city of Atlanta spent Sunday in hushed expectation. On Monday morning Dorsey finished, resummarizing the evidence, pitching to the jury as the noon hour neared, telling them, "[T]here can be but one verdict, and that is: We the jury find the defendant, Leo M. Frank, guilty!" At that moment, by design or marvelous chance, the bells of the nearby Church of the Immaculate Conception began their mournful count, and Dorsey repeated twelve more times, echoing each toll, "Guilty, guilty, guilty. . . ."[32]

By the time the jury began deliberations at 1:35 p.m., a crowd of 5,000 prowled the streets outside. Calls to lynch Frank could be heard through the open windows.[33] In the air of hostility against the defendant, Judge Roan and the attorneys agreed that Frank and his lead attorneys should not be present when the verdict was read, as their safety could not be assured.

The jurors took just four hours to come back with a verdict of guilty, and the news quickly spread:

> The tumultuous roar echoed from street to street. Trolley cars halted and their drivers and conductors jumped down to join in the jubilation. The result was posted on the scoreboard of the Atlanta Crackers' baseball game and the grandstand let out a roar. Spontaneous applause broke out at social functions. Hundreds joined hands and danced the cakewalk in front of the pencil factory. The telephone company handled three times as many calls as on any previous day in its history.[34]

The Atlanta newspapers kept pace. The first "extra" edition announcing Frank's guilt was on the street within three minutes of the announcement of the jury's verdict.[35]

Prosecutor Dorsey, riding a wave of fame that would carry him to the governor's house in 1916, on this occasion "reached no farther than the sidewalk. While mounted men rode like Cossacks through the human swarm, three muscular men slung Mr. Dorsey on their shoulders and passed him over the heads of the crowd across the street."[36]

The next day, August 25, 1913, Judge Roan sentenced Leo Frank to death.

In retrospect, looking back through the experienced lens of a full century, it is hard to understand how a jury could have convicted Leo Frank on the mendacious and sensational testimony of Jim Conley. Most of those involved doubted his story, including the police investigators and Conley's own lawyer, William Smith. Atlanta had not had a reputation of religious prejudice. But there was something oddly enthralling in Conley's telling, and something equally cold and unsympathetic in the icy demeanor of Frank. Added to the hostility that Atlantans felt for the starchly educated carpetbagger, the contrasts of rich and poor, Southerner and Northerner, Jew and gentile, and the loud and unceasing demand for justice trumpeted by the city's newspapers, deeply felt by each of the jurors, the conviction of Frank was unavoidable.

Anti-Semitism flared in its wake. With the trial concluded, the *Constitution,* the *Georgian,* and the *Journal* no longer covered the Phagan murder as daily headlines. In their place, populist firebrand Thomas Watson and his weekly *Jeffersonian* picked up the cause in dark and disturbing tones. Beginning in March of 1914, its steady stream of anti-Semitic, anti-privilege, and overtly violent reporting appeared on Atlanta's streets. The paper referred to Frank as "a foul degenerate" (April 23, 1914) and the "filthy and murderous Sodomite" (December 3, 1914).[37] Statements included "Does a Jew expect extraordinary favors and immunities because of his race?"[38] "It seems that negro[e]s are good enough to hold office, sleep in our beds, eat at our tables, marry our daughters, and mongrelize the Anglo-Saxon race, but are not good enough to bear testimony against a rich Jew."[39] "This campaign of lies, abuse, defamation and race hatred gets worse and worse. It must be costing the Chosen People a lot of money."[40]

Appeals followed in natural course. In October of 1913, Judge Roan denied the motion for a new trial, although he stated, "Gentlemen I have thought about this case more than any other I have ever tried. I am not certain of the man's guilt. . . . But I do not have to be convinced. The jury was convinced."[41] The Georgia Supreme Court voted four to two to uphold the conviction in February 1914. After the trial court rejected a second motion for retrial in November, the United States Supreme Court declined to review the case in December but not without misgivings. Justice Oliver Wendell Holmes, Jr., in ruling against Frank, nonetheless wrote,

> On these facts I very seriously doubt if the Petitioner [Frank] has had due process of law—not on the grounds of his absence when the verdict was rendered so much as because of the trial taking place in the presence of a hostile demonstration and seemingly dangerous crowd, thought by the presiding judge to be ready for violence unless a verdict of guilty was rendered.[42]

On April 19, 1915, the United States Supreme Court issued its final ruling against Frank, with two justices dissenting, including Justice Holmes, who wrote, "Mob law does not become due process of law by securing the assent of a terrorized jury."[43]

His appeals exhausted, Frank was scheduled to hang on June 22, 1915.

Calls began immediately for the death sentence to be reduced to life imprisonment. Over the previous twenty-four months, many of the prosecution's witnesses had recanted. The biologist who had testified at the trial now disclosed that subsequent tests showed the hair found on the second floor was not Phagan's. Albert McKnight, husband of the Franks' maid, admitted to having been bribed to testify to what his wife had said to him regarding the defendant's behavior on the night of the murder.[44] Newspaper boy George Epps, who testified that Frank had known and admired Phagan, withdrew his testimony. Nina Formby, the brothel-keeper, admitted that her allegations had also been entirely false. Other factory workers recanted as well. Witness C. Brutus Dalton, who had corroborated Conley's descriptions of Frank's Saturday meetings with other women, now confessed that his testimony was fabricated by the Atlanta police. The murder notes turned out to have been written on expired factory forms kept in the basement, not in Frank's office. Most revelatory, Conley's own attorney, William Smith, announced that he believed Conley to be guilty of Phagan's murder and Frank to be innocent.

Northern newspapers began to take up the cause. New York papers particularly saw the conviction of Frank as a miscarriage of justice perpetrated on a Northern Jew. The *New York Times*, Jewish-owned, was perhaps unsurprisingly vocal in support of Frank, but so too were the *World*, the *Herald*, and Hearst's *Journal*, all of which began to editorialize openly of Frank's innocence and for commutation of his sentence.

Watson and the *Jeffersonian* fired back. "If Frank's rich connections keep on lying about the case, SOMETHING BAD WILL HAPPEN"[45] and "[I]f the Prison Commission or the Governor undertake to undo—in whole or in part—what has been legally done by the courts that were established for that purpose, there will almost inevitably be the bloodiest riot ever known in the history of the South."[46]

Public demonstrations in support of Frank erupted in cities all through the North. In May of 1915, delegations arrived in Atlanta with petitions containing over two million signatures requesting clemency. Written pleas arrived bearing the signatures of senators from six states and the governors of eight.[47] In Georgia, however, particularly in Phagan's hometown of Marietta, protests demanding the death of Frank continued, with participants sometimes numbering in the thousands.

The Georgia Police Commission met on May 31, 1915 to consider commutation of the sentence, hearing evidence over two days. Submissions included a plea from Conley's lawyer, William Smith ("I swear to you that I believe Leo M. Frank to be innocent. With all the earnestness and seriousness of my life, I appeal to you not to let him die."[48]), and a written submission from trial judge Leonard S. Roan, who had succumbed to cancer six months earlier:

> After many months of continued deliberation, I am still uncertain of Frank's guilt. The state of uncertainty is largely due to the character of the negro Conley's testimony, by which the verdict was evidently reached. . . .
>
> The execution of any person whose guilt has not been satisfactorily proved to the constituted authorities is too horrible to contemplate . . . hence at the proper time I shall express and enlarge upon these views directly to the governor and the prison commission. However if for any cause I am prevented from doing this, you are at liberty to use this letter at the hearing.[49]

Despite all that it heard, on June 9, 1915, after eight days of deliberation, the commission ruled against Frank on a vote of two to one.

With thirteen days until Frank's execution date, the final

decision came to rest with Georgia governor John M. Slaton. Nothing could have been less welcome. A native Georgian, a lawyer by training, Slaton had only seventeen days remaining in his term. Pressures that had been building for months reached a crescendo in the days before Frank's scheduled hanging. Slaton received letters encouraging commutation of the sentence from citizens public and private, including US vice president Thomas Marshall, and from editors of newspapers across the country. William Randolph Hearst, whose *Georgian* had reported so loudly and consistently on the murder and subsequent trial, wrote,

> I have heard you say that any man could do the right thing in an ordinary situation, but the test of a really great and genuine man was to be able to do the right thing in an exceptionally critical and important situation.[50]

Slaton commenced hearing arguments in his office on Saturday, June 12. Frank's lawyers pleaded for the government to commute the sentence to life imprisonment, believing that additional time would lead to further evidence of his innocence and thus his freedom. Hugh Dorsey was present to press the prosecution's arguments. Slaton toured the factory and examined the basement where Phagan's body had been found. Then on Wednesday, June 16, with only six days until the date set for execution, he boxed up the records and testimony of the trial and retired to his sprawling estate outside of Atlanta to study. Over the next four days he left only once, to return to the factory to test the elevator.[51]

It all came down to the pile of human excrement that Conley admitted to leaving in the shaft of the elevator that Saturday morning before the murder.[52] It was observed as undisturbed when the police inspected the factory basement later that night when they were called to the murder scene. It was mashed the first time when police brought Frank down the elevator to inspect the premises early on the Sunday morning, several of the investigators recollecting the noxious odor when the elevator car reached the bottom. Unremarked at the time, it meant that the elevator had not been used on Saturday and that Conley had lied when he described how he and Frank had brought the body down the elevator from the second floor.

On Sunday, June 20, just before midnight, Governor Slaton had Frank moved under cover of darkness from the police station where he had been housed for more than two years to the state prison in Milledgeville. On Monday morning, Slaton summoned the press to his suburban estate and announced that he was commuting the sentence:

> All I ask is that the people of Georgia read my statement and consider calmly the reasons I have given for commuting Leo M. Frank's sentence. Feeling as I do about this case, I would be a murderer if I allowed that man to hang. I would rather be plowing in a field than to feel for the rest of my life that I had that man's blood on my hands.[53]

It was the end of his political career, and he knew it. Atlanta erupted in protest, and martial law was declared. Despite the efforts of the city's police, several thousand rioters descended on the governor's estate, only barely repulsed by militia with fixed bayonets. Furious Atlantans hung him in effigy in Atlanta's courthouse square with the sign "King of the Jews."[54] On his next appearance in town several days later, an attempt was made on Slaton's life.

His term up, Slaton and his wife left Georgia and didn't return for ten years. She had told him, "I would rather be the widow of a brave and honorable man than the wife of a coward."[55]

Frank's reprieve was not to last. Four weeks later, a fellow Milledgeville Prison inmate crept up on the sleeping Frank in the middle of the night and slashed his throat from ear to ear, narrowly missing his carotid artery.[56] Two fellow inmates, both doctors, immediately provided aid, and when the prison physician arrived the three operated for two hours to save his life. An investigation determined that the assailant was deranged and had acted alone. After seventy-two hours it became clear that Frank would survive, and he was moved to a private room to convalesce.[57] "I must live," he told the prison doctor. "I must vindicate myself."

Tom Watson and the *Jeffersonian* continued to pour invective, now openly calling for Frank to be lynched.

Watson's challenge was taken up. Late in the evening of August 16, a band of well-organized citizen-soldiers calling themselves the Knights of Mary Phagan fell on a surprised and slumbering Milledgeville Prison, disarming the guards without a shot, cutting telephone lines, and disabling the prison vehicles to avoid pursuit. They seized Frank from his bed and bundled him into a waiting automobile.

The Knights were no ordinary rabble. The twenty-five members included ringleaders Joseph Mackey Brown, a Harvard-trained lawyer and Georgia's governor preceding Slaton, E. P. Dobbs, mayor of Phagan's hometown of Marietta, and Eugene Herbert Clay, former mayor of Marietta and son of Georgia senator Alexander Stephens Clay. Other members included a judge, police officers, former sheriffs, lawyers, bankers, farmers, and merchants.

Frank was driven seven hours back to Frey's Gin, a wooded area just outside Marietta. Still wearing his night shirt, he was handcuffed, with his legs tied together at the ankles, a khaki cloth tied around his exposed midsection, and he was made to stand on a table. A noose was placed around his neck. Witnesses reported him to have been calm and possessed. Asked if he had anything to say, he responded, "I think more of my wife and mother than I do of my own life."[58] After agreeing to return Frank's wedding ring to his wife, the Knights hanged him.

Photographs of the lynching taken in the spreading morning light show Frank's body hanging from the tree, surrounded by spectators in shirtsleeves and boater hats making no effort to hide their identities. One man is holding a camera. In another, Judge Newton A. Morris, the Knight who had presided at the hanging and kicked the table out from under Frank's legs, looks on.[59]

That morning, thousands came to see the body.[60] Pieces of Frank's clothing were cut off by souvenir hunters. The body was taken down and crushed under booted heels. After the mutilated corpse was finally deposited at Greenberg & Bond's Mortuary, forty troopers were required to guard it from the crowds.[61] Frank was buried in an intimate ceremony at Mount Carmel Cemetery in Queens, New York, attended by his family.

In every corner of America outside the state of Georgia, the lynching of Leo Frank was condemned in the harshest possible terms, in newspapers, editorials, and pulpits, from the man on the street to President William Howard Taft, who called it "a damnable outrage."[62]

In Georgia, while the lynching was denounced by all of the leading newspapers, though not by the *Jeffersonian*, inquests into the death of Frank were stymied or misdirected. The coroner's grand jury was directed by one of the Knights, and the jury itself numbered seven more. Although thirty-five witnesses were called, and the perpetrators were well-known, not one was identified. The grand jury concluded, "We have been unable to connect anybody with the perpetrators of this offense or to identify anyone who was connected with it."[63]

The effects of Frank's conviction and death were far-reaching. In September of 1913, the B'nai B'rith created the Anti-Defamation League. In November of 1915, the Knights of Mary Phagan burned a gigantic cross at the top of Atlanta's Stone Mountain, inaugurating the revival of the Ku Klux Klan.

Following the lynching and in a new era of prejudice, approximately half of Georgia's three thousand Jews left the state.[64] The number did not include Frank's widow, Lucille, who returned from the funeral in New York to live quietly in Atlanta, where her husband's wedding ring, delivered as promised, awaited her. She worked the glove counter of the J. P. Allen store until her death in April of 1957, and never discussed the case publicly.

Conley's lawyer, William Smith, who had fought so hard to save Frank, no longer was able to practice law in Georgia. He went to work in a shipyard, then found employment in a detective agency in New York City. Five years later he passed the New York bar and started over.[65] Jim Conley went from celebrated Negro to oft-convicted drunk, disappearing from public records in 1941. There is no record of his death or burial.[66]

Prosecutor Hugh Dorsey became the next governor of Georgia, serving two terms, after which he sat as a state court judge until his death in 1948.

Tom Watson, who had called for and then celebrated the lynching of Leo Frank in the pages of the *Jeffersonian*, continued to influence public opinion in Georgia, and to profit from it. Circulation of the *Jeffersonian*, at five cents a copy, rose from 25,000 in March of 1914 to 87,000 in September of 1915. He was elected US senator in 1920 and Georgia governor the following year.

In 1982, eighty-five-year-old Alonzo Mann, Frank's one-time office boy, gave his deposition to lawyer John J. Hooker. He told the truth for the first time. On that Saturday morning, nearly seventy years before, he had walked into the National Pencil Company and seen Jim Conley, by himself, carrying the unconscious Mary Phagan. The sweeper threatened to kill him if he told anyone. Mann had, nonetheless, told his parents, and they had instructed him to say nothing about it. Thus he had kept his secret when interviewed by the police and when called to testify at Frank's trial.

In 1983 the Georgia State Board of Pardons and Paroles granted a pardon to Leo Frank. In its decision the board explained,

> Without attempting to address the question of guilt or inno-
> cence, and in recognition of the State's failure to protect the
> person of Leo M. Frank and thereby preserve his opportunity
> for continued legal appeal of his conviction, and in recogni-
> tion of the State's failure to bring his killers to justice, and as
> an effort to heal old wounds, the State Board of Pardons and
> Paroles, in compliance with its Constitutional and statutory
> authority, hereby grants to Leo M. Frank a Pardon.

The site of Frank's lynching at Frey's Gin has disappeared, buried beneath the concrete of Interstate 75 on its modern route north from Atlanta. Writes author Steve Oney,

> The ghosts still clamor to be heard and the trial refuses to
> end and the sons refight their fathers' battles and like a trans-
> figuring scar, the events that made up the saga have grown
> ever more vivid. Many swear that they know why this is so,
> and they speak of Jews and injustice and the vengeful magis-
> trate—Judge Lynch—who presided at the end. These argu-

ments all have their merits, but they ignore the conflicts that was there to begin with, the conflict between the future and the past that was dramatized so audaciously on April 26, 1913, the conflict that transformed murder into myth.[67]

CHAPTER 3

1920–1930:
"Fatty" Arbuckle and
the Dead Actress

The French called it "The Crazy Years" for the extraordinary social, economic, and artistic changes that occurred. The British called it "The Golden Age Twenties" for its years of economic boom. In America, it was the "The Roaring Twenties," and it was the decade in which the twentieth century came of age. The twenties brought peace and prosperity to most and a sense of social evolution. Charles Lindbergh piloted the *Spirit of St. Louis* from New York to Paris. Baseball was America's pastime and Babe Ruth its unquestioned king. Prohibition did little to slow the party atmosphere of jazz, flappers, and excess, which roared unabated until the stock market crash of October 1929. And above all, America went to the movies.

In 1921, Roscoe "Fatty" Arbuckle was the highest-paid film star in Hollywood. King of the two-reel comedies, he was beloved by millions for his pratfalls, his pie fights, and his innocent, angelic smile. Studios churned his movies out by the score, and excited ticket buyers across the country stood in line to watch them.

But all that came to an end on September 5, 1921. Coming off a punishing year-long schedule of back-to-back filming, Arbuckle drove with friends to San Francisco for rest and relaxation over the Labor Day weekend. Prohibition was in full swing, but liquor was available to those who could afford it, and Arbuckle certainly could. That weekend, after a drunken revel in his suite at the St. Francis Hotel, Arbuckle was wrongfully charged in the rape and death of bit-part actress Virginia Rappe. Rumors swirled of his callousness, brutishness, and sexual deviation, none of it true. Caught in a firestorm of ambitious politicians, rapacious studio owners, social reformers, and newspaper publishers, Arbuckle was tried in both the courts and the press. Three trials later he was acquitted, but the damage was done. He was blacklisted, financially ruined, and one of the most-reviled men in America.

Just thirty-four, his rise and fall in the world had been dizzying from every perspective. Born March 24, 1887, Arbuckle was one of five children in a poor farming family in Smith Center, Kansas. His father, William, presumed him to be the product of his wife's infidelity, and in revenge and derision he named him Roscoe Conkling Arbuckle, after controversial New York senator Roscoe Conkling, a notorious womanizer and a power broker in the unconventional election of Rutherford B. Hayes in 1876.[1]

Arbuckle's movie success was neither chance nor favor, but rather the result of talent and many years of hard work. His family had packed up their few worldly goods and trekked west by 1892, living in a rundown home in Santa Ana, California. That winter, Arbuckle's father walked out on the family. All of the Arbuckle children went to work, including five-year-old Roscoe. He dropped out of school at seven and began working in bars and vaudeville theaters until his mother's death in 1899, when he was packed off to his father, then living in San Jose.[2]

But his father never appeared at the station to pick him up. Twelve years old and with no family, friends, or money, Arbuckle found a job at a local hotel as a bell hop and janitor. He was big, even then 185 pounds, and people thought him older.

Roscoe "Fatty" Arbuckle. From the Library of Congress.

His first taste of show business came early. Arbuckle was in the habit of singing while he worked, and a hotel patron overheard him and invited him to perform in an amateur talent show at the Empire Theater in San Jose. The show consisted of the audience judging acts by clapping or jeering, with the worst of the performers pulled offstage by a large hook. Arbuckle's singing did not impress the audience, and they screamed for his removal. Light on his feet despite his size, when he saw the hook emerge from the wings he avoided it by dodging and dancing, eventually somersaulting into the orchestra pit. The audience loved it, and that night Arbuckle not only won the competition but began a career in vaudeville.[3]

In the spring of 1902, fifteen-year-old Arbuckle was offered a permanent job by David Grauman at his Unique Theater in San Jose, earning the then-decent salary of eighteen dollars per week. Grauman, father of impresario Sid Grauman who would go on to build the opulent Chinese and Egyptian motion-picture palaces in Hollywood, had followed Arbuckle's local performances and had privately encouraged him to continue to hone his singing and dancing skills.[4] Arbuckle stayed with Grauman for nearly two years, opening each night's show by singing, and filling in after with small acting parts. In 1904, Grauman moved Arbuckle to the Portola Café in San Francisco, which featured singing waiters and was evidently an improvement over small-town vaudeville. It was there that Grauman introduced Arbuckle to Alexander Pantages, the grand showman of the early-twentieth-century American stage, and the young singer soon joined Pantages's traveling troupe.[5]

What followed for Arbuckle were several years of extensive touring, initially for Pantages but eventually on his own with ever-changing acts and partners. His salary increased to fifty dollars per week, and he was no longer required to clean and sweep between shows. Arbuckle was a talented performer, capable of broad slapstick physical humor, dancing, and prat-falls. His humor and charm were popular with audiences. He played parts of every ethnicity and age. One night when the only female member of the troupe could not be found, Arbuckle went on in her place, dressed in her complete costume, wig, and makeup. Weighing in at 250 pounds and in an outfit padded where appropriate, he brought the house down, and his female character became a standard. Reteamed with Pan-tages, Arbuckle toured California, Canada, and Alaska.[6]

In 1908, now married to fellow tour member Araminta "Minta" Durfee, Arbuckle took the acting company to El Paso, Texas, where the picnicking troupe found themselves sur-rounded one afternoon by soldiers of Mexican revolutionary Pancho Villa. Arbuckle and Villa introduced themselves and, in a moment of sublime historical mischance, began in fun throwing fruit pies at each other.[7] When Arbuckle later introduced the gag in early films, the pie fight became a mainstay for him and scores of other comedians who adopted and perfected it.[8]

Arbuckle began his film career with Selig Polyscope Company in July 1909, appearing in *Ben's Kid.* The one-reeler, lasting approximately ten minutes, earned Arbuckle five dollars. Movie actors were held in low regard in 1909, often barred from rooming houses and stores, and certainly not accepted into polite society. To act in films was considered by many an admission of failure as a stage performer, but Arbuckle needed the money to support himself and Minta. He worked sporadically for Selig until he finally landed a permanent job with Keystone Studios, the seminal early movie studio in Los Angeles founded by Mack Sennett. Between 1912 and 1917, many Hollywood stars got their start at Keystone, including Charlie Chaplin, Harold Lloyd, Gloria Swanson, Mabel Normand, and Harry Langdon. Sennett, the son of Irish Catholic Canadian farmers, had an unerring feel for comedy, and his Keystone Kops, anchored at one end by the sizable girth of Arbuckle, have entered the American lexicon as any group that mismanages its affairs despite an excess of energy and activity. So recognizable were the disaster-prone Kops with their tall, British helmets that police departments throughout the United States quickly abandoned the headgear in favor of military-style officers' caps.[9]

Paired in films in 1914 with actress Mabel Normand, Arbuckle moved to Paramount Pictures for the then-unheard-of offer of $1,000 a day plus 25 percent of all profits and complete artistic control. The movies they made, primarily twenty-minute two-reelers, were so popular that Paramount signed Arbuckle to an unprecedented three-year, three-million-dollar contract, making him the highest-paid movie actor of his day.[10]

But by 1916, Arbuckle's weight and heavy drinking were impacting his health. Then age thirty, he tipped the scales at more than 300 pounds. Wherever he went he was known as "Fatty," and that nickname appeared everywhere: in articles, movie posters, and product promotions. But it was only a screen name, and Arbuckle never used it himself nor did his friends use it in conversations with him. He disliked anyone addressing him as "Fatty" in public, and when they did he responded, "I have a name, you know."[11]

His marriage to Minta cooled, and by 1916 they were separated, with Minta living in New York.[12] Though Arbuckle certainly lived the life of a visible and highly paid motion-picture actor, tales of a promiscuous and dissolute lifestyle are probably inaccurate. His much-discussed relationship with perennial costar Mabel Normand was close but not sexual. She was involved in her own stormy relationship with Mack Sennett, and Arbuckle once saved her life by taking her to a hospital after she was struck in the head with a vase in a particularly nasty episode in the Sennett home.[13]

Other rumors of his sexual excesses were similarly false. In 1917, Arbuckle went on a long promotional tour for the Paramount film *Mickey*, stopping at every major city across the United States and concluding in New York. Before the tour formally ended, a banquet hosted by Paramount was held in Boston at which an exhausted Arbuckle made a short appearance and then returned to his hotel to sleep. Unknown to him, Paramount executives left the reception to party at Mishawum Manor, a brothel in Woburn, Massachusetts. Many of the prostitutes were minors, and the scandal hit the national papers. The reputation of the studio and many of those present, including Adolph Zukor, Hiram Abrams, and Jesse Lasky, suffered in the reporting. The Paramount executives denied their own personal involvement but took no steps to make clear that Arbuckle had not attended.[14]

By the summer of 1921, Arbuckle was at the height of his success and popularity. His two-reel comedies played in every city and small town in America. He had paid the then-enormous sum of $250,000 to purchase the Theda Bara mansion on West Adams Boulevard in Los Angeles,[15] with another mansion for relaxation some twenty miles south on Ocean Avenue in Long Beach. Both homes were opulently furnished with antiques at a cost of hundreds of thousands of dollars, mostly bought on credit. He entertained often, spent freely, and saved nothing. He employed a butler and a chauffeur. He kept six cars, including a Rolls Royce.[16] In early September 1921, he bought a custom-built Pierce-Arrow touring car four times the size of an average car. Arbuckle told interviewers, "Of course my car is four times the size of anyone else's. I am four times as big as the average guy!"[17] At $25,000, the car cost one hundred times the average American's annual salary.

These excesses of Hollywood stirred the passions of the national press and caught the attention of politicians. Newspapers, particularly the Hearst dailies, ran editorials critical of movie actors, and calls came from many directions for the industry to police itself. It was in this charged environment that Arbuckle, exhausted from his work schedule, announced an "open" party at the St. Francis Hotel, loaded his Pierce-Arrow with supplies, and headed north to San Francisco.

Arbuckle left Los Angeles on Saturday morning, September 3, accompanied by his friends, actor Lowell Sherman and director Fred Fischbach. According to Arbuckle, they arrived in San Francisco late that afternoon, checked into the St. Francis, and after an early dinner went to bed.[18] The St. Francis was, even then, legendary for its luxury and clientele. Built in 1904 by the Crocker heirs, one of California's wealthiest families, during the 1920s it was the fashionable place to stay for politicians, celebrities, and film actors.

Arbuckle took three adjoining rooms: 1219 for himself and Fischbach, 1221 for Sherman, and the middle room, 1220, from which the bed had been removed, as the party room. Rooms 1219 and 1221 each had its own bathroom, but not 1220, which was only rented by the hotel as an adjoining room for either 1219 or 1221 to make a suite.

On Sunday, September 4, the three men did some sightseeing and visited friends across the bay.[19]

The following day was Monday, September 5, and the national holiday. Beginning in the morning, Arbuckle's suite began to fill with friends, and witnesses estimate that anywhere between fifteen and twenty people dropped by at various times throughout the day. Among them was a curious trio invited by Fischbach: petty criminal Maude Delmont, who described herself as a model, twenty-five-year-old bit-part actress Virginia Rappe, and

Rappe's manager, Al Semnacher. Arbuckle had never met any of them except in passing, and there is some dispute about what they were doing in San Francisco that weekend, but according to witnesses familiar with the individuals the young actress was in San Francisco to have an abortion.[20]

Young Virginia Rappe's brush with history is limited solely to the events of that day in Arbuckle's suite at the St. Francis. Born Virginia Rapp, she added the "e" to her last name because it sounded more elegant. According to interviews given after her death by her grandmother, Rappe was born out of wedlock following an affair between her mother, Mabel, and an English nobleman visiting Chicago where she lived. In an era where illegitimacy was still frowned upon, the pregnant Mabel moved to New York where her daughter was born, and where Mabel died eleven years later. Young Rappe then returned to Chicago to be raised by her grandmother.[21]

Growing up she was indiscriminate in her relationships. She had at least five abortions by the age of sixteen, and at age seventeen gave birth to an out-of-wedlock child, which she placed into foster care. Her good looks led to a modeling career in her teens, and she moved to San Francisco where she pursued that work. She was engaged to a dress designer named Robert Moscovitz, but he was killed in a trolley accident before their wedding. Distraught and in financial straits, Rappe moved to Los Angeles where she took a room with an aunt.[22]

In 1917, Rappe met and began dating Keystone Kops director Henry Lehrman, and he helped her find the roles in her four credited films, although it is likely that she supported herself by prostitution.[23] Rappe's stormy relationship with Lehrman was well-known in Hollywood and unpopular. The two were accused of spreading venereal disease and lice, and Mack Sennett once ordered them off the Keystone lot and had it fumigated.[24] Some people close to Rappe believed that in September 1921 she was pregnant by Lehrman and heading to San Francisco that Labor Day weekend to abort his child.[25]

Maude Delmont was a different kettle of fish entirely. Of uncertain age, her photo reveals her to be a woman of middle age with a dour expression. Using a string of aliases, she had an extensive police record, with at least fifty charges filed against her on crimes ranging from bigamy to extortion. She has been described as a professional corespondent, a woman hired to provide compromising photos or evidence in divorces.[26] How she met Semnacher is a matter of conjecture, but just the month before he had filed in San Francisco for divorce from his wife, and he admitted to having hired Delmont to obtain evidence of his wife's adultery. Delmont met Semnacher at his Hollywood home on Saturday, September 3, where she was introduced to Rappe, and the three drove north to San Francisco.

By midmorning on Monday, September 5, the party in Arbuckle's suite was in full swing. There was food, bootleg liquor, music and dancing, and a stream of guests coming and going. Fischbach, who had invited Semnacher, Delmont, and Rappe to the party, left to give someone a ride. Delmont retired with Sherman to his bedroom, evidently to have sex, leaving Arbuckle, Rappe, and the other guests in the party room. Rappe became extremely drunk, then inexplicably erupted into hysterics and ran through the suite ripping at her clothes. Startled witnesses believed she had been accidently kneed in the abdomen by Arbuckle while dancing.[27] When Arbuckle later attempted to use the bathroom in his room, the door was blocked. When he finally opened it sufficiently to allow him to enter, he found Rappe on her knees vomiting into the toilet. She was crying with pain, and he carried her to his bed in room 1219 for her to lie down. She continued to tear at her clothes.

Arbuckle left the bedroom and re-entered the party room to get some ice, believing, he later testified, that it would calm her down. He placed several pieces of ice on her stomach and held one against her thigh. When Delmont next entered the room she found Rappe disheveled and screaming, with Roscoe leaning over her. The clamor brought other guests into the room, including actresses Zey Prevon and Alice Blake, along with Fischbach who had returned from his errand. Delmont ordered those present to fill the bathtub with cold water to cool Rappe's fever. As Fischbach carried her, the young actress screamed at Arbuckle, "Stay away from me! I don't want you near me!"[28]

The cold bath apparently calmed Rappe down. Arbuckle and Fischbach located a vacant room, 1227, down the hall and took her there to lie down, Delmont following to keep an eye on her. Arbuckle phoned the hotel manager and asked for the physician on call, but he was busy with other guests. Eventually a Dr. Olav Kaarboe examined Rappe and determined that she was simply suffering from too much to drink.[29]

The party continued without Delmont or Rappe for the rest of the afternoon in high spirits, and with no other incidents. Arbuckle left for a few hours to make arrangements to ship the Pierce-Arrow back to Los Angeles, and when he returned to the hotel the primary hotel physician, Dr. Beardslee, had just arrived at room 1227 to examine Virginia. She was screaming again, and Dr. Beardslee gave her an injection of morphine.

The next day, Tuesday, September 6, Rappe was no better. Dr. Beardslee checked on her four times during the day and gave her additional injections of morphine. Convinced now that the pain in her abdomen was not the fault of too much drink, he inserted a catheter to drain her bladder. Delmont, who had taken over the supervision of Rappe, summoned another doctor, Melville Rumwell, a physician associated with the local Wakefield sanitarium. This was an unusual selection but perhaps telling, as Dr. Rumwell was a specialist in maternity, and Wakefield an institution with a reputation for performing abortions.[30]

Delmont now began telling people that Rappe's injuries were the result of a sexual assault by Arbuckle. Both Beardslee and Rumwell ignored Delmont's accusations, either because they were inconsistent with Rappe's injuries, or in the case of Rumwell because he knew differently. That afternoon, Arbuckle, Fischbach, and Sherman checked out of the St. Francis, Arbuckle picking up the tab for the entire weekend, including the bill for room 1227. They boarded the ferry *Harvard* for the trip south to Los Angeles. On Wednesday, September 7, Arbuckle returned to work.

Back in San Francisco, Rappe's condition continued to deteriorate. She was moved to the Wakefield sanitarium on Thursday afternoon. By then she was delirious with a high fever, her abdomen was distended, and Rumwell diagnosed her as suffering from peritonitis, an acute infection caused by a ruptured bladder. He felt her condition too delicate for an operation, and she died in the early afternoon of Friday, September 9.

In an unusual turn of events, Rumwell called in Dr. William Ophuls, a Stanford University professor in pathology, to assist in a postmortem examination. They performed an illegal autopsy without the consent of the coroner's office, removing and later destroying the bladder, uterus, rectum, and fallopian tubes.[31] With its reputation as an illicit abortion clinic, gossip suggested that Rappe had had her abortion at the clinic the day before the party, and that Rumwell had removed and disposed of her organs to destroy any evidence that her death was somehow a consequence of that operation.

After Rappe's death, Maude Delmont contacted the San Francisco Police Department and swore out a complaint against Arbuckle, swearing that he had dragged Rappe into his bedroom and raped her, either personally or with a Coca-Cola bottle, and that her death was the result of his assault.

The newspapers picked up the story immediately, with the first articles appearing on Saturday, September 10.[32]

Arbuckle did not even know that Rappe had died until two men from the San Francisco sheriff's office knocked on the door of his West Adams home and summoned him to San Francisco for questioning. Early Saturday morning, Arbuckle returned to San Francisco with an attorney, Frank Dominguez, and reported to the Hall of Justice, where he was questioned for three hours. Dominguez believed the matter of Rappe's death would be dispensed with easily and in due course, but was concerned about the consequences of Arbuckle's possession of bootleg liquor in contravention of the Volstead Act. He advised Arbuckle to remain silent. His concerns were seriously misplaced, and at about midnight that night, Saturday, September 10, Arbuckle was arrested and charged with first-degree murder.[33]

He spent the next eighteen days in jail, a celebrity even incarcerated, until the charges were reduced to manslaughter and bail was granted on September 28.[34]

That Arbuckle came to find himself in this fight for his life was the result of several colliding forces. First, Delmont's inexplicable fabrication of the assault on Rappe, given in the form of a sworn affidavit, could not be easily explained away or ignored by the authorities. Second, the new district attorney in San Francisco was forty-six-year-old Matthew Brady, a politically connected and ambitious lawyer now in his second year as prosecutor. Brady, despite his reservations about the quality of his complaining witness, saw the prosecution of Arbuckle as a stepping-stone to higher office. Finally, and importantly, the immediate focus of both the local and national Hearst papers was overwhelming and uniformly biased against Arbuckle.[35]

The coverage was all-pervasive. Beginning Monday, September 12, the Hearst dailies ran sensational front-page headlines every day. Those of Hearst's *Washington Times*, for example, splashed across six columns for each day that week, started with "Arbuckle's Wife Rushes to Aid" on September 12, and grew progressively more negative. On September 13 the headline read "Arbuckle Indictment Held Up," followed by "Fatty Faces Coroner's Jury,"[36] "Arbuckle Ready to Give Bail—Orgy Girl Offered Bribe to Keep Mum,"[37] and "Movieland Liquor Probe Started—40 Quarts Killed At Fatty's Big Party."[38] In the nation's capital where Hearst owned two dailies, the *Washington Herald* ran similar articles on Arbuckle every day.

So did papers all over the United States. Coverage in the *New York Tribune*, founded by Horace Greeley in 1841, was nearly continuous, as it was in papers across America. While some reporting was relatively balanced, this was the age of yellow journalism, and much of the content pilloried Arbuckle. On September 13, for example, the *Tulsa Daily World*, not a Hearst daily, ran a front-page headline that read "Fatty, Movie's Falstaff, Falls from Film Throne As Evidence Web Tightens."[39]

This kind of reporting was typical. The film star was routinely referred to as "Arbuckle" or "Fatty," while Rappe was always "Miss Rappe." The *San Francisco Examiner* ran an editorial cartoon featuring Arbuckle with liquor bottles in the middle of a giant spiderweb and seven women caught in the web.[40] On September 13, the *Washington Times* carried a Keystone photo of Arbuckle under the headline "Silly Mr. Arbuckle in Idiotic Pose," and captioned "Roscoe ('Fatty') Arbuckle, star of 'The Life of the Party,' as he appeared in one of his extremely foolish films."[41] On the same page a picture of Rappe under the headline "Miss Rappe Dressed for Afternoon Walk" shows her stylishly dressed and carried the caption "The picture of the dead actress in sporty street attire. She was considered the best dressed woman on the movie screen."[42]

On September 14, the *Washington Times* late edition carried dueling headlines, "Lead Quiet Life, Victim's Last Advice to Girls" and "Arbuckle's Fat and Rum Blamed By Psychoanalysts," with the article beginning, "If Roscoe Arbuckle committed the crime of which he is charged, he did it because he is fat."[43]

In contrast, prosecutor Matthew Brady was widely championed by the press. On September 16, the *Washington Times* late edition read,

> Lionized by a city to whose service he has given a greater portion of his life Brady is preparing for the biggest battle of his history. "I will get the truth." Behind these words of the district attorney there is a force at play, mighty and strong and irresistible.[44]

Between his release from jail in late September and the beginning of the trial in mid-November, Arbuckle withdrew from public view. His work for Paramount was suspended pending the hearing, and he made no public statements on advice of his attorney. He lived quietly with Minta in his West Adams house, while his attorneys prepared for what was going to be one of the most visible celebrity trials in history.

That trial commenced before the superior court judge Harold Louderback on Monday, November 14 with the voir dire of jurors. Arbuckle was now represented by attorney Gavin McNab, well-known for representing Hollywood celebrities and highly regarded in San Francisco politics, along with a team of four other respected attorneys. Matthew Brady was assisted by Milton U'Ren and Leo Friedman. After five days of questioning, a jury of seven men and five women was empaneled.[45]

Brady was working with weakening evidence and recalcitrant witnesses. Actresses Prevon and Blake had both been interviewed by the police immediately after Rappe's death, and had initially backed Delmont's story. While neither could say that they had seen Arbuckle personally assault Rappe, they did testify that the two had been alone in his room together for at least half an hour, and when Delmont attempted entrance the door was locked, facts that all of the men at the party had denied. They had both previously stated that they had heard Rappe accuse Arbuckle of assaulting her. But early on Prevon had recanted her testimony and refused to sign her statement.[46] At the coroner's inquest, she changed other parts of her testimony, denying that Rappe had named Arbuckle as her assailant. When Blake tried to do the same, Brady threatened both with perjury and confined them in protective custody until the trial started to prevent the defense from interviewing them.

But Brady's most difficult challenge was Maude Delmont. The charges were based largely on her claims, but not only was she a lifelong criminal, she had changed her story so many times that by the time the trial commenced both sides knew that she was a liar as well. Brady had elicited her damning testimony at the earlier inquests, and to make sure her testimony would not be contradicted by the defense at trial, he had her jailed on bigamy charges and refused to release her to testify. Defense requests to call her to the stand were turned down by the court.[47]

The prosecution called as its first witness Grace Halston, a nurse at the Wakefield sanitarium. She testified that Rappe's body was covered with bruises, and she had found numerous organ ruptures and that the injuries were caused by force. On cross-examination the defense elicited her testimony that the injuries could have been the result of natural causes.

Dr. Arthur Beardslee testified for the prosecution about the actress's injuries, which he also believed to have been inflicted by an outside force.

On Monday, November 21, the prosecution called Betty Campbell, a model who testified that she was a guest of the party at the St. Francis. She had arrived an hour after the incident and found Arbuckle, Sherman, Fischbach, Semnacher, and Prevon relaxing in the suite. Brady offered this to show that Arbuckle exhibited neither remorse nor concern for the condition of Rappe. On cross-examination, Campbell testified that Brady had threatened her with prison if she refused to testify against Arbuckle, and McNab presented sworn affidavits obtained from Campbell, Blake, and Prevon backing up claims of Brady's intimidation tactics.[48]

Brady was ordered by the court to bring Prevon to the stand to testify, and when she finally did so she informed the court that she was still being held a prisoner by the district attorney and had been repeatedly interrogated by Brady and his staff. She claimed that Brady kept insisting she sign a statement that Rappe had said, "He has killed me," even though she had already told the grand jury she was mistaken when she first made that statement and that it was not true.[49]

Prevon recounted to the jury the events leading up to Rappe's collapse, testifying only that the actress had said, "He hurt me," which could have referred to Fischbach manhandling her into the ice bath, or to the rumored abortion. Called next, Alice Blake reiterated Prevon's story. Neither actress testified that Rappe had accused Arbuckle of causing any injuries.[50]

Prosecution witnesses to follow included a studio security guard who testified to Arbuckle's having met Rappe two years before in 1919, a hotel chambermaid who testified to the rowdy nature of the St. Francis party, and a criminologist who testified that Arbuckle's fingerprints on the inside of his bedroom door obscured those of Rappe, suggesting that Rappe had struggled to open the door and that Arbuckle had forced it closed.[51]

The defense opened its case on Tuesday, November 22. Medical witnesses were called to demonstrate that Rappe's ruptured bladder could have been the result of disease. Three witnesses testified that they had witnessed Rappe on prior occasions drink to excess and run about tearing at her clothes, even running naked in the streets. Fischbach testified that Rappe had been his guest at the party, but witnessed nothing that could have caused her injuries or death.

Arbuckle was the final witness in his defense. His testimony was described as calm, lasting four hours. He recounted the events of the party and how he found Rappe on the floor of his bathroom in front of the toilet, carried her into room 1219, and put her on the bed. He described her distress, the screaming, and the tearing at her garments. He testified that it was Delmont who put the ice on Rappe and Fischbach who had carried her into the bathroom for her ice bath.[52]

The cross-examination was carried out by Assistant District Attorney Leo Friedman. He retraced Arbuckle's testimony but was unable to find chinks in his defense. It was clear that if a crime had been committed, no one had seen it and there was no physical evidence that pointed to Arbuckle.

Rebuttal witnesses were called, including medical experts, but the prosecution was unable to demonstrate that the rupture of Rappe's bladder was the result of external force.

Maude Delmont, with her black past and her shifting story, was never called as a witness.

Both sides made closing arguments, the defense portraying Arbuckle as a kind man who had sweetened the lives of millions of little children, and who was now needlessly suffering when no crime had been committed, and the prosecution calling the same defendant a "modern-day belshazzar and a moral leper" with whom no woman in America was safe.[53]

The jury retired for deliberation. After forty-one hours and twenty-two ballots, hopelessly deadlocked, the jury returned on December 4, unable to reach a verdict at 10–2 for acquittal.[54]

Arbuckle continued to protest his innocence. On December 31, he told *Movie Weekly*:

> The undisputed and uncontradicted testimony established that my only connection with this sad affair was one of merciful service, and the fact that ordinary human kindness should have brought upon me this tragedy has seemed a cruel wrong. I have sought to bring joy and gladness and merriment into the world, and why this great misfortune should have fallen upon me is a mystery that only God can, and will, some day reveal.[55]

A second trial commenced on January 11, 1922, before a new jury, again featuring Brady for the prosecution and McNab for the defense. Many of the same witnesses testified, and buoyed by his near success in the first trial McNab chose not to have Roscoe testify, focusing instead on a parade of witnesses who trashed Rappe's reputation. The strategy backfired, with nearly disastrous results. After two days of deliberation, the jury returned deadlocked again, but this time 10–2 for conviction.[56]

The third and final trial commenced on March 6, 1922. After the near-scare of the second jury, this time McNab left no stone unturned, carefully detailing both Rappe's sordid past and calling Arbuckle to testify in his own defense. After five weeks and only six witnesses called by the exhausted prosecution, the jury retired to deliberate on April 12.

It returned in less than five minutes. Not only did it vote unanimously for an acquittal, it took the few minutes behind closed doors to craft a written apology to Arbuckle, which it handed to the court. The jurors wrote,

> Acquittal is not enough for Roscoe Arbuckle. We feel that a great injustice has been done him. We feel also that it was only our plain duty to give him this exoneration, under the evidence, for there was not the slightest proof adduced to connect him in any way with the commission of a crime.
>
> We wish him success, and hope that the American people will take the judgment of fourteen men and women who have sat listening for thirty-one days to evidence, that Roscoe Arbuckle is entirely innocent and free from all blame.[57]

But the verdict of a single San Francisco jury, even one motivated to the extraordinary gesture of penning a written apology to the defendant, was not enough to save Arbuckle's career. Within a week of the death of Virginia Rappe, exhibitors in every city in America had withdrawn Arbuckle's films, and those that had been completed and ready for distribution were never released. His record-setting three-year three-million-dollar contract was canceled. The day after Arbuckle had been freed on bond pending the first trial, he received a telegram stating that he was in breach of his contract with Paramount and suspended until cleared. Throughout the early fall of 1921, spontaneous women's groups gathered to protest in front of any theater showing his films to shout at patrons who entered. Although the studio paid for much of his legal defense, without the ability to work Arbuckle was financially ruined.[58]

Delmont's part in Hollywood's history was also played out. Why she set the destructive storm in motion with her criminal complaint against Arbuckle is unknown. She had a history of procuring young women as party guests, then blackmailing wealthy men into silence, and perhaps she saw the opportunity to make some money. She is reputed in 1921 to have sent telegrams to attorneys in both San Diego and Los Angeles stating, "We have Roscoe Arbuckle in a hole here. Chance to make some money out of him."[59] "I believe that the whole trouble started," Minta Arbuckle wrote on Christmas Eve in 1921, "when someone who thought that Mr. Arbuckle would be an 'easy mark' . . . seized on Miss Rappe's death as the reason for wild statements and unfounded charges. It is difficult to discuss that point without making direct accusations, and that I prefer not to do. . . ."[60] Delmont disappears from the record after 1921.

Fueled by newspaper coverage, the groundswell of negative publicity continued to build. Amid a Hollywood lifestyle considered by most Americans to be out of control, Arbuckle was only the most visible example. In early 1922, other scandals set the newspaper presses running. On February 2, 1922, while the second trial was underway in San Francisco, prolific actor and Paramount director William Desmond Taylor was found murdered. His body was discovered inside his bungalow on Alvarado Street in the Westlake Park area near downtown Los Angeles, then a trendy and affluent neighborhood. He had been shot in the back. Numerous suspects were identified by both the police and the newspapers, including workers in his home, neighbors, employees of Paramount, women with whom he had rumored romantic liaisons, and Arbuckle's friend and costar actress Mabel Normand, but the crime was never solved. When word of Taylor's death was brought to Arbuckle as he sat at the counsel table awaiting the second jury's verdict in San Francisco, his eyes filled with tears.[61] In March, papers reported that movie heartthrob and Paramount star Wallace Reid was undergoing treatment for drug addiction. His treatment was unsuccessful, and he was dead within a year.

These scandals, along with the Arbuckle trials, led to the creation in 1922 of the Motion Picture Producers and Distributors of America, known as the Hays Office, under the dictatorial sway of Presbyterian elder and former postmaster general, Will Hays. Just as Major League Baseball hired Judge Kenesaw Mountain Landis as commissioner in 1921 to quell questions about the integrity of the sport following the 1919 World Series Black Sox scandal, so the movie industry the next year formed the Hays Office to deal with public backlash against a trail of broken lives and disgrace that threatened the young industry. One of Hays's first moves was to blacklist Roscoe Arbuckle, prohibiting him from working in films. After consultation with Hays, Adolph Zukor and Jesse Lasky canceled the distribution and showings of all of Arbuckle's films in April 1922. Although the ban was lifted eight months later in December 1922,[62] his career was finished.

Not everyone was sorry. William Jennings Bryan, devout Christian, perennial presidential candidate, and a chief proponent of Prohibition, wrote to Hays,

> His [Arbuckle's] acquittal only relieved him of the penalty that attaches to a crime. The evidence showed a depravity entirely independent of the question of actual murder. As long as his character must be measured by such orgies as that in which he played the leading part, there is no reason why he should be given another chance.[63]

The best of his friends stood by, including Buster Keaton, Al St. John, and his agent, Joe Schenck. When he couldn't act, he found some work directing. He couldn't use his own name, so he took credit as William Goodrich, his father's first two names. Keaton called him Will B. Good. Surprisingly, one of the directing jobs offered him was *The Red Mill*, bankrolled by

William Randolph Hearst to feature his companion, Marion Davies. The experience was a disaster for Arbuckle, and the film a box-office flop. Arbuckle did a little live performing on stage for Alexander Pantages, who had given him work when he was an unknown comic. In many places citizens objected to his appearances, forgetting the acquittal and remembering only the rumors of sexual depravity, and battles took place in city councils about whether he should be allowed to perform.[64]

In 1925, Minta, from whom he had been separated for nine years, divorced him.

He married twice more. In 1925 he wed actress Doris Deane, who he met for the first time on the fateful ferry ride home from San Francisco on September 6, 1921. He met her again during a stint doing an unaccredited cameo role for a feature called *Hollywood*, a send-up of the movie business in which dozens of famous Hollywood stars had cameos, including Charlie Chaplin, Cecil B. DeMille, Douglas Fairbanks, William S. Hart, Mary Pickford, and Will Rogers. The marriage was short-lived, exacerbated perhaps by Arbuckle's heavy drinking. They divorced four years later in 1929. He married again in 1933, wedding actress Addie Oakley Dukes McPhail, then twenty-six.[65]

Over the ten years that followed his acquittal, Arbuckle had small uncredited roles in only four films. He finally had an opportunity to return to pictures under his own name, appearing in six two-reelers between February 1932 and June 1933, but his art and style had not kept up with the public's taste. His broadly comic slapstick shorts were old-fashioned and forgettable in an industry now producing highbrow, full-length features. By contrast, in 1932 the Oscar-winning best film was *Grand Hotel*, the stylish period piece starring Greta Garbo, John Barrymore, and Joan Crawford. In 1933, movie audiences had a choice of Busby Berkeley's spectacular *42nd Street*, *A Farewell to Arms* starring Gary Cooper and Helen Hayes, and the comedy *She Done Him Wrong* with Mae West and Cary Grant. Katherine Hepburn won her first Best Actress Academy Award that year. Arbuckle's two-reelers simply didn't measure up, and it was clear that both his fans and his culture had abandoned him.

After a high-spirited dinner on June 29, 1933, to celebrate a just-received offer to appear in a feature-length film for Warner Brothers, Arbuckle and Addie returned to the Central Park Hotel at Fifty-Fifth Street and Seventh Avenue in Manhattan and went to bed. Arbuckle died in his sleep. He was forty-six.[66]

His films now largely unwatched, America has forgotten Arbuckle, once its darling. A century of innovation, from silent to sound, short to feature-length, black-and-white to color, faltering nitrate to sophisticated computer graphics, has relegated Arbuckle and his contributions to the back drawer of history. Scholars and critics may know him, but most Americans today will barely recognize his name, and those who do remember only vaguely the rape and rumored coke bottle, the legacy, obituary really, written for Arbuckle in the newspapers in the fall of 1921 when he was still a household name. Few in America have fallen so far or so fast. And few profited from that fall, except perhaps William Randolph Hearst, who once boasted to Buster Keaton that the Arbuckle trial sold more of his newspapers than the sinking of the Lusitania.[67]

"The sentiment of every church on Christmas Day," Arbuckle had written the December following his acquittal, "will be peace on earth and good will toward all mankind. What will be the attitude the day after Christmas to me?"[68]

CHAPTER 4

1930–1940:
Bruno Hauptmann and
the Lindbergh Baby

T he 1920s had been a decade of unbridled optimism, full of rapid economic growth, technological advancement, and unrestrained progress and productivity. Americans had flocked to movie theaters to see "talkies" and bought Ford Model Ts for the affordable price of $290 per car.[1] Patriotism had been at an all-time high after America's strong showing in the First World War.

But the stock market crash of 1929 and the Great Depression that followed ushered in a new and sober period for the country. The 1930s were a dark time for Americans, marked by unemployment, poverty, suicide, alcoholism, and crime. The man on the street was looking for distractions, and found it in Charles Lindbergh, world-famous aviator and inspiration to millions of Americans.

It was in this setting on a quiet spring night in 1932 that Charles Lindbergh was enjoying a relaxing evening with his wife, Anne, at their bucolic New Jersey estate. At some point during the evening, perhaps while they were eating dinner or chatting lightheartedly in the living room, their sleeping son, only twenty months old, was plucked from his crib in an upstairs nursery by a kidnapper who had ascended a homemade ladder and entered through an unlocked window. No one, not Charles nor Anne nor any of their domestic servants, heard the baby cry out nor did the family fox terrier bark in warning. The kidnapper made off into the night with the child, who, after an extraordinary country-wide search, was found dead and buried only miles from the Lindbergh home.

The kidnapping of the Lindbergh baby and the ensuing investigation, two-and-a-half-year manhunt, and eventual trial and execution of the kidnapper, Bruno Richard Hauptmann, brought not only the country but the entire world to a standstill. An enraged populace reacted in shock and horror to the brutal abduction of the child of one of the century's greatest heroes. The Lindbergh case, labeled the "crime of the century" even before the decade was out,[2] still elicits strong feelings and alternative theories from criminology enthusiasts and is remembered today as among the most-famous crimes in American history.

Born on February 4, 1902, Charles Lindbergh grew up on a farm in Minnesota before enrolling at the University of Wisconsin to study engineering. He dropped out of school in 1922 to pursue aviation, his true passion, and spent the next few years working as a barnstormer, or daredevil pilot, training as an Army Air Service Reserve pilot, and flying airmail between St. Louis and Chicago. He became a worldwide celebrity in May 1927 when he completed his historic flight from New York to Paris, making him the first person to ever fly solo across the Atlantic. He was showered with medals and commendations. He began touring the country in his famous plane, the *Spirit of St. Louis*, giving speeches, for which he received $2,500 a week from the Guggenheim Foundation. He wrote articles for the *New York Times* and the *Saturday Evening Post* as well as authored a book entitled *We* about his celebrated flight, which quickly became a national bestseller.[3] Tall, lean of frame, light-haired, and undeniably handsome, Charles Lindbergh was as recognizable to the average American as President Calvin Coolidge, Babe Ruth, and Charlie Chaplin.

Bruno Hauptmann in his jail cell. © AS400 DB/Corbis.

Charles met Anne Morrow on a diplomatic visit to Mexico in December 1927. Anne, a dark-haired and delicate-looking twenty-one-year-old recent graduate from Smith College, was the daughter of Dwight Morrow, the United States' ambassador to Mexico as well as a partner in the JP Morgan Company and one of the wealthiest men in America. Charles and Anne began dating and were married in May 1929. Though greatly mismatched in height and coloring, they made a very attractive couple. When they were not traveling, they lived on the Morrow estate in Englewood, New Jersey. Their first child, Charles Augustus Lindbergh Jr., was born on June 22, 1930.[4]

Charles had become, as one reporter called him, "the most worshipped hero in the western hemisphere."[5] Reporters constantly followed him and Anne, publicizing their daily activities. When they embarked on a transcontinental journey from Washington, DC, shortly after their marriage, for example, hundreds of people gathered to watch their plane take off.[6] The birth of Charles Jr. was nationwide news. The *New York Times* announced it on the front page, where it trumped Admiral Byrd's return from Antarctica, and the infant was celebrated by both friends and complete strangers. The Junior Optimist Club of Kenosha, Wisconsin, for instance, with no connection to the Lindberghs, awarded the infant membership in the highest standing.[7]

The Lindberghs found the attention from the press and the constant torrent of autograph hunters and fans to be unbearably intrusive. In the summer of 1930, they purchased a 390 acre tract of land near Hopewell, New Jersey, as the site of a new house. They hoped this home would be remote enough to afford them a greater level of privacy and quiet.[8] The estate was far from the highway, only approachable by unpaved country lanes, and a mile of driveway separated the nearest road from where the house would stand.[9]

The new home was completed in late 1931, and the Lindberghs began spending weekends at it in early 1932. They typically returned to Englewood on the Monday following each weekend, but on the last weekend in February 1932, Anne decided to extend their stay at Hopewell for a few days. Charles Jr. was sick with a cold, and she did not want him to travel. Instead, she arranged for his nursemaid, twenty-eight-year-old Betty Gow, to come to Hopewell from Englewood.[10]

Tuesday, March 1, passed like any other day at Hopewell. That evening, Anne and Betty together put Charles Jr. to bed in the nursery upstairs. They closed the doors and windows, except for the southeast window, the shutters of which were warped, making it too difficult to shut. Anne left the nursery at about seven thirty, leaving Betty to finish preparing the baby for bed. At about eight o'clock, when he fell asleep, Betty pinned his blanket to the crib mattress and left the room, stopping by the living room to inform Anne that the child was sleeping soundly.[11]

Charles returned home from New York City at about 8:25. After he quickly freshened up in the upstairs bathroom that adjoined the nursery, he and Anne took their dinner in the dining room, then adjourned to the living room for their routine after-dinner talk. Charles would later remember that, during this conversation, he heard a cracking noise that resembled the sound the slats of a wooden crate make when splitting, but he casually wrote it off as a "kitchen" sound and ignored it. The Lindberghs left the living room at about a quarter past nine. Both went upstairs, Anne to bathe and Charles to read in his study.[12]

At about ten that evening, as was her custom, Betty went to check on Charles Jr. Finding the crib empty, she nervously rushed to inform Anne. Anne hurried to the study, hopeful that the baby was with Charles, who was known to dabble in practical jokes. In the past, he had, in fact, hidden Charles Jr. simply to tease Betty. But Anne found Charles alone in the study. The Lindberghs were now panic-stricken. Charles called the local police and their personal lawyer, Henry Breckinridge, and the two frantically searched the premises.[13]

Within the hour, both the local Hopewell police and New Jersey state troopers arrived and began inspecting the home, starting with the nursery. The crib rail was still up, and the blanket was still pinned to the mattress, hinting that the baby had been removed by the head. The shutters on the southeast window were open, and they noticed clumps of soil beneath the windowsill.[14] Following these clues outside, they found two imprints in the mud below the nursery window and some footprints, which they traced in a southeastern direction. About seventy-five feet from the house, they came across a home-made ladder, broken up into three sections, which had obviously been used by the kidnapper to scale the house and climb through the nursery window. One of the rungs was broken.

They also found in the nursery a small white envelope that had been placed on the windowsill. It was dusted for fingerprints, but officials could make out no more than an indecipherable smudge. The envelope contained a note written in blue ink that read:

> Dear Sir!
>   Have 50,000$ redy 25000$ in 20$ bills 15000$ in 10$ bills and 10000$ in 5$ bills. After 2-4 days we will inform you were to deliver the Mony. We warn you for making anyding public or for notify the polise the child is in gute care. Indication for all letters are singnature and 3 holes.[15]

The note was signed with a strange symbol: two blue interlocking circles joined by a solid red mark. The design was pierced by three evenly spaced holes.[16]

It was now abundantly clear to the Lindberghs that their worst fear had become reality: their only child had been kidnapped and was being held for ransom. The police, in an effort to halt the kidnappers from taking the child out of the state, ordered that every major bridge, tunnel, and highway that led from New Jersey to New York be blockaded and that all outgoing cars be stopped and searched. They also advised every hospital in the state to be on the lookout for the baby.[17]

The following day marked the beginning of the official investigation, which, for a variety of reasons, can only be described as a fiasco. For one, the case was a jurisdictional nightmare. Kidnapping had, tragically, become extremely commonplace throughout the country in the preceding years. In the year prior to Charles Jr.'s abduction, there had been 279 reported kidnapping cases as well as an estimated 600 that went unreported. The stock market crash and the following depression had made violence a means of economic survival and had ushered in a wave of gangs, bootleggers, and professional criminals. Kidnapping for ransom was an effective method for criminals to profit from wealthy Americans like the Lindberghs. It had become a remarkably organized business.[18]

Yet, despite its growing prevalence, the laws regarding kidnapping were highly inconsistent. In New Jersey, for example, it was punishable by thirty years in prison, but in New York a convicted kidnapper only faced five to fifteen years.[19] The ease and availability of transportation had made it common practice for kidnappers to jump state lines, yet the crime still was not a federal offense and state police could only arrest a suspected kidnapper in the state in which the crime was committed. As a result, just which branch of law enforcement would take the lead in a kidnapping investigation was anything but clear, and, due to the high profile of this particular victim, almost every level of law enforcement wanted to be involved. The investigation was officially led by Colonel H. Norman Schwarzkopf, the superintendent of the New Jersey State Police, and his state troopers, but an astonishing 35,000 local officers were involved in the search, as were countless New York City police officers.[20] Henry Breckinridge even placed a call to his friend J. Edgar Hoover, the director of the FBI, who promised the help of his agents as well.[21] These local, state, and national agencies all bitterly wrestled for authority, which resulted in excessive confusion and a failure to share information.

To make matters worse, the general public was also overly involved in the investigation. News of the kidnapping had gone out over the wires and radio stations overnight, and it was front-page news nationwide on March 2. The headline of the *New York Times* read "Lindbergh Baby Kidnapped From Home of Parents on Farm Near Princeton; Taken From His Crib; Wide Search On" with an accompanying story that took up most of page one and all of page two. The *Chicago Daily Tribune* trumpeted "Lindbergh Baby is Stolen," and the *Pittsburgh Sun Telegram* led with "Lindbergh Baby Kidnapped, Abductors Demand Ransom." It was the first time that a crime other than the assassination of a national leader made such an impression on the front pages of America.[22]

Learning about it over their morning coffee or daily commute, readers were shocked by the news. This baby, the son of a genuine American hero, represented all things innocent and pure, and his kidnapping seemed an inordinately despicable act. As one New York psychiatrist commented at the time, there was "an intense feeling of individual and personal affront at this crime against the adored citizen of the world,"[23] and it seemed that the entire county, if not the world, wanted to help look for the missing Lindbergh baby. The president of Princeton University volunteered his services as well as those of the school's students to help in the search. So did countless troops of Boy Scouts. Even several foreign prime ministers expressed their condolences, and Al Capone, writing from prison, offered his assistance to help find the kidnapper.[24] Law enforcement units in every state began looking for any out-of-place babies or shifty characters. One Trenton native who was driving across the country was stopped and questioned 107 times simply because his car had New Jersey license plates.[25]

The nationwide outpouring of sympathy, while comforting, was problematic for the investigation. The Lindberghs' home was overrun with reporters, cameramen, local residents, and curious onlookers before the crime scene could be properly assessed and documented, and it is unknown how many foot-prints, tracks, and other pieces of evidence were destroyed by this mob.[26] The Lindberghs received hundreds of letters and sympathy cards each day as well as tips and reports of suspicious-looking people carrying blond babies, all of which had to be meticulously examined and assessed for validity. This process was extremely time- and resource-consuming, and almost every potential lead proved to be false.[27]

Several facts became evident from the beginning of the investigation: the kidnappers had been wearing gloves, which suggested that they were a gang of professionals, and they were aware of the Lindberghs' daily schedule. They knew that, in spite of their usual habits, the Lindberghs were still at Hopewell midweek. Schwarzkopf and his men spent their time following the most promising of the public's tips and questioning the Lindbergh and Morrow staff members, despite Charles's ardent objections. They interviewed Betty Gow, the baby's nurse, and Oliver and Elsie Whately, the Lindberghs' caretaker and house-maid, as well as the twenty-nine members of the Morrow staff who worked at Englewood, several of whom aroused suspicion.[28] A neighbor remembered seeing the car of Betty Gow's boyfriend, Red Johnson, on the night of the kidnapping, in the back of which police found an empty milk bottle. Violet Sharpe, a twenty-eight-year-old Englewood maid, was particularly evasive during the interview, and her story only became more convoluted and far-fetched as questioning continued. However, Johnson had an alibi for the night of March 1, and Sharpe, although she was mentally unstable and later committed suicide by drinking cyanide crystals to avoid being questioned, was eventually cleared of any involvement in the kidnapping.[29]

Charles, on the other hand, was conducting his own investigation. Countless people called Hopewell, claiming to have found the baby, and Charles took every phone call personally.[30] He made pleas to the kidnappers on the open wire and in newspapers, assuring them that he and Anne would comply with their demands, and he hired a local racketeer named Morris "Mickey" Rosner to contact professional criminals on his behalf.[31] He also used his tremendous stature to influence the conduct of the investigators at the crime scene. He would not allow police to listen in on his phone calls, perform lie detector tests on his staff, or do anything that he felt would jeopardize his son's safe return. He even convinced Governor Moore of New Jersey to revoke his offer of a $25,000 reward to anyone who could safely return the baby, thinking it would anger the kidnappers.[32]

The only real development that occurred in the early days of the investigation was the receipt of a new note from the kidnappers on March 4. The letter, mailed from Brooklyn, New York, chastised Charles for involving the police and the press. It assured him that the baby was safe but that they would not inform him of where to deliver the money until the police and the media were silenced. It also claimed that this heist had been planned for a year and that they were "preparet for everything." It was signed with the same geometric symbol. A similar letter was mailed to Breckinridge's office on the chance, presumably, that the police were interfering with the Lindberghs' mail. Charles responded with a message in the papers authorizing two bootleggers, "Salvy" Spitale and Irving Bitz, to act as intermediaries and promising the kidnappers once again that he would cooperate in every way to assure the safe return of his child.[33]

Meanwhile, the media was running wild with the case. Reporters obsessively chased even the smallest leads like hungry cats chasing mice. They swarmed on Hopewell, filling the local hotel and even taking rooms in private homes. The local telephone exchange was forced to triple in size to accommodate the calls,[34] and the railroad station became an unofficial news headquarters.[35] Newspapers and tabloids published stories on the kidnapping every day, even if there was nothing new to report. The Associated Press issued 10,000 words on the story daily, only to be outdone by the Hearst Corporation, which published almost 30,000 words. Entire pages were devoted to the Lindbergh case, and the public was kept apprised of every minor development and false lead in the investigation. Stories ranged from the relevant ("Authorities Clear Nurse of Suspicion: Declare Miss Gow Blameless in Kidnapping of the Baby After Questioning Her"[36]) to the irrelevant ("Kidnappers Puzzle to Psychiatrists: One Group of Criminals That Experts Are Unable to Classify"[37]) to the plainly fictional ("Baby Expected Back Today"[38]). The *New York Times* managed to publish a story on Anne Lindbergh's behavior despite being banned from the Lindbergh estate,[39] and Charles Jr.'s face graced the cover of *Time* magazine.[40]

Public sentiment was similarly high. The *New York Times* commented that the entire "world waits hopefully" for news of the baby's whereabouts.[41] The five hundred orphans of St. Michael's Orphanage in New York prayed daily for his safe return, as did clergymen from a variety of faiths.[42] Referees interrupted a boxing match at Madison Square Garden so the entire stadium could stand and collectively pray for the child, and even President and Mrs. Herbert Hoover expressed their extreme sorrow and anxiety over the kidnapping.[43] Offers to help with the investigation continued to come from all sectors of society, sometimes at the expense of common decency. Anne would later write that "there were people who fluttered around the flame of publicity, politicians who came and posed for pictures next to the kidnapper's ladder," remarking particularly how "there was one city official, acting as a self-appointed investigator, who woke me up in the middle of the night and asked me to re-enact his theory of the crime, which ended with the imaginary throwing of a baby into a furnace."[44]

The course of the investigation shifted dramatically on March 8 when Dr. John F. Condon, a seventy-two-year-old retired schoolteacher who lived in the Bronx and lectured part-time at Fordham University, published his own offer of aid in the *Bronx Home News*. A fervently patriotic citizen, Condon worshiped Charles Lindbergh and believed the kidnapping to be a national tragedy. In his message, he pledged to do whatever was necessary, including contributing $1,000 of his own money, to ensure the safe return of Charles Jr. and offered his services as an intermediary to the kidnappers. The very next day, he received a letter postmarked from Station T in New York City; the kidnappers had seen his letter in the paper and were accepting his offer. They instructed him to deliver an enclosed envelope to Charles Lindbergh and, when he had received the ransom money, place a message in the *New York American* that would read "Mony is redy" then await further instructions. It was marked with the same geometric symbol.[45]

Condon telephoned Hopewell and described the letter to Charles Lindbergh who, upon hearing of the geometric signature, insisted that he come to Hopewell immediately. As they talked late into the night, Charles became convinced that Condon was indeed in touch with the kidnappers. They placed the message in the *New York American* the next day under the code name "Jafsie," the phonetic sound made by Condon's initials—J. F. C. They also began accumulating the ransom money and assembling a box for it according to specific instructions laid out in the kidnappers' recent letter.[46]

Condon soon received a phone call from a man with a thick German accent advising him to be at home every night between 6:00 and midnight, and at 8:30 on March 12, a taxi driver rang Condon's doorbell. He handed Condon a letter and explained that a man with a German accent had hired him to take this letter to Condon's address. The letter instructed Condon to bring the money to an empty frankfurter stand at a specified subway station, where he would find another note with more precise directions. Although the money was not yet ready, he obeyed and followed the directions found at the frankfurter stand into nearby Woodlawn Cemetery, where he was met by a man in a dark overcoat and a felt hat who called himself John. The two men spoke for over an hour, during which John, who henceforth became known as "Cemetery John," assured Condon that the baby was alive but, without the money, very little could be done. They parted company.[47]

As Lindbergh worked on accumulating the ransom money, Condon and Cemetery John continued to exchange messages; Condon would place ads in the *Bronx Home News* and the *New York American*, all under the "Jafsie" code name, and the kidnappers would respond via mail. On March 17, in an effort to reassure the Lindberghs that their son was still alive, the kidnappers sent a package that contained the baby's sleeping suit, although it came with a price—they now demanded $70,000 in ransom.[48]

With the aid of Elmer Irey of the IRS, Charles finalized the two ransom packages, one that contained $50,000 and a smaller package that held the additional $20,000 that would not fit in the original box. The majority of the ransom money was in gold notes, a stroke of genius on the part of Irey considering the country would be going off the gold standard within a year and any use of gold notes, which bore a round yellow seal, would become conspicuous. The IRS also recorded the serial number of each bill so that they could be tracked when spent.[49]

On April 2, Condon received a note from the kidnappers instructing him to bring the money to St. Raymond's Cemetery in the northeast Bronx. Upon arrival, he found Cemetery John and handed over the larger package of ransom money (he told John that Charles could not raise the additional $20,000) and in return was given a note informing him that the baby was on a boat called *Nelly* that was sailing between Martha's Vineyard and the Elizabeth Islands. Charles spent the entire night flying above the area but found no such boat. Condon continued to place ads in the *Bronx Home News* throughout the month of April, begging John for further clarification, but never received a response. The kidnappers had taken the money and disappeared.[50]

Charles and Anne, refusing to give up hope, continued looking into other leads. But on May 12, a truck driver, who had stopped on his route to relieve himself in the woods, found the body of a baby buried beneath leaves and dirt no more than five miles southeast of the Lindbergh home. Despite some decomposition, the baby was identified by both Charles and Betty Gow as Charles Jr. Fractures in the skull, when combined with the broken rung on the kidnap ladder, suggested that the kidnapper had fallen when descending and that the baby had been dead since the night he was kidnapped.[51]

The news of the baby's death reached the public instantly.

It was broadcast on the radio by CBS and NBC a mere eighteen minutes after New Jersey's Governor Moore made a formal announcement of the discovery. Within the next three hours, the *New York Times* received over 3,000 telephone calls from civilians asking for more information.[52]

Everyone involved with the search was devastated, and for many months the investigation floundered. Schwarzkopf ordered a re-enactment of the crime, questioned the staff again, had the wood of the ladder inspected and traced to its source, and even interviewed Condon, who had now fallen under suspicion and was so harassed by press that he was forced to leave and enter his home in disguise. No new information was uncovered.

The press echoed the loss and hatred felt by the American masses. The *New York Times* called the killing of the baby the "most merciless, perfidious, and despicable of deeds" and claimed that those responsible would be shunned by even the "fallen angels in hell."[53] With no real new information, newspapers published a variety of both plausible and implausible theories. As one historian has noted, they were "novelists in search of the perfect crime."[54]

However, the indisputable loss of the baby did not slake the public's interest in the kidnapping. While Americans certainly grieved, they remained as obsessed with the Lindbergh case as ever. On the night the baby was found, countless people rushed to the woods with their cameras to see the spot where the body was uncovered. So many spectators came that local merchants began selling peanuts, popcorn, and hot dogs as well as postcards of the nearby Lindbergh house. Other observers stood all night outside the funeral home where Charles had identified the body of his son. One photographer who managed to slip inside and take a photo of the corpse sold copies on the street for five dollars apiece.[55]

The lack of leads initially frustrated the public and the police, but excitement returned when the kidnappers began spending the ransom money. The police methodically tracked the bills as they appeared in two particular areas of New York City: along Lexington and Third Avenues in upper Manhattan and in the German-speaking neighborhood of Yorkville. Each bill tendered was folded in the same manner, into eight segments, and every cashier remembered the individual who passed the note as a man of about forty years of age with small features and a triangular face and of medium height and weight. He was often described as wearing a felt hat.[56] But police were unable to find this mysterious man until September 1934, two and a half years after the baby had been kidnapped, when a gas station attendant, convinced that a customer had given him a counterfeit twenty-dollar gold note, wrote the man's license plate number on the side of the bill before he drove away. A few days later, the bill was identified as part of the ransom and the car's owner was arrested. He was Bronx resident Bruno Richard Hauptmann.[57]

Hauptmann, thirty-five at the time of his arrest in 1934, was born and raised in Saxony, Germany, where he studied carpentry, drawing, and architecture. He had committed a series of crimes, several of which were uncannily similar to the Lindbergh kidnapping. He had, for instance, entered and robbed the town mayor's home by climbing a ladder into the second story and had mugged two women with baby carriages. After his third arrest, he escaped from jail and stowed away on a passenger ship to the United States, arriving in New York in 1923. He married his wife, Anna Schoeffler, in 1924, and the couple had one son. Hauptmann had spent the last few years working as a carpenter but also made money manipulating the stock market. He had an athletic frame but boyish qualities and delicate features.[58]

After his arrest, Hauptmann was taken to the precinct on

Manhattan's lower west side, where he was questioned at length by police. He immediately denied any involvement, claiming that he had been picking up his wife from the bakery where she worked at 9:00 on the night of the kidnapping and that he was at home with a friend on the night Condon met Cemetery John at St. Raymond's Cemetery.[59]

But Hauptmann's denial and supposed alibis convinced no one. As investigators searched his home, they found a wealth of incredibly damning circumstantial evidence. They discovered $14,600 worth of ransom bills hidden in his garage, handmade sketches of two windows and a ladder that resembled the one found at the scene of the crime, paper that matched the paper of the ransom note, several maps of New Jersey, and a small bottle marked "ether."[60] One of the rails of the ladder left at the Lindbergh home fit perfectly into a hole in the attic floor, and Condon's address and phone number were scribbled on the wall inside Hauptmann's closet. The bills in the billfold Hauptmann had on him when arrested were folded in the same signature eight-part fashion, and his latest purchases evidenced a recent dramatic increase in his personal finances. His handwriting and grammar matched that of the kidnapper, and he was identified in a lineup by the cab driver he had paid to deliver a message to Condon, the gas station attendant who wrote down his license plate number, two Hopewell residents who had seen a man driving a car with a ladder in the back on the day of the kidnapping, and a cashier from the Loew's Sheridan, where a ransom note had been passed.[61]

Hauptmann's arrest and each accompanying development were reported at length in the daily papers and on the radio. Reporters, photographers, and sensation seekers rushed to his home in the Bronx, rifled through the excess lumber the investigators had found, and questioned his neighbors.[62]

Based on the considerable evidence, the grand jury of Hunterdon County, New Jersey, voted on October 8 to indict Hauptmann for the murder of Charles Lindbergh Jr. He was extradited to New Jersey, protected from the public by a seven-car, two-motorcycle motorcade, to await trial, which was set to begin on January 2, 1935, at the Hunterdon County Court-house in the small town of Flemington.[63]

The prosecution would be led by David T. Wilentz, New Jersey's thirty-eight-year-old attorney general. Small, thin, stylish, and extremely quick-witted, Wilentz was a graduate of New York University Law School and a highly experienced lawyer, but had never tried a criminal case before. He would be assisted by Anthony Hauk, Joseph Lanigan, Robert Peacock, and George Large.[64] Hauptmann was trusting his defense to Edward J. Reilly, the fifty-two-year-old, larger-than-life, wildly famous defense attorney who was, in every way, Wilentz's polar opposite. Big and boisterous and never in court without a white carnation tucked into his jacket buttonhole, Reilly, who was sometimes referred to as "Big Ed" or "the bull of Brooklyn," had represented over two thousand defendants and had an excellent record of achieving acquittals. He replaced Haupt-mann's first attorney, the court-appointed James Fawcett, when the Hearst Corporation offered Anna Hauptmann $25,000 to help pay the defense in exchange for exclusive interview rights.[65] Reilly chose as his assistants three New Jersey attorneys: Frederick Pope, Egbert Rosecrans, and Flemington native C. Lloyd Fisher.[66] The trial would be presided over by the Honor-able Thomas W. Trenchard, a seventy-one-year-old judge with twenty-eight years of experience on the bench and a reputation as being fair, patient, and paternal.[67]

The trial began as scheduled on January 2 with jury selec-tion, which ran very smoothly. The prosecution opened its case after lunch on January 3. In his opening statement, Wilentz pledged to prove that Hauptmann was guilty of kidnapping and murder and, despite the consistent use of "we" in the ransom notes, had acted alone for the sole purpose of exhorting money from the Lindberghs. He told the jury that before he finished he would ask for the death penalty.[68] As the trial proceeded, he was calm, organized, and presented an overwhelming amount of meticulously researched evidence. Testimony from seventy-nine witnesses began with Anne Lindbergh, who outlined the events of the day of the kidnapping and identified the sleeping suit that Condon received in the mail as the one worn by her son. Charles Lindbergh, who took the stand next, told of the initial investigation on the night of the kidnapping, his identification of the baby's body, and the ransom note, which Wilentz read into the record.

Charles was followed by members of the Hopewell, New Jersey, and New York police departments, who discussed the crime scene at the home and the investigation of Hauptmann's house, and the eyewitnesses who had identified Hauptmann in the lineup. Next came Dr. Condon, who testified as to his position as Lindbergh's go-between, the ransom negotiations, and the cemetery meetings. He also identified Hauptmann as the man he knew as Cemetery John. All the ransom letters were entered into the record as was the kidnap ladder and the autopsy. Testimony also came from, among others, Henry Breckenridge, Colonel Schwarzkopf, Betty Gow, and Elsie Whately, as well as an IRS agent who identified the money found in Hauptmann's home as ransom money, eight handwriting experts who each claimed Hauptmann's handwriting samples matched that on the ransom notes, and a wood expert who demonstrated not only how the ladder rail fit perfectly into the gap in Hauptmann's attic floor, nail holes and all, and came from the same type of wood, but also how it had definitively been planed by a tool found in his garage.

Reilly, who seemed slow and cumbersome in comparison to Wilentz, was able to establish very little on cross-examination other than that some members of law enforcement had made mistakes at the crime scene, such as forgetting to measure the footprints found under the window. He spent much of his examinations suggesting that the kidnapping had been carried out by a member of the Lindbergh staff or by Condon. As the prosecution rested, the prevailing feeling throughout the courtroom was that Wilentz had buried Hauptmann under a mountain of evidence that would be impossible to get out from under.[69]

The first witness Reilly called when he began his defense was Hauptmann himself, who swore under oath that he was innocent. He had alibis for the night of the kidnapping and the night the ransom was exchanged, and he claimed that the money in his house had been left in his keeping by a friend named Isidor Fisch, who subsequently moved back overseas and had recently died and who, he implied, was the true kidnapper. Hauptmann denied writing the ransom notes and testified that the spelling in his handwriting samples matched that in the notes only because he had been tricked by police during questioning. But nothing about Hauptmann's story nor his expressionless face and metallic-sounding voice were believable or even interesting, much to the dismay of the massive crowds of spectators who stood six-deep in the aisles and had fought a major snowstorm and closed roads to be in Flemington to see him defend himself.[70]

Hauptmann's testimony was followed by that of his wife, Anna. She corroborated his story that he had been at home with a friend on the night the ransom was exchanged and that Fisch had stored some items at their home, but on cross-examination she became deflated and unconvincing, especially with regard to Fisch's belongings. The subsequent witnesses were even worse. Reilly put several people on the stand who claimed to have seen and interacted with Hauptmann on the night of the murder, thus proving his alibi, as well as some supposed expert witnesses. But when cross-examined, Wilentz exposed many of them as professional witnesses, petty criminals, bootleggers, and drunks. One even had a history of mental instability. Any credibility they had was shattered.[71] With very little accomplished, Reilly rested.

Despite the defense's lackluster performance, the prosecution came back with no less than twenty rebuttal witnesses. They testified that they had interacted with Fisch on the night of the kidnapping, giving him an alibi and making it seem unlikely that he had given Hauptmann the ransom money, and that the housemaid Violet Sharpe, whose involvement Reilly had questioned throughout the trial, had not left the Englewood estate until 8:00 that evening.[72]

Both sides made their closing statements; Wilentz strongly maintained that Hauptmann had acted alone while Reilly focused on mistakes police had made during the investigation and his theory that the entire undertaking had been an inside job committed by the Lindbergh staff or Dr. Condon. Finally, on Wednesday February 13, after over a month of trial that featured 162 witnesses and 381 exhibits, Judge Trenchard instructed and charged the jury, reminding them that, according to New Jersey law, a verdict of murder in the first degree automatically mandated the death penalty. They deliberated all afternoon and evening and returned at 10:30 that night to deliver their verdict: Hauptmann was guilty of murder in the first degree.[73]

The verdict was plastered across the headlines of every major newspaper in America on February 14. The press, as expected, had been on hand throughout the trial, which was described as "conceivably the largest media event ever."[74] Seven hundred reporters flocked to Flemington, many of them famous authors and celebrated columnists like Walter Winchell, Arthur Brisbane, Kathleen Norris, and Alexander Woollcott. The facilities of this small town, with its population of only 2,700 and its quiet Main Street, were completely overwhelmed.[75] Its Union Hotel only had fifty rooms, several of which were reserved for jury members, so countless members of the press were forced to find lodging with accommodating local homeowners. One New York newspaper took over the town's country club to house its staff. Others who were less fortunate commuted every day from Manhattan or Trenton.[76]

Every major American paper was represented as well as several international publications, including the *Paris-Soir* and the *London Daily Mail.* The Hearst Corporation alone sent two hundred staff members. Reporters, who were issued tickets for courthouse admittance, sent reports on the trial to their publications via 168 telephone lines that were installed to supplement the existing communications system. Space was cleared in the courthouse for forty telegraph and cable operators. It was estimated that such a system could adequately serve a city with a population of a million people and that the press used it to transmit over a million words each day, a true journalistic feat.[77] An airfield was built on the edge of town for the sole purpose of flying film out for next-day publication.[78]

Americans were a people obsessed. Flemington became a popular vacation spot during the trial as spectators rushed to get in on the action. Starting in October, the Union Hotel received some nine hundred letters from people all over the world requesting accommodations for the length of the trial.[79] By the trial's end, hundreds of thousands of people had visited Flem-

ington, among them movie stars, famous singers, and socialites, including Ginger Rogers, Jack Benny, Lynn Fontanne, Jack
Dempsey, and Elsa Maxwell.[80] A few lucky hundred rushed into
the small, historic courthouse when the doors opened at nine
each morning and found seats in the supplied folding chairs,
squeezed into the aisles and window recesses, or stood on radi-
ators and tables. Thousands of others who were less fortunate
crowded the street outside, despite the frigid weather. Authorities were hardly able to control the masses.[81] For those who could
not make it to Flemington, newsreel films of the trial screened at
theatres in New York and New Jersey. A vaudeville agent offered
each jury member three hundred dollars a week to go on tour in
New England when the trial was finished.[82]

The environment in Flemington, shockingly, was one of con-
viviality and amusement. Vendors sold all sorts of souvenirs—
replicas of the ladder, bookends shaped like the courthouse,
pictures of the Lindberghs with counterfeit signatures, even
pieces of blond hair that one salesman claimed came from the
baby's head (as the trial progressed, the blond salesman himself
became conspicuously more and more bald).[83] Women pinned
miniature ladders to their lapels and wore them around their
necks.[84] Spectators visited the jail where Hauptmann was kept
and the homes of jury members. They toured the courtroom
during the weekends, led by the local chapter of the American
Legion, and waited in line to be photographed sitting in Lindbergh's, Hauptmann's, and Trenchard's chairs.[85] In a makeshift
bar at the Union Hotel, patrons changed the lyrics of a German
folk song popular in beer halls in New York to reflect the goings-
on in the trial and sang along enthusiastically.[86] One restaurant
on Main Street served what it called a "special trial lunch," which
consisted of Lindbergh Steak, Hauptmann Beans, Trenchard
Roast, Jafsie Chops, Gow Goulash, Jury Pie, and Reilly Pudding.[87]

So over the top was the atmosphere that author Edna Ferber, covering the trial for the *New York Times*, penned an article titled "Vultures at the Trial," describing how it was considered "chic" to go to the Hauptmann trial and equating the scene in front of the Union Hotel to a Manhattan party, with its mink coats and its Cossack hats. "Hel-lo darling? Isn't it divine! Have you had lunch?" she writes, as the voice of the crowd, whom she compares to the sansculottes of the French Revolution. The entire scene, she disparaged, "made you want to resign as a member of the human race."[88]

After hearing his fate, Hauptmann was led out of the courthouse through the crowd of onlookers that had gathered outside, now more than seven thousand strong, and taken back to his cell.[89] A few days later he was transferred to the New Jersey State Prison at Trenton, escorted by fourteen state troopers and followed closely by countless members of the press. The date for his execution was set as March 18, and appeals began immediately.[90] Hauptmann dismissed Reilly, whose services he deemed not only too expensive but unsatisfactory, and hired Fisher as his chief counsel. The first trial having depleted his personal finances and the money from the *Journal*, Hauptmann was declared a pauper, and appeals were financed partially by the state and partially by the Hauptmann Defense Fund, a charity set up to raise money for his legal fees. The fund was spearheaded by Hauptmann's wife, Anna, who spoke at rallies across the country, proclaiming his innocence and trying to raise public sympathy. Their home in the Bronx was also opened for tours and was visited by as many as a thousand people each day.[91]

Fisher argued on appeal that the unrestrained press coverage and atmosphere in Flemington had prejudiced the jury and made it impossible for Hauptmann to receive a fair trial, but the New Jersey Court of Errors and Appeals upheld the conviction, the United States Supreme Court abstained from reviewing the decision, and the New Jersey Court of Pardons sustained his sentence. Despite the brief promise of a reprieve from New Jersey's governor Harold G. Hoffman, Hauptmann was executed on April 3, 1936, having never confessed to the crime,[92] while a Hauptmann execution party took place at the nearby Stacy-Trent Hotel.[93] His death was front-page news nationwide the following day, and his funeral, held on April 6 in Queens, was mobbed by almost a thousand people.[94]

Anna Hauptmann continued unsuccessfully to try to clear her husband's name until her death in 1994. Charles and Anne Lindbergh, in an attempt to escape the constant hounding of the press and the occasional threats on the life of their new young son Jon, set sail for England shortly after the trial concluded. Charles reportedly said that "it was impossible for [him or his] family to lead a normal life because of the tremendous public hysteria" and that they "couldn't go to a theater, a store, or even for a stroll without being surrounded, stared at and harassed."[95] They stayed abroad for several years, returning to the United States during the war, then lived in a variety of places, including Europe and Hawaii, attempting to forget the tragedy of Hopewell. Charles died in 1974 after a life of personal controversy; he had several illegitimate children with a German woman, and many believed he had harbored Nazi sympathies. Anne died in 2001.[96]

Yet, in spite of these attempts at closure, the Lindbergh kidnapping truly became, as one recent book calls it, "the case that never dies." One of the most-famous episodes in the history of American criminal justice, it has been studied extensively by many and, at the very least, heard of by all. It is perhaps the most heralded "trial of the century" and still, after over eighty years, maintains a surprising level of cultural relevance. Several movies have been made about the case, one starring Anthony Hopkins as Bruno Hauptmann and another actually called *Crime of the Century*. It has inspired several pieces of literature, from Agatha Christie's 1934 novel *Murder on the Orient Express*, which is about the kidnapping of a wealthy baby girl and a member of the staff that commits suicide in the aftermath, to *Outside Over There*, a children's picture book about a girl who finds that her younger sister has been kidnapped from her crib and taken through a second-story window. In this tale, the kidnappers leave an ice sculpture of a baby in the crib, the illustration of which was based on photographs of the Lindbergh baby. The Spanish slang expression "estar mas perdido que el hijo de Lindbergh," used to imply that one is clueless, literally translates as "to be more lost than Lindbergh's child."[97]

In the end, people are still drawn to the investigation. Despite a consistently upheld conviction, something about the case, perhaps the lack of a confession or the reliance on circumstantial evidence, makes countless amateurs and criminal justice professionals alike believe that something is still missing. In 1935, after the verdict was announced, the *New York Times* published a piece claiming that "the long trial at Flemington, the charge of the judge and the verdict of the jury established a crime but did not clear away a mystery" and that "we do not yet know exactly what happened on that tragic night in Hopewell." The *Times* called the case an "unsolved mystery" that was "one of the most puzzling in criminal annals."[98] Fifty years later, John F. Keenan, a federal judge reviewing a recent book about the trial, described this phenomenon aptly when he wrote that doubt remains "where there is no confession, no apprehension at the scene with the smoking gun, no video or audio tape, no ultimate acknowledgement of guilt." He comments on the tendency of such defendants to "become martyrs or victims to observers" and the prosecutors and investigators to be "put under a retroactive microscope."[99]

Many still view Hauptmann in this way. Over the past eighty years, people have continued to pore over details and pen alternative theories of what really happened at Hopewell. One such theorist wrote a book in which he aims to prove that Hauptmann had an accomplice, a deli worker named John Knoll. Lloyd Gardner, in his book *The Case that Never Died,* purports that Charles Lindbergh himself, a proponent of eugenics, orchestrated the kidnapping to cover up the fact that his son had rickets. A recent PBS documentary entitled *Who Killed Lindbergh's Baby?* follows an investigator attempting to "finally solve the crime of the century."[100] The Internet is littered with discussion boards and chat rooms in which people espouse their own theories about Hauptmann's guilt or innocence. Dozens of people, men and women alike, have come forward over the years claiming to be the lost Lindbergh baby.[101] Even the Red Mill Village Museum of Hunterdon County, not far from where the trial itself was held, recently hosted a presentation called "12 Theories of Who Kidnapped the Lindbergh Baby."[102]

Despite the varying degrees of thoroughness and validity in these theories, one criticism does ring true. Regardless of whether or not he was guilty, it is difficult to support the contention that Hauptmann truly had a fair trial. The press coverage in 1935 was undeniably out of control. Several potential jurors had to be dismissed during voir dire because they openly admitted that they had been influenced by the writings of Walter Winchell of the *New York Daily Mirror* who had all but legally convicted Hauptmann.[103] Moreover, the public was calling for blood. The crowd in the streets of Flemington chanted "kill Hauptman!" as they waited for the verdict.[104] Is it possible that a jury could have given him a fair chance? Unfortunately, however, nothing could be done to improve the situation. The press coverage of the case was so pervasive and far-reaching that there was no place far removed enough to be a more fitting setting. The atmosphere would most likely have been the same anywhere the trial might have been moved to.

A fanatical press, a lynch mob public, and the absence of a confession made the Lindbergh kidnapping a standout episode in criminal justice history. Interest in it today is almost as strong as it was eighty years ago, and it shows no signs of relinquishing its coveted position among the most-recognized trials in American history. The most famous man of his generation, hunted and haunted, Charles Lindbergh is now as famous for the death of his child as for his pioneering aerial exploration.

CHAPTER 5

1940–1950:
WAYNE LONERGAN AND THE
BLUDGEONED HEIRESS

The 1940s were the glory days of the "café society," that collection of wealthy, beautiful people living luxuriously in the world's biggest and brightest cities. This crowd dined at the fanciest restaurants, danced at exclusive nightclubs, vacationed in exotic locales, and hosted glamorous parties. Patricia Burton Lonergan was a prime example of this set, the classic New York socialite. Heiress to a brewing fortune, at age fifteen she was living in a villa in Cannes, with neighbors that included acclaimed novelist Somerset Maugham and the Aga Kahn. At age eighteen, she was a resident of the Ritz Tower on Park Avenue in New York City. At age twenty, she was a fixture on elite charity committees and habitually dined, drank, and danced at the city's most exclusive and glamorous nightclubs and restaurants. And at age twenty-two, she was dead, bludgeoned and strangled in her bedroom by her charming, handsome husband.[1]

The murder of Patricia by Wayne Lonergan on October 24, 1943, referred to even by newspapers of the day as "New York's greatest murder thriller in recent years,"[2] and the accompanying investigation and trials were front-page stories and dining room–table fodder for months. In the midst of a world war, not only New York but an entire nation found distraction in the dramatic case, which involved love gone wrong, aberrant sexual behavior, New York City's glamorous "café society," and a multimillion-dollar fortune.[3]

Patricia Burton Lonergan's regrettably short life began in Long Branch, New Jersey, where she was born to William and Lucille Burton on September 1, 1921.[4] Though he sometimes dabbled in painting, her father truly derived his income from the Burton family fortune. He was the only son of Max Bernheimer (the family later shortened Bernheimer to Burton) of the Chicago-based Bernheimer and Schwartz Brewing Company, which operated one of the largest breweries in the world, and, upon the passing of his mother, he was set to inherit a seven-million-dollar trust fund. Patricia, as an only child, would be next in line for the fortune. This money, which in today's economy would be an estimated seventy million dollars, gave the family the freedom to maintain a truly extravagant lifestyle. William's mother once threw a dinner party in which she required all of her guests to sit on the table and eat off their chairs and began the meal with dessert and ended it with soup. Max Bernheimer left the Metropolitan Museum of Art a stamp collection that was said to rival that of the king of England.[5]

Only a few weeks after she was born, Patricia and her parents moved to Paris, where they lived for five years before William and Lucille divorced. They were separated for four years, during which Patricia lived with Lucille, but decided in 1930 to give their union another chance because, according to Lucille, they "worshipped the child." They lived in Cannes from 1930 through 1939, where they maintained a luxurious villa and guesthouse, in which Patricia lived with her governess, as well as a yacht large enough to sail across the Atlantic. They wanted for nothing, and even as a child Patricia, who was sometimes called "Pat" or "Patsy," had an extensive jewelry collection.[6] William and Lucille divorced for a second time in 1939, at which point Patricia and her father returned to New York and took up residence in a suite at the Ritz Tower. William died of a heart attack in 1940, and Patricia lived with a chaperon for a few months until her mother returned from France.[7] She had matured into an attractive and slender nineteen-year-old with dark, curly hair and a classically pretty face.

Patricia and Wayne Lonergan. © Bettmann/Corbis.

Wayne Lonergan experienced a very different upbringing. The youngest of three children, he was born in Toronto in 1919 to an American mother and a Canadian father. He attended Catholic primary school, St. Michael's College in Toronto, and a Canadian business school, but he never found a professional calling. At various points, he was a police constable, a lifeguard, and a survey worker for a mining company. He also seemed to have a knack for finding legal trouble.[8]

He journeyed to New York City in the spring of 1939 with no particular plan or agenda, only intending to stay for a weekend. But he greatly enjoyed New York and, deciding to extend his visit, obtained a job at the World's Fair. According to some accounts, he was a dispatcher for Greyhound, but others maintain that he pushed a rickshaw.[9] After the fair, he worked briefly at Abercrombie and Fitch and for photographer Anton Bruehl but eventually quit in 1941 because, by this point, he had managed to fall in with the city's most fashionable and wealthy crowd. He was attending opening nights on Broadway, dining in famous supper clubs, and playing squash at the Princeton club.[10] He was quick-witted, and any money he needed he made by gambling and playing cards. It was not unheard of for him to make two hundred dollars in one afternoon.[11]

Wayne Lonergan first met the Burtons in 1939, when he was working at the World's Fair, although it was William, not Patricia, whom he first encountered. That William Burton was gay was an oft-heard rumor, and, upon their meeting at the World's Fair, Wayne, who was 6'3" and handsome with a slim face and neatly manicured hair, became his lover. For several months he was a frequent guest of William's at the Ritz Tower, but the relationship was short-lived, ending prior to William's death in 1940.[12]

Wayne first met Patricia, whom he remembers as being quite shy at the time, in the fall of 1939 at a dinner party at the George Washington Hotel hosted by her father. They chatted amiably throughout dinner, and at one point Patricia confessed to Wayne that she had recently been denied entry to the Stork Club, a swanky and exclusive club in midtown Manhattan. Wayne insisted that they leave the party and go to the Stork Club immediately. When they arrived, the maître d', who knew Wayne by name, admitted them without delay. They had a drink before returning to the dinner party.[13] The excursion left quite an impression on Patricia.

Wayne and Patricia began casually dating that winter and continued to see each other throughout 1940.[14] Patricia was taken with Wayne, despite the fact that he had been previously involved with her father. She would reportedly say "if he was good enough for my father, he's good enough for me."[15]

Lucille, on the other hand, did not approve of Patricia and Wayne's relationship. In her opinion, Wayne was "completely selfish . . . and totally heartless."[16] In the summer of 1941, she took Patricia to stay with family in Santa Barbara, California, in the hope that she would meet a nice, wealthy man out west and forget all about Wayne. Her plan backfired. At Patricia's request, Wayne flew out to California, and the two eloped to Las Vegas.[17]

When they returned to New York, the newlyweds subleased a large apartment at 983 Park Avenue. Wayne was unemployed, but they were able to support themselves with Patricia's small trust (she would not obtain the rest of the fortune until the death of her grandmother). Their son, William Wayne Lonergan, was born in the late spring of 1942.[18]

Wayne and Patricia, as regular members of New York's cafe society, were constantly going out and entertaining. While Wayne's enthusiasm for social outings was wavering, Patricia's was on the rise. Although some of Patricia's friends remembered her as being "confused by the café-society atmosphere in which she grew up," others recall her as being "a party girl, wild and ready for anything."[19] She was a favorite on charity committees. She loved having engagements in her calendar for every night of the week and staying out until the early hours of the morning.[20] The Lonergans were rich and beautiful, and they became minor celebrities, occasionally appearing in gossip columns and frequently spotted at the Stork Club, El Morocco, and the city's other hot spots.[21]

But Wayne and Patricia found marriage to be extremely trying. Patricia was willful and spoiled. Billy Livingstone, the producer and boyfriend of famous debutante Brenda Frazier, knew the couple at the time and recalled Patricia as constantly nagging and whining. He described her as "pathetic" and claimed that "if Wayne hadn't killed her, [he] could have." He also remembered that "Wayne was having dalliances during the marriage."[22]

They fought constantly from the beginning. Reginald Wright, a friend of the couple, alleged that "they fought like cats and dogs" and that "there was never any peace between them." Patricia used to call Wayne a "heel," and during one argument she exclaimed, "that's to be expected when a girl marries a man who is beneath her." Wright remembered that Wayne "had a few choice words for her, too."[23] They separated in 1943 when Patricia sublet a townhouse in Beekman Hill. With the Second World War in full swing, Wayne joined the Royal Canadian Air Force, moving to Toronto on September 6, 1943, with the understanding that he would come back to New York on his leaves to see his son.[24] Although they were not legally divorced, it seemed unlikely that they would ever reconcile, and during this separation Patricia removed Wayne as a beneficiary from her will. Their son would now be the only heir to the Burton family fortune.[25]

Patricia was murdered on the morning of Sunday, October 24, 1943.

Wayne had been granted a forty-eight-hour leave from the RCAF on that weekend. He flew into New York City in the very early morning of Saturday, October 23 and went straight to the apartment of a friend, John Harjes, with whom he planned to stay. Harjes told him that he was going to the country for the weekend but that Wayne was welcome to remain at his apartment. Wayne had a busy day, which included lunch with some lady friends, a doctor's appointment, and a trip to F. A. O. Schwartz to buy a toy elephant for his son. At about six o'clock, he went to Patricia's apartment and visited with his son for nearly an hour, although he did not see Patricia, who was not at home. He left her townhouse and returned to Harjes's apartment, where he met Mrs. Jean Murphy Jaburg. Mrs. Jaburg, who was also separated from her spouse, lived in the same building, and Harjes had arranged for her to go out with Wayne that evening. The two went to see a show, followed by dinner and drinks, returning about three thirty in the morning.[26]

Wayne was next seen at about ten thirty, when he ordered breakfast from Harjes's butler, Emil Peters. He then ran a few errands, went to the apartment of one of the women he had lunched with on Saturday, where he had accidentally left the toy elephant. He then took the toy to Patricia's apartment, leaving it outside the front door with a note saying "for Billy." He returned to Mrs. Jaburg's apartment, having made plans with her the previous night to have lunch together on Sunday, and took her and her nine-year-old son to lunch at the Plaza Hotel. He spent the rest of the day with them before he flew back to Toronto that evening.[27]

Patricia had also been out on a date on Saturday night, in the company of Italian interior designer Mario Enzo Gabellini, with whom she had been out several times before. On this particular night, they met friend Thomas Farrell and his date, Jean Goodman, for dinner and drinks at the Peter Cooper Bar, after which they went dancing at the Stork Club. When the nightclub closed, all four went back to Farrell's suite at the Peter Cooper for a nightcap before Gabellini took Patricia home in a taxi at about six o'clock in the morning. Entering her apartment in those early-morning hours, she was seen alive for the last time.[28]

Patricia's body was found in her bedroom some twelve hours later on Sunday evening. The only other adult resident of the house, Elizabeth Black, little Billy's nurse, had knocked on her door to rouse her multiple times throughout the day but was not surprised when there was no movement inside; it was common for Patricia to stay out late and sleep all day on the weekends. Ms. Black had taken Billy to see his grand-mother that afternoon, and when she returned about five thirty in the evening and found Patricia still silent in her bedroom, she became concerned. She telephoned Patricia's mother and asked her to please come over and check on her daughter. When Lucille arrived and found the bedroom door locked, she called Peter Elser, a captain in the Marine Corps Reserve and a friend with whom Patricia had scheduled a date that evening. He arrived at the townhouse and was able to break down the bedroom door.[29]

The gruesome scene they found behind the closed door would be described in vivid detail in newspapers in the days to come. The room showed the obvious signs of a struggle. Patricia had sustained several forceful blows to the head. Her body was naked and sprawled across her bed, which was covered in blood. A heavy candlestick was found, dented and partially broken, on the bed, and its mate lay nearby on the floor.[30] There were traces of blood around a second door into the bedroom, which led to an outside hallway and the build-ing's public staircase, and there was residue of flesh beneath her fingernails, indicating that she had fought back against her attacker.[31] One reporter would write that the setting was "almost unreal, almost like something out of Dashiell Hammett or Rex Stout."[32]

Detectives arrived at the scene by nine o'clock that evening and began their investigation, led by Acting Deputy Chief Inspector Patrick Kenny and Assistant District Attorney John Loehr. The autopsy, carried out by Assistant Medical Examiner Milton Helpern, revealed that death had been caused by asphyxia by strangulation, together with lacerations of the scalp, possible fracture of the skull, and concussion of the brain.

Having learned how Patricia spent her last evening, the detectives first suspected Gabellini, whom they questioned for over twelve hours.[33] Gabellini, however, had a strong alibi. When he brought Patricia home after their date, he had asked the cab driver to wait for him while he walked her inside. The driver would attest that he had only been inside the building for three to five minutes before he returned to the taxi and directed him to a nearby coffee shop, where Gabellini treated him to coffee and donuts.[34]

The detectives quickly learned that Wayne had been in New York over the weekend but had flown back to Toronto late Sunday night. Early Monday morning, members of the Toronto police arrived at his residence and began questioning him about his wife's murder, but Wayne maintained that he was not involved and had only learned of it from the morning papers.[35] Eager to have him back in their jurisdiction, Loehr, accompanied by two New York detectives, flew to Toronto on Tuesday to accompany Wayne back to New York. He willingly waived extradition, claiming that he had "absolutely nothing" to do with the murder and that he simply wanted to be at Patricia's funeral and see his son. He also said he was going to New York "to help the authorities." The party arrived in New York on Wednesday evening and went directly to the district attorney's office, where questioning was resumed and continued well into Thursday.[36]

As the investigation proceeded throughout the week, suspicion began to fall strongly on Wayne. Two peculiar circumstances seemed to point heavily to his guilt. First, the RCAF uniform he had been wearing when he arrived in New York was missing. When he flew home from New York on Sunday evening, he had been wearing an ill-fitted, mismatched suit belonging to Harjes, and he was similarly wearing civilian clothes when picked up for questioning on Monday.[37] A note had been found in Harjes's apartment that read,

> John: Thank you so much for the use of your flat. Due to a slight case of mistaken trust, I lost my uniform and borrowed a jacket and trousers from you. I will return it on my arrival in Toronto. I'll call you up and tell you about it.
>   Yours, Wayne.[38]

Despite this note, the prevailing police theory was that the uniform had been stained with blood during Patricia's murder and that Wayne had been forced to dispose of it.

Second, Wayne had two very obvious scratches on his chin and lower face. It was believed that these scratches had been sustained during the murder and had been the source of the flesh found beneath Patricia's fingernails.[39]

Wayne consistently maintained his innocence throughout questioning. He told police that after he had left Mrs. Jaburg on Saturday night he had met an American soldier named Maurice Worcester on the street outside Harjes's building. He claimed the man had been looking for a room to rent for the night and that he had invited him to stay at Harjes's apartment. He implied that they had shared a sexual encounter but that he awakened in the middle of night to find the soldier robbing him. They fought, and the soldier ran off with his uniform and one hundred dollars, thus explaining the missing uniform and the scratches to his face.[40] However, Harjes's butler, Peters, denied that anyone had stayed at the apartment other than Wayne.[41] Assistant District Attorney Jacob Grumet, who would eventually lead the prosecution team, summed up police sentiment when he called this account a "cock-and-bull story" and "fantastic."[42]

The story was published widely in newspapers and tabloids, as was, among other salacious details, the newly uncovered fact that Wayne had been rejected from the US Armed Forces because of his homosexuality.[43] Seeing these stories in the papers, a former army private who resided in Bridgeport, Connecticut, named Maurice Worcester appeared at the district attorney's office. He refuted the story, claiming that he had never met Wayne Lonergan and that he wanted to clear his name for the sake of his children. Lonergan was brought in to see this Maurice Worcester and showed no recognition of him.[44]

On Thursday afternoon, after being told that he had not recognized the principal character of his alibi, Wayne changed his tune and gave police a long, detailed admission of how he had, in fact, killed Patricia. In his confession, which proceeded in a question and answer format and took three hours to tell, he told how he had gone to Patricia's apartment around nine in the morning and that she had woken up and let him in, still undressed. They argued, him calling her a "tart" and criticizing her for being the "belle of El Morocco" and "behaving like a drunken sailor" and she calling him a "son-of-bitch" and a "dirty bastard" and getting angry over his having a date later that day. He told of how, when he turned to get his hat and gloves from the sideboard, she threatened that he would "never see the baby again" and how, enraged, he had picked up the candlestick next to his belongings and rushed at her, striking her on the head. The candlestick broke, and he reached for its mate and struck her with that as well. She fought back, kicking and scratching, which, he confirmed, was the source of the marks on his face. He seized her by the neck and strangled her until she lost consciousness.[45]

Wayne explained that afterward he went back to Harjes's apartment and, noticing that his uniform was splattered with blood, cut it up and put it in a duffel bag, into which he also placed a dumbbell that he found in the apartment. He changed into one of Harjes's suits and ordered breakfast from the butler, Peters, but only ate a small portion, hiding the rest in a desk drawer. He told of how he then took the duffel bag along Seventy-Ninth Street to the East River and threw it into the water. On his way back, he purchased some makeup at a drug store to cover the scratches on his face. He then carried on with the rest of his day as he had previously claimed; he bought some newspapers, cashed a check, picked up the toy elephant and brought it to Patricia's townhouse, and took Mrs. Jaburg to lunch.[46] When his story was complete, the police asked how he felt. "Not so good," he replied.[47]

His confession taken down, Wayne was escorted to the East 51st Street Station for booking and then to the East River so that he could show detectives where he had thrown his duffel bag. Finally he was placed in a detention cell at Police Headquarters.[48]

Wayne was indicted on Friday, October 29, for first-degree murder. According to New York law, he would be required to plead not guilty, as the state's punishment for murder in the first degree was death by electric chair. A conviction of first-degree murder would mean that he was guilty of murder with premeditation, deliberation, and intent to kill as opposed to second-degree murder, meaning murder with intent to kill but without premeditation or deliberation, or manslaughter,

meaning the killing of a person without premeditation, deliberation, or intent.[49]

Wayne was held in the Tombs prison without bail until his
trial, for which preparations commenced immediately.[50] The
case was assigned to Assistant District Attorney Grumet, a tall,
slim, mustached Columbia Law graduate who had been with
the district attorney's office since 1935. An experienced prosecutor, he had worked on several cases involving racketeering
and organized crime. Grumet began by contacting many of the
names in Patricia's and Wayne's address books and by sending
divers into the East River in the hope of retrieving the lost
duffel bag, which was never found.[51]

The court assigned three lawyers to serve as Wayne's defense
team: Millard H. Ellison, Abraham J. Halperin, and Edward V.
Broderick. Ellison and Halperin had no experience in criminal
law, but Broderick, who would act as chief counsel, was a seasoned criminal trial attorney with an excellent track record.[52]
A big, thickset man remembered as always having a cigar in his
mouth, he was also a graduate of Columbia Law School. Over
the years, he had represented thirty-seven first-degree murder
defendants, thirty-four of which were acquitted, and three of
which were ultimately only convicted of the lesser crime of
manslaughter.[53]

There were immediate problems among the members of
the defense team. Broderick, Ellison, and Halperin bickered
constantly and would rarely meet with Wayne as a group,
instead visiting the Tombs individually, which caused confusion
in their defense strategy. Eventually, Wayne fired all three attorneys and rehired only Broderick at his own expense.[54]

In many respects, the trial was a circus. Broderick's primary
tactic seemed to be to stall for time. The trial was initially set for
January 31, 1944, but Broderick managed to achieve multiple

postponements in light of what he called new "European com-plications" to the case (of which there were none). When the trial eventually began on February 23, Broderick was in Canada gathering more evidence, a fact that enraged the presiding judge, John Freschi. Broderick was ordered to return to New York immediately but was still missing the following day. The judge threatened to hold him in contempt for his absence, but he had no choice but to postpone the case until the following Monday, February 28.[55] Jury selection began on that date, but only five potential jurors were questioned and all were excused.[56]

Broderick was also excessively provocative and antagonistic toward the press, the Burton family, and the prosecution team. Despite Judge Freschi's requests that he refrain from "use[ing] this courtroom for a vaudeville stage" and the chastisements for his "unwarranted excitement and ungentlemanly conduct," Broderick constantly launched into long, angry diatribes and made exclamations like "the Bernheimer-Burton seven-mil-lion-dollar estate and the *New York Times* have ganged up on me" and "the administration of justice is on trial." He criti-cized Grumet's performance as an attorney, saying that he was "responding to the pressure of the Bernheimer-Burton mil-lions," and accused him of taking the case too lightly as if it were a "cream-puff game." Grumet angrily fought back, crying that there were "too many shenanigans going on in this case" and causing Judge Freschi to ask one afternoon "can't we elimi-nate all this? Otherwise, the jurors could go home and I could go to my chambers, and leave you two lawyers to fight it out."[57]

On Thursday, March 2, Grumet asked the judge to revisit a prior motion by Broderick to discharge the jury panel. Brod-erick had argued that the proceedings of the court so far had made it impossible for Wayne to receive a fair trial, but Grumet had other reasons. Showing, if nothing else, the excessive intrusion of the press in this case, he cited an article that had appeared in the *Daily Mirror* stating that the defense had in its arsenal "bizarre" pictures of Patricia. Grumet questioned Broderick's role in the publication of this story. Such conduct by the defense attorney, he asserted, stood in the way of a fair trial.[58] Despite Broderick's adamant protestations that he had no involvement in the news story, Judge Freschi consented to reconsider the motion and, on Friday, March 3, declared a mistrial. He reasoned that Broderick's conduct had been

> [A]dequate in [his] mind to raise the question whether his statements, demeanor, and entire attitude have not so beclouded the issues in this case that there is a danger that the jurors ultimately selected from this panel might find it difficult to evaluate the evidence and the relevant facts, and therefore the defendant might be prejudiced.[59]

Freschi set an upcoming date for Broderick's contempt hearings and adjourned the proceedings, lamenting that he hoped the case would come before a different presiding judge.[60]

The second trial began on Monday, March 20, before a new judge, James Garrett Wallace. The same attorneys were in attendance, but the proceedings ran much more smoothly than they had a few weeks prior. A jury was selected within two days, and testimony began.[61]

The prosecution brought forward a wealth of testimony, starting with an engineer who submitted into evidence a detailed layout of Patricia's apartment and a police officer who showed photographs of the crime scene. Medical Examiner Helpern, who had performed the autopsy, then testified to the circumstances of Patricia's death. He described her head wounds and opined that, although it had been hard to pinpoint an exact time because of how little she had eaten and how much she drank the night before her death, he could say with confidence that she was killed sometime between six in the morning and two in the afternoon.[62]

Grumet introduced the two ornate candlesticks found at the scene as the murder weapons and then began reconstructing the events of Sunday, October 24. He introduced Elizabeth Black, little Billy Lonergan's nurse, who testified that she had tried to wake Patricia at several points throughout the day before telephoning Lucille Burton when she became concerned. She admitted to waking at roughly eight that morning but said she heard nothing that would have hinted at a struggle. Lucille took the stand next and described how she arrived at the townhouse, followed by Elser, who testified as to how he had broken the door down, found Patricia dead, and called the police.[63]

Dr. Hadley Ashley of the Toronto police force testified to seeing the scratches on Wayne's chin. Harjes was then called to tell of Wayne's arrival in New York. He also identified the note Wayne had left at his apartment, the jacket and pants Wayne borrowed from him, a Max Factor makeup kit that he had found in his apartment, and the model dumbbell of which he had owned four but now could find only three.[64] Harjes was followed on the stand by Detective Wall of Toronto who read the transcript of the questioning Wayne had undergone there.[65]

Grumet then tried to introduce into evidence Wayne's October 28 confession, but Broderick vigorously objected, arguing that the confession had been made under duress and was inadmissible. Refusing to actually refer to it as a confession, he brought a variety of Canadian and American law enforcement officials, including Grumet, to the stand and questioned them thoroughly about any sort of coercion that may have occurred. Broderick claimed that they had threatened Wayne, physically abused him, kept him drunk throughout questioning, made him false promises about attending Patricia's funeral, forced him to stay awake for days at a time, and ignored his requests for a lawyer, all of which were avidly denied by each witness. With no other witnesses to question, Broderick was forced to consent to the reading of the confession, which would be the most decisive piece of evidence in the case.[66]

The confession was followed by testimony from Annalisa Schoenberg, a nurse who was employed by Patricia's upstairs neighbors. She had been on duty that Sunday morning and told of how, as she ventured out into the building's common hallway to retrieve the newspaper at approximately 8:55, she had heard a woman scream when she passed by the door to Patricia's bedroom. She heard some additional screams when she returned to the apartment, but at no point did she call the authorities or check on the downstairs neighbors.[67]

The final witnesses called by Grumet were Jean Murphy Jaburg, who testified to her evening with Wayne and her lunch with him the following day, at which, she claimed, she did not notice any obvious scratches on his face; Max Levinson, a drug-store owner who identified Wayne as the man who bought a pancake makeup kit from him at 11:30 Sunday morning; and Ruth Forster, a neighbor of Harjes's who was acquainted with the Lonergans and testified to seeing Wayne exiting Harjes's apartment with a duffel bag at about eleven o'clock Sunday morning.[68] After almost a week of testimony, the prosecution rested its case on March 28, 1944.

It was now Broderick's turn to present evidence. He began by making several motions to dismiss the indictment and to reduce the charges to second-degree murder. When denied, he opened with the testimony of Dr. Michel, who Wayne had seen on his weekend in the city, but much of this testimony was ruled inadmissible.[69] He then called Mario Gabellini, Patricia's date of the prior evening, and Felix Guiffre, the cab driver who had dropped her off the morning she died, attempting to demonstrate that Patricia had been wildly drunk, but both witnesses testified that she was quite functional, despite her many drinks. With that, having proved very little, he shocked those present by announcing that the defense would rest.[70]

Closing statements began on March 30. Broderick's summation was a mess. He was persuasive when he discussed the physical evidence, such as how awkward the candlesticks were as murder weapons and how Jaburg had not seen the scratches on Wayne's face, but swiftly deteriorated into an unconvincing and inappropriate diatribe. He spent much of his time verbally assaulting the prosecution team, and he even implied that Patricia's murder was not a murder at all but simply the unintended and unfortunate consequence of a clumsy, drunken accident. He argued that Wayne's confession had been coerced and portrayed him as a simple country boy who had been swept away by big-city life.[71]

Grumet followed with his closing statement, and, at 12:46 in the afternoon on Friday, March 31, the jury retired to deliberate. It returned at 10:20 that evening to deliver its verdict: second-degree murder, for which Wayne was sentenced to thirty-five years in prison. He was admitted swiftly thereafter to Sing Sing prison as prisoner number 103,124.[72]

The press coverage of Patricia's murder and the ensuing trial was phenomenal and immediate. On October 25, the day following the discovery of Patricia's body, the *New York Times* detailed how she had been "bludgeoned to death in her locked bedroom, apparently with one of a pair of antique bed lamps." The story, and others like it, described how "the body was nude" and that "no evidence of a struggle was discovered," setting the stage for widespread intrigue in the case.[73]

The story quickly became a sensation. Newspapers and tabloids reported on every new lead and ran full-page stories that outlined even the most minor details of the crime, from Wayne and Patricia's separation and their respective Saturday nights out on the town to the layout of Patricia's apartment and the fact that Ms. Black was hard of hearing. There was nothing about the crime that newspaper readers did not know.[74]

When Wayne became the primary suspect, the press became fixated on him. With so much evidence pointing toward his guilt, most publications portrayed him as the obvious culprit even before he confessed. Newspapers chronicled his journey from Toronto to New York, and, when he arrived at La Guardia airport, he was met with reporters who hounded him with "why did you kill her, Wayne? Where's the uniform? Who's the other woman?" and told him to "hold up the hand you choked her with."[75] He was described as calm, collected, and completely unaffected by his wife's murder, giving him a distinct air of villainy. One newspaper described him as he arrived at La Guardia as having a face that "betrayed no emotion" except for "once or twice, as flash-light bulbs exploded near him, his lips curled."[76] He was described as a "playboy" in countless articles, and, after the news broke of his homosexuality, the coverage turned even more negative. One piece in the *Journal-American* called him the "sex-twisted, 25-year-old Café Society playboy with the crew hair-cut and the easy sneer."[77]

Wayne's confession ran as a front-page eight-column spread entitled "Lonergan Confesses" in an extra edition of the *Journal-American*, which went to press even before he had finished confessing on that October afternoon. An article in *Time* magazine claimed that "it took no Sherlock Holmes to untangle a crime whose tawdry details petered out into unprintable and nearly unprintable gossip."[78]

Newspaper coverage from that point on documented trial

preparations and lingering investigations. Many postulated on who would testify and why, and whether there was enough evidence to prove that the murder was premeditated. Reports offered quotes from handwriting analysts, who claimed that "his handwriting would indicate the cause was uncontrollable emotion rather than a planned act," and murder novelists and uninvolved criminal attorneys, many of whom were eager to provide an opinion.[79] Papers also printed untrue conjectures and rumors, such as the one that became popular, despite Grumet's denial, that there had been another person in Patricia's bedroom with Wayne at the time of the murder.[80]

When the trial began, the press again went wild. One columnist, commenting on the reporters covering the Lonergan case, wrote that "you'd think the Lonergan murder had been committed for their special convenience."[81] Judge Freschi accredited 160 newsman for the first trial, some of whom were reporting internationally, all the way to Europe and South Africa. Seventy temporary telephone stations were installed in the courthouse so that stories could be transmitted as quickly as possible, and press seating overflowed into space that was normally reserved for spectators. More reporters were present at the first day of the proceedings than were covering the action on the Italian war front.[82] The case was front-page news on the opening day of the second trial, beating out the story that, on the very same day, Russia's first and second armies of the Ukraine had forced German troops into a retreat into Rumania.[83] The guilty verdict was announced nationwide by countless publications, as were Wayne's many appeals.

The reporters covering this episode were simply catering to their audience, a nation rabid for every morsel of information about this case. Not only New Yorkers but Americans all over the country were fixated on the Lonergan murder. They voraciously consumed news stories as fast as the papers could print them. One historian remembers following the case as a teenager and sneaking out of his boarding school every afternoon during gym class to read the latest news at the local drug store.[84] People lined up at the courthouse to get a glimpse of Wayne when he arrived at his trial,[85] and a crowd of people hundreds strong flocked to see him enter the car, a bulletproof limousine, that took him to Sing Sing. A group of children at a public school across from the Tombs waited outside for him, chanting "we want Lonergan."[86] Thyra Samter Winslow, who covered the case for the *Mirror*, summed up the pervasive interest in the case when she wrote that "folks ask the same questions—from members of the press to people you meet at dinner parties: 'which side are you on?'"[87]

The widespread public interest in the case was driven by multiple factors, beginning with the crime's sleazy undertones, which were apparent from the start. On the morning following the murder, the *New York Times* claimed that "the police said much of the information in their hands seemed to indicate the whole background of the case was somewhat sordid, with more than the usual amount of unpleasant relationships developed in sex crimes."[88] As more details began to unfold—Patricia's nude body, the fact that Wayne had been William Burton's companion, Wayne's dismissal from the military, and his alleged night with an American soldier—they all gave the case a heightened level of intrigue and its followers something to talk about. Winslow, in the same article mentioned above, wrote that when "the subject of sex aberrations arise[s] . . . all are at attention" and that "most of the important murder trials of the past—as well as this one—wouldn't be so interesting if sex weren't involved."[89]

Additionally, the victim and the suspect were both widely recognized socialites. Those who had read about them in the gossip columns in years prior loved seeing their pictures on the front page now. Those who had known them personally had even stronger reactions. Ms. Winslow, who had met the couple at cocktail parties, wrote in her column that it was a "recipe for the creeps! To see, on the first day of his trial for murder, a man you knew socially!"[90]

Not to be overlooked is the pervasive, class-crossing fascination with the café society. The beautiful Lonergans, with their posh Beekman Hill apartment and their nights at El Morocco and the Stork Club, were the perfect embodiments of this crowd. America had entered into the Second World War following the Japanese attack on Pearl Harbor on December 7, 1941, and the majority of Americans, who were rationing their gasoline and groceries and starting victory gardens in their backyards, could never dream of living this lifestyle. They were entirely mesmerized by it, just as people of the aughts were captivated by the affluence of the Gilded Age elite and people today are fascinated by the fast-living lifestyles of rock stars. But for most, this fascination was mixed with disapproval. One newsman summed up the general public's mixed enthrallment and repulsion of this set when he wrote that "they get around too much, these members of what must be called the Younger Generation, ever to lose their aplomb completely. At seven they know which fork to use. At thirteen they know the difference between a daiquiri and a Bacardi. At twenty they've lived a harsh lifetime."[91] Judge Freschi, in a statement he made condemning the case's widespread publicity, denounced what he called the "morbid curiosity" that had taken hold of so many New Yorkers with regard to this case. He felt that "what people should have more of are the details of decent living and the simple virtues of life and of wholesome instincts and habits of piety, rather than the worthless and aimless monotony of some of those who have been called in this case the café society."[92]

Regardless of whether they admired or hated them, the everyday American found pleasure in the fast-living Wayne getting his comeuppance. An article published after Wayne was arraigned and placed in the Tombs to await trial asserted that he "who experienced the glitter of café society and knew the life of a Broadway playboy, was left alone and friendless in his cell today."[93]

Finally, the Lonergan case came at a time when many Americans were looking for a distraction from the harsh realities and persistent concerns of the Second World War. The drama provided a welcome diversion, and many latched on to it, treating it as a piece of entertainment. Winslow of the *Mirror* wrote that "there's nothing like a real good murder," and one reporter actually compared the whole trial to a Hollywood production, remarking, for example, that Broderick "seemed miscast."[94] Wayne himself provided the perfect textbook villain, and he became as easy to hate as a Hollywood heavy.[95] One reporter, describing the case in 1950, summed up the situation perfectly when she said,

> The blithe exchange of partners which saw Lonergan dating a blond divorcee while his wife went out with a self-styled interior designer, the overtones of sexual perversion, the luxurious setting in which the crime was committed and the insouciant craftiness of the killer, all gave the case a hothouse, out-of-the-ordinary aura which was just what a war-weary world needed to "tsk-tsk" over in disapproval of such lurid goings-on.[96]

Wayne served over twenty years in prison, split between Sing Sing and a facility upstate in Dannemora, New York. He initiated several unsuccessful appeals, the most promising of which was a state appellate court review of his case in November 1944 in light of the landmark US Supreme Court case of *McNabb v. State of Tennessee*. In that case, the defendant was held and questioned for eleven hours before arraignment and before being allowed to speak with an attorney. The Supreme Court overturned McNabb's conviction in 1943 and created what would later become known as the McNabb-Mallory rule, which holds that if there is an unreasonably long delay between a defendant's arrest and preliminary hearing any confession made in that time is inadmissible.[97] The New York appellate court determined, however, that the McNabb decision did not require a reversal of Wayne's conviction, and the decision was upheld.[98] Another promising appeal was made in June 1964 following the US Supreme Court's ruling that a judge rather than a jury can conclude whether a confession was voluntary or coerced, but this appeal ended similarly, with the judge maintaining that Wayne's October 28 confession had been voluntary.[99]

Throughout his life, Wayne adamantly denied any involvement in Patricia's murder. He was quoted as telling a probation officer, "I did not murder my wife. I am innocent. The so-called confession is false."[100] He claimed that, when he was being questioned, not only was he threatened and physically beaten, but, at one point, an investigator presented him with a copy of the *Journal-American*, with a front-page story about his case, and told him to think about the negative effects the publicity was bound to have on his son. The officer told him that if he confessed to second-degree manslaughter, for which he would only serve a few years, "everything [would be] turned off" and "in two weeks . . . it'll be all forgotten." Wayne maintained that the promise of media abatement and a charge of manslaughter rather than murder were the only reasons that he made his confession.[101]

In the years following his conviction, however, Wayne did admit that his story about the encounter with the American soldier was fabricated. He alleged that he was so certain that the New York police would solve the case and find him innocent that he simply told false stories or agreed with what police suggested in an attempt to buy time. According to his account, he originally gave the soldier the name "Piggy Worcester" after a character in a P. G. Wodehouse story he had recently read and the police warped the name from Piggy to Murray to Maurice, and he made no attempt to correct them. On other occasions, he claimed that he told such an elaborate tale in order to preserve the reputation of a young woman with whom he actually spent those hours.[102] No woman ever came forward to identify herself.

Wayne was paroled in December 1965 under the explicit conditions that he return to Canada and never re-enter the United States without permission from US authorities.[103] In his first week in Toronto, he met and moved in with a wealthy female executive and, following their separation, dated actress Barbara Hamilton, whom he lived with for fourteen years.[104] Wayne died of cancer on January 2, 1986.[105]

With one parent dead and another incarcerated, young Billy Lonergan was placed in the custody of Lucille Burton and his name was legally changed to William Anthony Burton.[106] Some interest followed the boy in the immediate aftermath of the case, and it was not uncommon for his governess to be followed by photographers as she took him for walks in his carriage, but his celebrity was very short-lived. He attended a prestigious private primary school in New York and then Harvard University, after which he launched a career as a television producer for an advertising company. He lived in New York for several years before moving to the West Coast.[107]

The boy knew little of his parents' legacy until he was eleven years old. A reporter stopped him on his way home from school to tell this boy, who, according to the news story, "since infancy had regarded himself as an orphan," that "his mother was the victim of one of the most sensational slayings in New York history" and that "his father [was] not dead but imprisoned for the crime." The occasion for the renewed interest in the Lonergan case was the death of Stella Housman, Max Bernheimer's first wife. With her passing, Billy became the sole beneficiary of the Burton family fortune.[108]

When Wayne was paroled and returned to Canada, he attempted to reach out to his estranged son. He spoke with him on the phone on multiple occasions and asked him to visit him in Canada, explaining that he was not permitted to return to the United States. Billy never visited, and Wayne received an attorney's warning to cease contact with his son. Billy moved soon after, and Wayne hired a private detective in an attempt to obtain his new phone number. It proved too difficult to find. They never spoke again.[109]

For his behavior in the trial, Broderick faced contempt hearings and was charged by Judge Freschi with a $250 fine and thirty days in jail, although the sentence was later reduced to only the fine. Freschi cited a variety of behavior that was "unbecoming of a lawyer in the defense of his client" and maintained that he had "never heard of conduct so unprofessional."[110]

As for Patricia, she was buried at the Salem Field Cemetery in Brooklyn.[111]

Although one of the lesser-known trials of this American century, the Lonergan case was long remembered by those who were alive to witness it, and, even today, removed from its wartime context, it is a wildly captivating tale. With its salacious undertones, the involvement of a million-dollar fortune, an easily detestable villain who denied his involvement in the crime to his dying day, and a crime scene reminiscent of the Milton Bradley board game Clue, it is easy to understand why the press and the general public ran wild with this story.

CHAPTER 6

1950–1960:
WHO KILLED MARILYN?—
THE SAM SHEPPARD CASE

O n September 4, 1951, President Harry Truman spoke to the nation on television, and for the first time a broadcast was watched by viewers coast to coast at the same time. America, and especially its media, had come of age.

The 1950s represented a decade of unprecedented prosperity, progress, and optimism. Inflation stayed low, and Americans found jobs. Suburbs boomed. Passenger jets entered service, and Americans traveled. The ravages of polio became a dark horror of the past, and Disneyland a beacon of the future. Bing Crosby and Perry Como gave way to Elvis Presley and Chuck Berry. The launch of Sputnik and the Cold War were coming, but those celebrating the Fourth of July in 1954 felt part of a new and youthful era.

The murder of Marilyn Sheppard in her bedroom during the early-morning hours of July 4, 1954, remains one of America's most-notorious unsolved crimes. Young and beautiful, she was the mother of one child and pregnant with another, and her bludgeoning death transfixed a nation. Every circumstance of her death and the nine-week trial of her husband that followed became fodder for an unprecedented crush of newspaper coverage. In what the US Supreme Court later called "a carnival," hundreds of reporters took up every inch of the Cleveland courtroom, reporting every line of testimony and tracking the judge, jury, lawyers, and witnesses from home to court and back again. No one moved in the corridors without being questioned. Newsmen handled the evidence as it was offered during the proceedings. They set up a television station in a room next to the jury.[1]

On trial was not just Marilyn's physician husband but the image of America's newfound suburban lifestyle, with its privilege, comfort, and infidelity. Purveyors of America's exploding postwar ambition and optimism needed an outlet in the 1950s, and the national media found it in the trial of Dr. Sam Sheppard.

Sam and Marilyn were both raised in Cleveland, Ohio, and had known each other since childhood. Born in 1923, Sam was the youngest of three sons of Dr. Richard Allen Sheppard. His father and both of his older brothers were doctors of osteopathic medicine, and his father ran a prominent Cleveland medical clinic. Good-looking and personable, Sam was elected president of virtually every club he joined and was voted class president for all three years he was in high school. He lettered in varsity football, basketball, and track, and at graduation he was awarded Most Valuable Athlete.[2]

Dark-haired and beautiful, Marilyn was the elder of the two by eighteen months, graduating high school a year before Sam and attending Skidmore College in New York. Sam in his turn enrolled in Hanover College in Indiana, then took supplementary courses at Western Reserve University in Cleveland. Following in the footsteps of his father and brothers, he moved to Los Angeles to finish his education at the Los Angeles Osteopathic School of Physicians and Surgeons, was awarded the D. O. degree, and commenced internship and residency in neurosurgery at Los Angeles County General Hospital. He asked Marilyn to join him in Los Angeles, and they were married on February 21, 1945. Returning to Ohio in 1950, they bought a waterfront home on Lake Road in Bay Village, along the shore of Lake Erie.[3]

Sam Sheppard. © Bettmann/Corbis.

Bay Village was in the 1950s an upscale middle-class suburb of west Cleveland, with quiet streets and nice houses, everything that the postwar boom in America promised in its advertising and movies. Village neighbors knew each other and shopped in local stores. Its small five-man police force rarely handled more than accidents and disturbances; until July 4, 1954, it had not investigated a murder. The Sheppard family of physicians was popular and prominent in the small town, and their clinic, Bay View Hospital, was the only hospital in Bay Village.

Sam and Marilyn settled down to what to all appearances was an ideal suburban marriage. In the summer of 1954, Sam was working at the family-owned Bay View Hospital while Marilyn stayed home with their seven-year-old son, Sam Reese Sheppard, then called "Chip." In July she was four months pregnant.

But all was not ideal in the Sheppard home. Initially denied by him, evidence of Sam's infidelity was eventually proven at the trial, although the degree of the infidelity was in some doubt. Certainly, he was carrying on a torrid, three-year-long extramarital affair with Susan Hayes, a former nurse at the clinic. According to some, Marilyn was at least resigned to his affairs, if not happy.[4] To others their marital discord was obvious by the summer of 1954.[5]

Saturday, July 3, 1954, was a busy one for Sam. A father brought a young son into the emergency room after the boy had been hit by a utility truck. Sam rushed the small child to the operating room, cut open his chest, massaged his heart, and attempted other resuscitation efforts. None were successful, and the boy died. An exhausted Sam left the hospital that afternoon, stopped to visit his parents, and headed home.[6]

That evening Sam and Marilyn were hosting their neighbors Don and Nancy Ahern and their two children who lived five houses up the lane. The families arranged to meet first for cocktails at the Ahern home, but before they could move on to the Sheppard's for dinner, another emergency called Sam back to the hospital, where he treated another young boy hurt in an accident.[7]

Both families eventually reconvened for dinner at the Sheppard home that evening. After dinner, Don Ahern took his children home and then returned. Young Chip went up to bed about ten o'clock. Sam and Marilyn Sheppard and Don and Nancy Ahern settled in for the evening to watch a movie on television, but before it was done, Sam stretched out on a daybed in the room and fell asleep. The Aherns left some time after midnight, and Marilyn told Sam that she was going up to bed.

What happened next has spawned thousands of newspaper articles, numerous books, a network television series, and a major motion picture. Marilyn was found in the upstairs bedroom she shared with Sam, dead from the injuries received in a savage beating. There was blood everywhere. She was lying on her back at the foot of her bed, feet dangling to the floor. Her pajama bottoms were removed and her pajama top pushed up over her breasts, her open legs pinned by the horizontal bars of the foot-board. It was later determined that she had suffered some thirty-five blows, mostly to the head, with a blunt instrument.[8]

Sam was questioned that morning. He claimed to have been sleeping on the daybed in the living room when he was awakened sometime in the night by Marilyn calling his name. When he reached the top of the stairs by the door to the bedroom, he saw in the dim light a large form with tall, bushy hair and light-colored clothing. Sam testified that he was struck in the back of the neck and lost consciousness.

He regained consciousness an uncertain number of minutes later. In his testimony he explained what happened next:

I looked at my wife, I believed I took her pulse and felt that she was gone. I believed that I thereafter instinctively or subconsciously ran into my youngster's room next door and somehow determined that he was all right, I am not sure how I determined this. After that, I thought that I heard a noise downstairs. . . .[9]

He testified that he ran back downstairs and chased the bushy-haired intruder down to the Lake Erie beach below his house, struggled with him, and was again knocked out. When he awoke a second time, he was bare from the waist up, his pants and shoes were wet, and light was breaking.

Sam returned to the house and called a friend and neighbor, Spencer Houk, the mayor of Bay Village. "My God, Spen, get over here quick. I think they've killed Marilyn." Mayor Houk and his wife came over at once, finding Sam slumped in an easy chair downstairs and asked, "What happened?" Sam replied, "I don't know but somebody ought to try to do something for Marilyn." Mrs. Houk immediately went up to the bedroom, and Sam told Mayor Houk his story. When Mrs. Houk returned, the mayor called the local police, Sam's brother Richard, and the Aherns.[10]

The local police were the first to arrive. They in turn notified the local coroner, Dr. Sam Gerber, and the Cleveland city police. Dr. Richard Sheppard then arrived, determined that Marilyn was dead, examined his brother's injuries, and removed him to the nearby hospital operated by the family. When the coroner, the Cleveland police, and other officials arrived, the house and surrounding area were searched, the rooms of the house were photographed, and many persons, including the Houks and the Aherns, were interviewed. The Sheppard home and premises were taken into protective custody and remained so until after the trial.[11]

From the beginning, officials focused their suspicions on Sam, and to some the circumstances warranted it. The excessive number of blows suggested an enraged husband rather than an intruder. While the position of Marilyn's pajamas implied a sexual assault, there was no evidence of one; her pajamas were unbuttoned rather than ripped, and the position of her legs between the horizontal footrails of the bed made a sexual assault impossible. The house had the appearance of being ransacked, but "tidily," with drawers pulled out of desks and carefully stacked on the floor, rather than thrown about. Sam's shotguns were not taken. There were no signs of forced entry to the home, and nothing of value was missing, suggesting a staged burglary. There were no signs of a struggle on the beach. Sam was bare-chested, and his shirt was missing, perhaps to hide bloodstains. And the family dog, Koko, had not barked. The coroner, Dr. Gerber, is reported to have told his men, "Well, it is evident the doctor did this, so let's go get the confession out of him." Later that afternoon, the Cleveland police interrogated Sam at some length, at the end of which an officer told him, "I think you killed your wife."[12]

The Cleveland press followed soon after the police, and the frenzy began. Incredibly, they were given free roam of the house that morning, with photographers even allowed into the murder room while Marilyn's body still lay there.[13] The media coverage was immediate and overwhelming; over a period of six months the *Cleveland Press* printed 399 articles about Sam and the death of Marilyn.[14]

And from the beginning the newspapers trumpeted Sam's guilt. On July 7, the day of Marilyn's funeral, a newspaper story appeared in which Assistant County Attorney John Mahon, later the chief prosecutor in Sam's trial, sharply criticized the refusal of the Sheppard family to permit Sam's immediate questioning. This was simply untrue. Sam had been interrogated by the police four times on July 4, the day of the murder, and again on July 5 and sixth. On July 8, Coroner Gerber and four police officers went to the hospital to interview Sam, and the visit was reported by the newspapers under the headline "Testify Now In Death, Bay Doctor Is Ordered." On July 9, at the request of the coroner, Sam re-enacted the events at his home before the coroner, police officers, and a group of newsmen, who apparently were invited by the coroner. His performance was reported in detail by the news media accompanied by photographs of the proceeding.[15] On July 10, Sam spent all day at the sheriff's office being repeatedly questioned and signed a several-page formal statement.

During this same week the newspapers also played up Sam's refusal to take a lie detector test. A front-page newspaper headline on July 10 announced "Doctor Balks At Lie Test; Retells Story." The next day, another headline story disclosed that Sam had again refused to take a lie detector test and quoted an assistant county attorney as authority for that story. At the same time, the newspaper reported that other possible suspects had been "cleared" by lie detector tests. One of these persons was quoted as saying that he could not understand why an innocent man would refuse to take such a test. More stories appeared when Sheppard would not allow authorities to inject him with "truth serum."[16]

On July 20, a front-page editorial in the *Cleveland Press* entitled "Getting Away With Murder" condemned what it deemed the slow pace at which police were investigating, stating,

> In the background of this case are friendships, relationships, hired lawyers, a husband who ought to have been subjected instantly to the same third-degree to which any other person under similar circumstances is subjected, and a whole

string of special and bewildering extra-privileged courtesies that should never be extended by authorities investigating a murder—the most serious, and sickening crime of all.[17]

The following day, another page-one editorial was headed "Why No Inquest? Do It Now, Dr. Gerber," demanding that the coroner call an inquest and subpoena Sam to testify.[18] Smarting from the challenge, Dr. Gerber commenced the inquest the next day in the gymnasium of Normandy High School in Bay Village, and the three-day session was filled with public spectators, press, and high drama. In the front of the room was a long table occupied by reporters, television and radio personnel, and broadcasting equipment. Microphones were placed in front of the coroner and on the witness stand. Crowds lined up outside the school to get seats, and reporters and photographers chronicled all of the testimony. For the first two days, Coroner Gerber elicited the testimony of police officers, family members, and neighbors, including the sixteen-year-old son of Mayor Houk who with other local teenagers had been enlisted by the police to help search the lakefront yard of the Sheppard home.[19]

On the third day of the inquest, Sam was called to testify. Before a swarm of reporters and photographers, he was brought into the gymnasium by police and searched in full view of the spectators, who by then numbered several hundred. Sam's attorneys were present during the three-day inquest but not permitted to participate. When his principal attorney, William J. Corrigan, attempted to place documents in the record, he was forcibly ejected from the gymnasium. "Remove him," the coroner ordered, and Corrigan was hauled from the gymnasium while cameras rolled. The *Cleveland Plain Dealer* reported on its front page,

> Spectators cheered wildly yesterday as William J. Corrigan, criminal lawyer representing Dr. Samuel H. Sheppard, was half dragged from the room in the closing moments of the Marilyn Sheppard murder inquest in Bay Village.[20]

Afterward the coroner received hugs and kisses from ladies in the audience.[21]

At the inquest, Sam made the mistake that would haunt him at his trial: he denied his extramarital affair with Susan Hayes. Hayes was a lab technician at Bay View Hospital who had left in 1953 to move to California. Officers quickly tracked her down, and after first denying her relationship with Sam she later admitted all, the officers suggesting that if she did not she would face criminal charges for adultery, then still a crime in Ohio.[22] Susan described the affair to officers, including her many sexual encounters with Sam in his car, in the Bay View Hospital, and on his visits to California. All became fodder for the newspapers.

Media coverage continued to do more than report the case; it influenced and even directed the course of the administration of justice. Just as the Cleveland papers had compelled the coroner to hold the inquest, now the same papers demanded in front-page editorials to know why Sam was not jailed. A July 28 editorial in the *Cleveland Press* entitled "Why Don't Police Quiz Top Suspect" remarked of Sam,

> Now proved under oath to be a liar, still free to go about his business, shielded by this family, protected by a smart lawyer who has made monkeys of the police and authorities, carrying a gun part of the time, left free to do whatever he pleases as he pleases, Sam Sheppard still hasn't been taken to Headquarters.[23]

Two days later the *Cleveland Press*, in a front-page editorial headlined "Why Isn't Sam Sheppard in Jail?", demanded action against Sam:

> A murder has been committed. You know who the chief suspect is. You have the obligation to question him—question him thoroughly and searchingly—from beginning to end, and not at his hospital, not at his home, not in some secluded spot out of the country. But at Police Headquarters—just as you do every other person suspected in a murder case. What the people of Cuyahoga County cannot understand, and The Press cannot understand, is why you are showing Sam Sheppard so much more consideration as a murder suspect than any other person who has ever before been suspected in a murder case. Why?[24]

In response, police arrested Sam late that night at his father's house. He was taken to the Bay Village City Hall, where despite the hour hundreds of people, reporters, and photographers were waiting. He was immediately arraigned, denied a delay to secure presence of counsel, and bound over to the grand jury.[25]

A preliminary hearing was finally held before Judge William Thomas on August 16. Presented with no evidence by the prosecutor, he ordered Sam released on bail. The newspapers howled. The following day the prosecutor sought an indictment from the grand jury, and the newspapers printed the grand jury testimony, normally sealed. Even more, the pictures, names, and addresses of grand jury members were published in the *Cleveland Press*. Jurors found themselves telephoned and stopped on the street. The grand jury obediently returned an indictment against Sam, and grand jury foreman Bert R. Winston was quoted as saying, "The pressure on us has been enormous."[26]

Sam's trial commenced in October 1954 amid this circus of media attention. It was also two weeks before the November general election of 1954, at which the prosecutor Mahon was a candidate for judge and the trial judge, Edward Blythin, was up for re-election. Twenty-five days earlier, seventy-five individuals were called as prospective jurors. All three Cleveland newspapers published their names and addresses, so that when eighteen days of jury selection began on October 18, 1954, every prospective juror told the court that they had received letters and telephone calls, both known and anonymous, regarding the trial.[27]

From the beginning the press had free range of the courtroom. The courtroom itself was a modest 1,200 square feet, including four rows of seats behind the railing, or bar, that separated the spectators from the judge, jury box, and the well, where the prosecution and defense were seated. The first three rows of audience seats were assigned to the press, and only the last row assigned to family. When those three rows proved insufficient for all of the media representatives that clamored for seats, the extraordinary remedy was adopted of placing a twenty-foot-long temporary table in the space between the bar and the tables occupied by the prosecution and defense, and packing that table with reporters. Seated where they were, the press could hear the lawyers talk to each other and to Sam, and view and handle all of the evidence. One end of the extemporary press table ended only three feet from the jury box.[28]

Representatives of the news media also used every room on the courthouse floor, including the room where cases were ordinarily called and assigned for trial. Private telephone lines and telegraphic equipment were installed in these rooms so that reports from the trial could be speeded to the papers. Station WSRS was permitted to set up broadcasting facilities on the third floor of the courthouse next to the jury room, where the jury rested during recesses in the trial. Newscasts were made from this room throughout the trial, even while the jury deliberated.[29]

The tenor of the news reporting continued to be highly prejudicial to Sam, especially in light of the fact that the jury consisted of unsequestered townsfolk who knew his story and read the daily papers. On October 23, as the trial got underway, the *Cleveland Press* printed a page-one broadside against Sam:

BUT WHO WILL SPEAK FOR MARILYN?

It's perfect, you think at first, as you look over the setting for the Big Trial. The courtroom is just the size to give a feeling of coziness and to put the actors close enough to each other so that in moments of stress the antagonists can stand jaw to jaw and in moments of relaxation can exchange soft words of camaraderie. . . . These provide the perfect background for the most perfect character of all—the accused. Was there ever more perfect typing? Was there ever a more perfect face for the enigma that is the Big Trial? . . . Is he the one? Did he do it? Plus of course, the other characters. The accused's two brothers. Prosperous, poised. His two sisters-in-law. Smart, chic, well-groomed. His elderly father. Courtly, reserved. A perfect type for the patriarch of a staunch clan.

Then it hits you again. No there's something—and someone missing.

There is no grieving mother—she died when Marilyn was very young. There's no revenge-seeking brother nor sorrowing sister. Marilyn was an only child. Her father is not here. Why is his own personal business.

What then, you wonder, will be the other side. . . .

Here is the complete story of Marilyn Reese Sheppard. How she lived, how, we think, she died. Her story will come into this courtroom through our witnesses. Here is how it starts: Marilyn Sheppard, nee Reese, age 30, height 5 feet, 7 inches, weight 125 pounds, brown hair, hazel eyes. On the morning of July 4 she was murdered in her bedroom.

Then you realize how what and who is missing from the perfect setting will be supplied. How in the Big Case justice will be done. Justice to Sam Sheppard. And to Marilyn Sheppard.[30]

At twenty-eight days of witness testimony, the trial of Sam Sheppard was said to have been the longest criminal trial on record in the United States at the time.[31] Sam was represented by the legal team of Corrigan, Corrigan's young son Bill Jr., recently graduated from law school, and attorneys Fred Garmone and Arthur Petersilge. The prosecution team included Mahon, who was elected to a judgeship in the middle of the trial, Gertrude Bauer, whom Mahon would marry days after the trial ended, and Saul S. Danaceau and Thomas J. Parrino, both later judges. Also at the prosecution table was Cleveland Police Inspector James McArthur. His pretrial statements that there was no proof of anyone else being in the Sheppard house at the time of the murder had been published by the local newspapers.

The prosecution began with photos of Marilyn's murder projected on a screen in the courtroom, accompanied by testimony by Dr. Lester Adelson, the chief pathologist in the coroner's office who had conducted the autopsy on Marilyn and testified about the injuries she suffered. A wax model of Marilyn's head was used to demonstrate the murder blows. Neighbors Don and Nancy Ahern each testified how Sam had fallen asleep while they watched a movie the evening before the murder, still wearing his jacket, which he was not wearing after his fight with the intruder. The jacket was found neatly folded on the daybed, a fact the prosecution offered as evidence that Sam's actions on the night of the murder were calm and unhurried. Nancy Ahern testified that Marilyn had confided to her a rumor that she had heard that Sam was considering a divorce but had decided against it.[32]

Esther and Spen Houk were called to testify regarding their meetings with Sam on the morning of July 4. Esther was asked if Sam's shoulder was dry when she touched it, and she answered that it was, to the point that he was not wet when he returned from his altercation with the bushy-haired assailant at the beach. Mayor Houk, over objections, was allowed to testify that he had voluntarily taken a lie detector test in the days that followed Marilyn's murder, in sharp contrast to Sam's well-published refusal to do the same. Their son, Larry Houk, testified about finding a green bag in the Sheppard yard that contained Sam's watch and jewelry, which the prosecution considered a ruse.

The Houks were followed to the witness stand by Bay Village police officers Fred Drenkhan, Jay Hubach, and John Eaton, and firemen Richard Callihan and Richard Sommer. Then came Cleveland officers Henry Dombrowski, Jerry Poelking, Michael Grabowski, Pat Gareau, and Robert Schottke, along with county deputy sheriffs Carl Rossbach and Dave Yettra. The officers testified as to their actions on the morning of the murder, and that there was no sign of forcible entry to the Sheppard home.

Coroner Dr. Gerber then came to the stand, and he dropped a bombshell. He testified that his examination of the bloodstains on a pillow case on Marilyn's bed were made by the imprint of a long, hinged, two-pronged weapon, which he identified as a surgical instrument. Because no such weapon or instrument had been found in or outside the house despite an intensive search, including the dredging of Lake Erie in front of the Sheppard's home, he could not describe the instrument with greater particularity. Nevertheless, his testimony strongly implicated Marilyn's surgeon husband as the perpetrator.[33]

Then came Susan Hayes, who testified regarding her affair with Sam, with its damaging effect on his credibility after his denial of the relationship with her.

The defense's presentation, in turn, was light on scientific evidence. The law in 1954 did not require prosecutors to turn over evidence in a trial to the defense team, and the Sheppard home had been sealed against examination by experts hired by Sam and his attorneys. Evidence of the presence of a third-party intruder that might have cast doubt on Sam's guilt, including a trail of blood left by the assailant, was inaccessible to those experts. Though bleeding profusely, Marilyn had never escaped the bedroom, and Sam had no open wounds.[34]

Instead, the defense featured medical witnesses who testified that Sam's injuries the morning of the murder were of a type inconsistent with the struggle that Marilyn may have put up, and character witnesses who testified in Sam's defense. Dr. Charles Elkin, who had examined Sam on the first days following the murder, and five other doctors, a dentist, and several nurses were called by the defense for a thorough detailing of Sam's injuries, which included injuries to his spine and swelling at the base of the skull. The prosecution in response characterized those injuries as self-inflicted. Members of Sam's family testified. A long string of character witnesses testified to Sam's good nature and the general normality of his relationship with Marilyn. Members of her family also testified as to her buoyant mental state in the days preceding the murder in an attempt to deflect any suggestion of marital discord.[35]

Next the defense elicited the testimony of people who had been in the area the night of the murder. Various neighbors testified as to when lights went on and off at the residence. Fishermen from the lake testified to seeing teenage boys on the park pier early in the morning, and teenagers testified as to activities and movements in the immediate area. Drivers who had seen a stranger walking on Lake Road in the morning were called to give their testimony.

Then Sam testified on his own behalf, taking the stand for three days. Under cross-examination from the prosecution, his story of the events of that night did not change.[36] Both sides made their closing arguments, prosecutor Mahon concluding, "Why, this house was full of phantoms that night, I think, ladies and gentlemen. . . ."

During the course of the trial, all three Cleveland newspapers maintained their relentless call for Sam's conviction. Banner headlines included:[37]

SAM CALLED A JEKYLL-HYDE BY MARILYN,
COUSIN TO TESTIFY

CALLS DR. SAM LOVE SLAYER, ASKS DEATH

LAB MEN READY ATTACK ON SAM

STORY OF ILLICIT ROMANCE WILL CLIMAX TRIAL

DR. SAM FACES ATTACK ON LOVES

SAM FAKED BURGLARY TO COVER UP MURDER

At one point, a picture of Marilyn's bloodstained pillow was published on the front page, after having been doctored to more clearly show the imprint of the alleged "surgical instrument."[38]

Syndicated columns and news agency reports made the case almost as well-known in every community of the nation as it was in Cleveland. Dorothy Kilgallen, known for her celebrity role on the television game show *What's My Line?*, covered the trial and later expressed shock at the guilty verdict. But it wasn't until years later that Kilgallen also described how the judge called her into his chambers on the first day of the trial. They shook hands, and he asked her, "What brings you to Cleveland?" She replied that she was there to cover the trial and told Judge Blythin that she was intrigued by the mystery of who had committed the murder. The judge responded, "Mystery? It's an open and shut case. . . . He is guilty as hell. There is no question about it."[39]

In the middle of the trial, national broadcaster Walter Winchell aired a story about a woman under arrest in New York who claimed she had a child by Sam. It turned out to be false.[40]

After five days of deliberation, on December 21 the jurors came back with a verdict of second-degree murder, intentional but without premeditation.

The Sheppard family was, as expected, crushed and distraught by the jury's verdict. Sam's mother, Ethel, shot herself to death three weeks later. His father, Richard, died of stomach cancer eleven days after Ethel. By contrast, the prosecutors Bauer and Mahon, the latter now a judge-elect, were able to celebrate. The two married before Christmas.[41]

But mostly, the trial was a bonanza for the local newspapers. Before the murder, from March 1953 to March 1954, the *Cleveland Press* had suffered a circulation decline.[42] But all three Cleveland newspapers reported extraordinary circulation gains during the Sheppard trial, and the *Cleveland Press* sold 30,000 extra copies on the day of the verdict.[43]

Sam Sheppard spent ten years in a maximum-security state penitentiary in Columbus, Ohio, in all of which time his remaining family and legal team sought to overturn his conviction. On January 3, 1955, the trial court overruled the motion for a new trial, which had been based on numerous decisions of error occurring during the trial and deliberation, including Sam's arraignment before trial on a capital charge in the absence of counsel, the inability of Corrigan to represent him during the inquest, the refusal of the court to change the venue of the trial in the face of massive adverse publicity, the publication of the list of potential jury members in advance of the trial, the failure to sequester the jurors during the trial, the trial judge's decision to set aside the major portion of the courtroom to representatives of the news media, the police seizure of Sam's house and excluding him and his representatives from it for the duration of the trial, and other claims. On May 9, 1955, the trial court denied a supplemental motion for a new trial on the grounds that Sam's retained experts had since investigated the house and could demonstrate the presence of blood in the house that did not come from either Marilyn or Sam. In July 1955, the Court of Appeals affirmed the conviction and the denial of the motion for a new trial. On May 31, 1956, the Ohio Supreme Court affirmed the Court of Appeals, with two judges dissenting. On November 14, 1956, the US Supreme Court denied a petition for certiorari and subsequently denied an application for a rehearing. On September 5, 1960, the Ohio Supreme Court denied an application for habeas corpus.[44]

After six years of fighting on Sam's behalf, defense lawyer William Corrigan died in July 1961, and attorney F. Lee Bailey, just a year out of law school, was selected by Sam's brother Stephen to prosecute the appeal. Bailey was then in his early thirties. Brilliant, talented, and always controversial, he had studied at Harvard but had dropped out in 1952 to join the Marine Corps, where he received aviator wings in 1954. He received his law degree from Boston University, ranked first in his graduating class in 1960.[45]

By 1963, Sam and Bailey had moved their arguments to the federal courts. On April 11, 1963, they filed a petition for a writ of habeas corpus in the US District Court, contending that he had not received a fair trial. The court granted the writ, but the United States Court of Appeals reversed it. The matter finally reached the United States Supreme Court in 1966 and the now-famous decision in *Sheppard v. Maxwell*[46] handed down, the court ruling,

> Since the state trial judge did not perform his duty to protect Sheppard from the inherently prejudicial publicity which saturated the community and to control disruptive influences in the courtroom, we must reverse the denial of the habeas petition. The case is remanded to the district courtroom with instructions to issue the writ and order that Sheppard be released from custody unless the State puts him to its charges again within a reasonable time.[47]

The US Supreme Court awarded Sam a retrial. The case established Bailey's reputation as a skilled defense attorney and was the first of many high-profile cases, including the defense of the confessed Boston Strangler, the defense of US Army Captain Ernest Medina in the My Lai Massacre court-martial in 1971, the unsuccessful defense of Patty Hearst in her prosecution for armed bank robbery after being kidnapped by the Symbionese Liberation Army, and the acquittal of O. J. Simpson in 1995.

The State of Ohio did retry Sam soon after. At his new arraignment on September 8, 1966, Sheppard loudly pleaded "not guilty," with attorney Bailey by his side. Unlike in the original trial, this time neither Sheppard nor Susan Hayes took the stand, a strategy that proved to be successful when a not guilty verdict was returned on November 16, 1966.[48]

Sam's life never returned to the normality that it had before the early-morning hours of July 4, 1954. Days after his release from prison following the Supreme Court's decision in the summer of 1966, Sam married Ariane Tebbenjohanns, a German divorcee who had corresponded with him during his time in prison. Tebbenjohanns endured her own bit of controversy shortly after her relationship with Sam was announced, confirming that her half-sister was Magda Ritschel, the wife of Nazi propaganda chief Joseph Goebbels. Tebbenjohanns emphasized that she held no Nazi views. Their marriage short-lived, Sam and Tebbenjohanns divorced on October 7, 1969.[49]

After his acquittal, Sam coauthored *Endure and Conquer*, presenting his side of the case and giving insight into his years in prison. F. Lee Bailey wrote the foreword. Sam also returned briefly to medicine in Youngstown, Ohio, but was sued twice for medical malpractice by the estates of dead patients and left the practice.[50] Later, Sheppard enjoyed a brief career as a professional wrestler, going by the name The Killer, teamed with partner George Strickland in matches across the United States. Just six months before his death, Sheppard married George's daughter, Colleen Strickland.[51]

Sam died of liver failure on April 6, 1970, having by the end of his life become an alcoholic drinking as much as two-fifths of liquor a day. He was forty-six and had enjoyed his liberty for only four years. He was buried in Forest Lawn Memorial Gardens in Columbus, Ohio, where his body remained until 1997 when it was exhumed for DNA testing as part of the lawsuit brought by his son, Sam Reese Sheppard, to clear his father's name. After the tests, the body was cremated, and the ashes were laid to rest in a mausoleum at Knollwood Cemetery in Mayfield Heights, Ohio, next to those of Marilyn.

In 1963, ABC premiered *The Fugitive*, the drama series

created by Roy Huggins, starring David Janssen as Richard Kimble, a doctor falsely accused of his wife's murder and given the death penalty. While Kimble is en route to death row, his train derails and crashes, allowing him to escape and begin a cross-country search for the real killer, a one-armed man played in the series by Bill Raisch. The series was a hit and ran for four seasons, ranked as one of *TV Guide*'s 50 Greatest TV Shows of All Time. As originally conceived, the story called for the murder of Dr. Kimble's wife to have been committed by a "red-haired" man, but studio lawyers told Huggins that it was too similar to the "bushy-haired" intruder described by Sam.[52]

Huggins denied basing the series on Sam Sheppard, although the show's music supervisor, Ken Wilhoit, was married to Susan Hayes, Sam's lover and the star witness in the 1954 trial.

The series was remade as a 1993 feature film starring Harrison Ford as Dr. Richard Kimble. Grossing $368,000,000 in box-office business from a $44,000,000 budget, the film was a major financial success and was nominated for seven Academy Awards, including Best Picture.[53]

With the acquittal of Sam Sheppard in the second trial in 1966 came renewed interest in who else might have committed the crime. There were many people, particularly in the Cleveland area, who were convinced that Sam was nonetheless guilty. Those who prosecuted Sam clearly believe him to be the murderer, notwithstanding his acquittal.[54] But a number of other suspects raised speculation. In the weeks and months that followed the crime, numerous tips had been received and several people actually confessed to Marilyn's bludgeoning, but all were dismissed as either attention seekers or individuals with psychiatric problems. There was some interest in a hitchhiking drifter named Donald Joseph Wedler who was in Bay Village on the night of the murder and confessed to have beaten a woman to death with a pipe. Although several aspects of his statement matched the circumstances of Marilyn's murder, many did not, including the number of blows inflicted. He was not charged with the crime.[55]

Soon after Sam's acquittal, F. Lee Bailey compelled a grand jury to hear witnesses regarding his favorite perpetrators, Spencer and Esther Houk. Bailey recounted the testimony of Jack Krakan, a bread delivery man who had testified that he had seen Spencer Houk embracing and kissing Marilyn. On one occasion, he said, he had observed Marilyn give Houk a key to the house, which fit well with the police's theory that there was no evidence of a break-in. The grand jury heard a few witnesses, including Mayor Houk, but took no action.[56]

Sixteen years later, in November 1982, the new owners of the Houk residence on Lake Road in Bay Village found a buried pair of fireplace thongs, which matched the description Dr. Sam Gerber gave in the first trial of the instrument that left the bloody image on Marilyn's pillow. Both of the Houks were by then deceased, and the evidence was not considered conclusive.

But as a result of a lawsuit filed against the State of Ohio by Sam Reese Sheppard to clear his father's name in October 1995, more than forty years after the murder and twenty-five years after Sam's death, renewed attention focused on Richard Eberling, a petty thief and convicted murderer who boasted in prison that he had killed Marilyn and beaten Sam when he tried to interfere. Eberling had been employed in the village as a window washer in the summer of 1954, and had been in the Sheppard home on the second or third of July.[57]

Eberling was a behaviorally handicapped young man raised in a series of foster homes, eventually placed with George and Christine Eberling, an older couple who farmed in Bay Village,

Ohio. As early as his childhood, deaths began to occur around him. In 1946, while Eberling was still living with his foster parents, George Eberling died while suffering from pneumonia, but it was discovered that he had ingested poison left on his bedside nightstand. After reaching adulthood, Eberling started a window washing business, covering a long string of petty thefts from the homes he serviced. When he was arrested in 1959 on charges of theft, he was in possession of one of Marilyn's rings. In his examination, he told investigators that while cleaning the windows in the Sheppard house on either July 2 or July 3 he had cut himself, and that was why his blood was present on the floors of the house. Despite the suspicious nature of his confession, Eberling was not charged, Sam already having been convicted and more than four years into his sentence.

There were other surprising coincidences between Marilyn's murder and Eberling. Barbara Kinzel, a nurse at the Sheppard's Bay View Hospital, died while riding as a passenger in her Ford convertible when it veered off a Michigan highway and struck a parked vehicle. Eberling was driving. Kinzel, who had cared for Sam following Marilyn's murder, claimed that she felt Sam was innocent based on the severity of his injuries, and after her comments had been circulated in newspapers, Eberling began calling on her, and the two started dating. An autopsy performed on Kinzel raised questions as to the nature of her injuries, including a broken neck, which were inconsistent with the circumstances of the accident, but Eberling was not charged.

By 1962 Eberling had inserted himself into the life of one Ethel May Durkin, a wealthy, childless widow who lived in Lakewood, Ohio. Durkin's sister, Myrtle Fray, took an instant dislike to Eberling, and she was found savagely beaten about the head and strangled in her apartment on May 20, 1962, after she had gone to bed. Thirty years later, Eberling wrote that Fray was killed in the same manner as Marilyn Sheppard.[58] Another of Durkin's sisters died under suspect conditions in March 1970 while living with Durkin in her Lakewood home. This time the death was attributed to injuries sustained in a fall down basement steps that broke both legs and arms. By the time of this second death, Eberling was systematically looting Durkin's assets. Soon after, Durkin also began having a number of accidents that resulted in injuries, including falls down flights of stairs. On November 15, 1983, paramedics were called to the Durkin home, and they found her facedown on a hardwood floor. Eberling claimed that she had fallen while rising from a chair. X-rays revealed that her neck had been broken, and Durkin died from her injuries six weeks later. Her will, which had been forged by Eberling, left the bulk of her estate to him. Also in the will were instructions that she was to be buried with her jewelry and her favorite mink coat, but before the casket was sealed Eberling removed both the jewelry and the mink coat from her body. When Durkin's corpse was exhumed for examination, an autopsy revealed that Durkin had been struck in the neck from behind, and Eberling was charged with her murder and convicted in July 1989. In the investigation, Kathy Wagner, a health aide hired by Eberling, quoted him as confiding that he had killed Marilyn and struck Sam in the head with a steel pail, adding, "You didn't hear that." Eberling died in prison on July 25, 1998.

In 1995 Sam's son, Sam Reese Sheppard, used his father's estate to file a lawsuit against the State of Ohio for Sam's wrongful imprisonment. Under state law, Sheppard had to prove that his father was innocent, a far more difficult legal standard than that of Sam's retrial, where acquittal was required unless he was found guilty beyond a reasonable doubt. Young Sheppard and his lawyers focused their case on Eberling, claiming that recently performed DNA testing concluded that the blood found in the Sheppard home on the night of Marilyn's murder was his. Sam Reese Sheppard had his father's remains exhumed in order to conduct DNA testing and exclude Sam's blood from the blood-stains found in the home. In response, the State of Ohio had the bodies of Marilyn and the fetus she was carrying exhumed in 1999 so that they could perform their own DNA tests.

The wrongful imprisonment civil trial commenced in February of 2000, with lawyers for Sam Reese Sheppard attempting to prove that Eberling had committed the murder and prosecutors for the State of Ohio maintaining that Sam had killed his wife. F. Lee Bailey was the first witness. After two months of testimony, seventy-six witnesses, and hundreds of exhibits, the jury deliberated just three hours on April 12, 2000 before returning a verdict in the favor of the State of Ohio.[59] In February 2002, the Eighth District Court of Appeals ruled in favor of the State on the procedural grounds that a wrongful imprisonment claim could be made only by the person actually imprisoned, and not by a family member such as Sam Reese Sheppard. Legal standing to bring such a claim, the court of appeals found, died with the person who had been imprisoned. The appeals court decision was affirmed by the Supreme Court of Ohio later that year.[60]

Nearly fifty years after Marilyn's brutal murder, the trials finally came to an end. After tens of thousands of transcript pages in the numerous trials, ten books, thousands of newspaper articles, a television series, and a major motion picture, no one knows who killed her.

The bludgeoning death of Marilyn Sheppard and the spiraling descent of her husband from respected physician to prisoner, wrestler, and finally ignominious death have fascinated Americans for two generations. Something intangible about the Sheppards, other than just celebrity, combines into an elixir that continues to enthrall. And in that mix it's impossible to separate the story from the storyteller, to determine if the national media found a story of interest to its readers and reported it, or if they fanned a tiny ember into an undeserved firestorm. Jack P. DeSario and William Mason in *Dr. Sam Sheppard On Trial,* their recounting of the 2000 trial of the civil suit filed by Sam Reese Sheppard, in which Mason was lead counsel for the State of Ohio, write that when the pretrial proceedings got underway in 1999, the prosecutor's office was handling several gruesome cases, including that of Mary Jo Pesho, a Parma wife and mother who had been abducted at a mall and tortured, raped, and murdered in the back of a van, and that of Thomas McCarthy, a serial rapist who broke into a young woman's home, hung her up by her thumbs, and tortured and raped her. Either of these stories would have warranted extensive media coverage, yet when Marilyn's casket was transported that same year to the coroner's office for DNA testing, the drive turned into a public spectacle, with fleets of satellite trucks, television vans, and helicopters.[61]

Ohio Supreme Court Justice James Finley Bell Jr. captured it well in the opening paragraph of his decision in 1956:

> Murder and mystery, society, sex and suspense were combined in this case in such a manner as to intrigue and captivate the public fancy to a degree perhaps unparalleled in recent annals. Throughout the preindictment investigation, the subsequent legal skirmishes and the nine-week trial, circulation-conscious editors catered to the insatiable interest of the American public in the bizarre. . . . In this atmosphere of a "Roman Holiday" for the news media, Sam Sheppard stood trial for his life.[62]

CHAPTER 7

1960–1970:
EIGHT DEAD STUDENT NURSES
AND THE TEXAS DRIFTER

I t is impossible to look back on the 1960s with dispassion. It was a decade of rebellion and free love, of expectation and heartbreak. The youthful optimism that began with the inauguration of John Kennedy in 1961 died with him two years later in Dealey Plaza, followed by the assassinations of Martin Luther King Jr., Robert F. Kennedy, and the leaders of at least five other nations. America's undeclared war in Vietnam brought protesters to the streets in towns of every state, while others without viewpoints tuned in, turned on, and dropped out. Radio stations rang with protest songs. And all over the country poor and disadvantaged minorities launched a war for equal civil rights, galvanizing liberals and conservatives alike, filling nightly news with horrifying scenes of dogs, lynchings, and water cannons turned on marchers, tearing at the fabric of American culture and community.

In the early evening of Wednesday, July 13, 1966, as Chicago reeled from race riots and the National Guard patrolled its streets, Richard Oliva, on leave from Vietnam, was drinking beer and shooting pool with the Walsh brothers, Patrick, Jim, and Michael, at the Shipyard Inn. It was a working-class tavern on Chicago's South Side, catering to workers of the nearby factories and Lake Michigan shipyards. Looking up from his game, Oliva noticed a young man entering the bar. Over six feet, approximately 160 pounds, he had close-cropped sandy hair, a deeply pockmarked face, and numerous tattoos, including one reading "Born To Raise Hell." Ordering a drink at the bar, the man casually let a black switchblade fall to the floor with a clatter, and then slowly, unconcerned, he retrieved it and put it back in his pocket. Shortly after, standing at the jukebox, the man lifted his shirt to show off a second long knife hanging in a sheath at his belt.[1]

The stranger was Richard Franklin Speck, a twenty-four-year-old drifter from Texas, who had taken a room in the cheap hotel upstairs. Born near Monmouth, Illinois, he had moved at age eight with his mother and younger sister to Dallas to live with a hard-drinking stepfather who despised him and told him so. In his thirteen years in Dallas he was arrested forty-one times for a wide variety of crimes, spending two years in a Texas penitentiary. Following a March break-in of a Dallas grocery, Speck had fled Texas and returned to Monmouth, where in April he was suspected in the rape of an elderly woman and the murder of a barmaid.[2] Quickly leaving again, he had landed with an older sister and her family in a northwest Chicago neighborhood near Wrigley Field. Two days ago, the welcome expired, his brother-in-law had given him some money and dropped him off at the National Maritime Union Hall on East 100th Street, a little over a mile from the Shipyard Inn, and told him to find work.[3]

Now sitting in a booth at the Shipyard, Patrick Walsh noticed Speck staring at him. Walsh asked if they knew each other. In response, Speck pulled a black pistol from his waistband and pointed it at Walsh under the table. Walsh stood his ground, berating the stranger, and Speck put the gun away. The two struck up a conversation. For Patrick Walsh, and later for his brother Michael, Speck told wholly fabricated stories of seamanship, Vietnam, and bar fights. When the Walshes left the bar after ten, Speck went upstairs to change his clothes and set out on a murderous night's work.

Richard Speck enters court. © Bettmann/Corbis.

Just west across Cranden Avenue from the Maritime Union Hall on East 100th Street were three two-story attached townhomes used by South Chicago Community Hospital to house its student nurses. In one of the townhomes lived eight young women ranging in age from twenty to twenty-four. Three of them, Valentina Pasion, Merlita Gargullo, and Corazon "Cora" Amurao, were exchange students from the Philippines. The remaining five, Gloria Davy, Patricia Matusek, Nina Jo Schmale, Suzanne Farris, and Pamela Wilkening, were local girls. The eight slept upstairs in three cramped bedrooms and used a single bath. Downstairs were a kitchen and living area.

Speck had watched the student nurses come and go over the last two days as he waited for work at the Union Hall.[4] This evening he approached the townhouse from the rear, dressed in black pants and a black jacket zipped up to hide a white T-shirt. He opened a downstairs window using the switchblade and reached in and unlocked the back door. It was about 11:30 p.m. On that hot July night, just six of the students were home, Suzanne and Gloria still out until the 12:30 curfew. Upstairs, Speck knocked on the door of the bedroom shared by Cora and Merlita, and Cora opened it. He pointed the gun at her. Then he forced them at gunpoint down the short hallway to the large bedroom at the rear of the townhouse where Patricia, Pamela, and Nina were in bed, gathering Valentina from her room along the way. He instructed all six students to sit in a semicircle facing him, assuring them that he was not going to hurt them. He only wanted money to get to New Orleans.

At 11:45 Gloria was dropped off by her boyfriend and entered the townhouse downstairs. Speck stood by the bedroom door, and when she entered he held up the gun and ordered her to join the others on the floor. Then he pulled the sheet from one of the beds, used his switchblade to tear it into long strips, and began tying each student's ankles and wrists. "Don't be afraid," he told them, "I'm not going to kill you."

When he was done he looked them over. Selecting Pamela, he untied her ankles, pulled her to her feet, and with the gun in her back marched her to the unoccupied northeast bedroom. There he gagged and spread-eagled her on the floor. But as he stood over her, the last of the students, Suzanne, unexpectedly entered the room accompanied by Mary Ann Jordan, a fellow nursing student who lived at home with her parents but who had come to spend the night at the townhome. Taking in Speck and the prostrate Pamela, they turned and fled. He blocked the access to the stairs, and they burst into the south bedroom where they found the remaining six students hog-tied and seated on the floor. Here they were trapped, and Speck marched them at gunpoint back to the northeast bedroom, where Pamela still lay on the floor. There the two girls apparently turned and fought. The six students sitting tied in the south bedroom heard the commotion. The strong and fit Speck made quick work of Suzanne and Mary Ann. Suzanne was stabbed eighteen times, eleven times in the chest and seven in the back. Mary Ann was stabbed three times in the chest and once in the eye. Pamela, still immobilized on the floor, was stabbed once exactly in the heart.[5]

If they thought before that they were not going to be harmed, the remaining six students in the south bedroom now knew better. But tied hand and foot, all they could do was crawl away and try to hide.

Over the next two hours, Speck took the students one by one from the big south bedroom and murdered them. Nina was next, then Valentina, Merlita, and Pat. Each time he was gone for at least thirty minutes, torturing, strangling, abusing. After each victim, the fastidious Speck went into the bathroom and washed the blood from his hands, several times changing into a clean white T-shirt from a supply that he had brought with him. When he came for Gloria, his eighth victim, at 2:30 in the morning only Cora was left, hiding under the bed. Speck put Gloria on the bed, removed her jeans and underpants, and raped her, while Cora cowered below. At one point, Cora heard Speck ask Gloria in his soft Texas drawl, "Will you please put your legs behind my back?" When he was done, he carried her down the stairs, ripping off her blouse and scattering buttons as he went, and murdered her on the couch downstairs.[6]

Speck may have lost count. There were eight nurses living in the house, and there were eight bodies, but because Mary Ann had come home with Suzanne, Cora remained hidden under the bed.[7] Speck picked up any money he could find, and at 3:30 a.m. he left the townhouse, returning to his room over the Shipyard Inn to sleep. Crossing over the Calumet River bridge on his way, he tossed the switchblade into the water.[8]

Cora stayed hidden until 5:00 a.m., then crawled from the house and screamed for help. Police came quickly, first patrolmen and then investigators. What they discovered shocked even the most hardened of them. They found Gloria first on the downstairs sofa, naked and tightly bound. In the northeast bedroom, Pamela, Suzanne, and Mary Ann were lying in pools of blood, dead of multiple stab wounds. Nina, Valentina, and Merlita were in the northwest bedroom. Nina was on the bed, strangled and cut, her nightgown up above her waist. Valentina and Merlita were on the floor, covered with a bloodstained bedspread. They found Patricia on the bathroom floor, also partially naked, and covered in blood.[9]

The next day was Thursday, July 14. Speck spent the morning drinking in a local bar, Pete's Tap, while police fanned out from the townhouse with the physical description that a hysterical

Cora had given them, including his distinctive Southern drawl and tattoos. By midday, police teams had traced Speck back to the Maritime Union Hall and had his name and the address of his sister in North Chicago. Investigators contacted the Coast Guard in an attempt to get Speck's photograph, and while they waited for it they spent the next hours canvassing local joints and flophouses looking for him. Speck moved lazily from bar to bar, and at the Ebb Tide, he overheard the bartender and a customer discussing the murders. He remarked to them, "It must have been a sex maniac to have done something like that."[10] He was sitting at the Soko-Grad when the television broadcast a special report on the murder of the eight student nurses. Speck learned for the first time that he had left a survivor.[11]

Speck immediately collected his things from the Shipyard Inn, called a cab, and had himself driven to Old Town on the north side, another rundown and seedy Chicago neighborhood. Walking the blocks, he eventually checked into the decrepit Raleigh Hotel on North Dearborn. He spent the evening drinking in bars on nearby North Clark Street. He took a prostitute back to his room, and when she left she told the desk clerk about the gun, and he called the police. Two officers came to interview Speck in his room, but because his description had not yet been widely disseminated, they simply confiscated the gun and left. They had other things on their minds. For several days rioting had consumed Chicago's West Side; the Rev. Martin Luther King was in Chicago in an attempt to stem the violence.[12]

By Friday morning, July 15, the Coast Guard had finally provided a picture of Speck to the Chicago police. Cora identified him immediately, and the dragnet began in earnest. Speck was traced to the Shipyard Inn, where police learned that he had been taken away by taxi. After talking to the driver, the search moved to Old Town. Scores of policemen took to the streets in search of him. Speck spent that afternoon in the lobby of the Raleigh Hotel, watching the news of the murder on the television and chatting about it with the desk clerk, Otha Hullinger.[13]

Speck's instincts told him to move again. He went upstairs, packed his clothing into bags, and at 9:00 p.m. he left the Raleigh, telling the desk clerk that he was going to the Laundromat. Fifteen minutes later the police arrived and showed Speck's picture to Hullinger. "Oh, my god," she said. "It's him. It's Richard. He just left."[14]

Speck moved a few blocks southwest to the Starr Hotel, an even more decrepit flophouse, where he registered under a false name. Speck spent the rest of the evening drinking cheap wine on the fire escape with two transients he met, while police searched for him on the streets below. He tried to convince them to help him to hop a freight in the morning, but they didn't want to leave Chicago.[15]

The next day, Saturday, July 16, the police called a press conference, at which Chicago Police Superintendent O. W. Wilson identified Speck as the killer, based both on Cora's identification and on Speck's fingerprints obtained from the townhouse.[16] Wilson distributed Speck's photo and description, including his tattoos. Every Chicago paper featured the story on its front page, and by midafternoon Speck, carrying several papers and a bottle of muscatel, retired to the Starr Hotel. There he slashed his wrists with the shards of the broken bottle, collapsed into the room of another transient, and the police once more were called. Again, the responding officers did not recognize Speck.[17]

But the physician at Cook County Hospital, twenty-six-year-old Dr. Leroy Smith, had read about Speck just that afternoon and thought the unknown patient looked familiar. He asked the nurse on duty to fetch the newspapers he had been reading. He scrubbed the blood from Speck's arm and saw the tattoo "Born to Raise Hell," described by Wilson in his press conference earlier that day. Smith leaned down to ask the patient his name, and received the barely audible response: "Richard Speck." Smith summoned Patrolman Alan Schulman, who was in the corridor guarding another patient, and Schulman excitedly relayed the news to his commanders. Within minutes fifty police cars converged on the hospital. Speck was placed in irons and chained to his gurney.[18]

His arrest was, not surprisingly, the lead story that Sunday and for some days thereafter. Because of the late hour, most of the Chicago papers ran Sunday editions that still described Speck as at large. But radio reported the arrest, and by Monday morning the papers carried Speck's capture in full. And the story did not abate. All four Chicago newspapers continued to report on the crime without interruption in the months that followed, as did many national papers.

The prosecutor charged with the task of convicting Speck was William J. Martin, a graduate of Loyola Law School, now a Cook County assistant state's attorney assigned to the Criminal Division. Of medium height, with large, dark-rimmed glasses, he looked older than his twenty-eight years. Defending Speck was fifty-three-year-old Gerald F. Getty, one of Chicago's most-experienced public defenders. Canny and effective, he had tried hundreds of capital cases and never lost a defendant to Illinois's electric chair.[19] Both Martin and Getty were assisted by teams of lawyers and investigators. Appointed to preside over the case was well-respected judge Herbert Paschen.

And for perhaps the first time in a high-profile national case, the judge and both lawyers sought to proactively protect themselves and their case from the potential damage from the intrusive media coverage. Two recent cases caused them to worry. First, just thirty days before the murder of the eight student nurses, the United States Supreme Court had issued its decision in *Miranda v. Arizona*.[20] In a narrow 5–4 ruling, the Court overturned the conviction of Ernesto Miranda for the rape of a seventeen-year-old Phoenix girl, a conviction that was largely based on Miranda's jailhouse confession following his arrest. In its ruling, the Court held that a citizen's Fifth Amendment right against self-incrimination is violated unless the suspect is advised of a right to remain silent and to be represented by an attorney. Now familiar as the Miranda warning, the new rule was still being adjusted to by police departments and prosecutors across the country in July 1966; to protect their case against Speck in the summer of 1966, he was not questioned by prosecutors for three weeks following his arrest.

Speck did not confess, but neither did he assert an alibi. Instead, he professed to having had too much to drink, to having injected himself with drugs, and as a result claimed to have no memory of the events of July 13, of the townhouse, the nurses, or their murder.[21] But even without his confession, based on the eyewitness testimony of Cora and his fingerprints in the townhouse, he was indicted on eight counts of murder on July 25. After a thorough examination by a panel of psychiatric experts selected by both sides, on October 22 he was declared mentally competent to stand trial.[22]

The second case that worried the prosecutors was that of Sam Sheppard. His conviction for Marilyn's murder had been overturned just the month before the murders, and Sheppard's retrial was actually taking place in Cleveland, Ohio, in October 1966 as Speck awaited his own trial. The prosecutors understood well the lesson of the Sheppard case that pretrial press coverage could be so pervasive that it would be impossible to find and retain an impartial jury in the community where the crime took place. They were particularly worried about the impact of the press conference held by the police on Saturday morning, July 16, in which Police Superintendent Wilson had held up the photo of Speck and identified him as the killer. Wilson had told the reporters, "As far as I'm concerned, there is no question that he is the murderer."[23]

The morning after the Wilson press conference, every Chicago paper, yet unaware of Speck's capture in the early hours, had carried banner headlines with Speck's name and photograph. Beneath the front-page headline "Slaying Suspect-Man on Run," the *Chicago Tribune* opened with,

> Richard Franklin Speck, the ex-convict being hunted for Chicago's mass murder, has been on the run from police in two states for four and one-half months.[24]

The article gave an in-depth description of his life of crime, including the recent murder and rape in Monmouth of which Speck was now credibly suspected. A companion article on page two interviewed relatives of the victims and asked each what he or she thought of Speck, with predictable responses.[25]

National papers also picked up the sensational story. A front-page article in the *Washington Post* datelined Saturday, July 16, identified Speck as the killer of the eight nurses, fully reporting Wilson's press conference and giving a detailed description of Speck, including his photograph and tattoos.[26] Even the *New York Times* that Sunday covered the press conference in its "Major Events of the Day," ranked in national importance after the Chicago race riots but before a labor strike against the nation's airlines.[27]

The issue for the judge and lawyers tasked with prosecuting

Speck was not what Superintendent Wilson described, but that his belief in Speck's guilt was reported by the papers as settled fact: "I think the information I gave to the Chicago public was information they should have, and I saw no reason for with-holding this information. He is the killer."[28]

This reporting left no doubt in the minds of readers, who were to soon be jurors, that Speck had in fact killed the eight nurses. As early as Monday, July 18, the *Boston Globe* was reporting that the Wilson press conference hindered Speck's chances at a fair trial.[29]

Prosecutors were also desperately worried about Cora. National magazines were pursuing her for her story, offering compensation that would make the poor Filipina and her family fabulously rich by the standards of her country. If she told her story in the media before the trial, there might be no commu-nity in America where twelve impartial jurors could be found. It was not beyond imagination that the US Supreme Court of the 1960s, led by Chief Justice Earl Warren, champion of the rights of the accused, could rule that a criminal suspect's right to a fair trial could be so infringed that no trial was possible. To protect their primary witness from the media, prosecutors whisked Cora into hiding. First in hotels and finally in an apart-ment in downtown Chicago, Cora and her visiting family lived for the next seven months under assumed names and 24-hour police protection.[30]

Setting a foundation for grounds of eventual appeal, Getty filed a motion on November 16 to move the trial from Cook County, citing the overwhelmingly negative pretrial publicity. Collecting boxes of articles and press clippings, which he pre-sented to the court, Getty argued that Speck could not receive a fair trial in Chicago. No criminal trial in Illinois had ever been moved based on pretrial publicity, and Getty did not expect his motion to be granted, making it only to preserve the potential argument for appeal. To everyone's surprise, Martin made no objection to moving the trial, thus depriving Speck of a significant appellate argument. After a review of the capabilities of all remaining Illinois counties, the case was transferred 150 miles southwest to a reluctant Peoria, and trial tentatively set for February 6. The Illinois Supreme Court ordered Judge Paschen to continue presiding over the trial.[31]

But the ruling in the US Supreme Court's decision in *Sheppard* dealt not only with the pretrial publicity, which Marilyn Sheppard's murder had generated, but also with the intrusive presence of the press in the courtroom during the trial. In the environment condemned by the courts as a "Roman holiday," the local and national reporters occupied nearly every seat in the gallery of the Sheppard trial, and an additional long table was set up in the well of the courtroom immediately behind counsel table and within an arm's reach of the jury; the reporters handled the trial exhibits as offered, identified and harassed the unsequestered jurors as they traveled to and from the courtroom, and set up a web of telephone, telex, and television lines in the courthouse itself.

To make sure that this behavior did not occur in the Speck trial, on February 14, six days before the commencement of the trial, Judge Paschen issued a draconian set of orders that drastically restricted media access. No cameras, recording devices, or other electronic equipment were allowed on courthouse premises, and the sheriff was ordered to search every person entering the building for forbidden recording devices. No artist's sketches were permitted. No teletype or telephone lines were to be installed in the courthouse. No photographs of any kind of the jurors were permitted, nor were their names or addresses to be released or published until after the verdict.

Witnesses, jurors, lawyers, staff, court personnel, and police officers were forbidden from making any statements of any kind concerning the case until after a verdict was returned in open court. The respective attorneys were forbidden to make their case in the media, either publicly or by leaked leads, information, or other statements. Only twenty-five press credentials were issued, Judge Paschen rejecting requests from more than 200 others who sought attendance in the courtroom. No one would be permitted to enter or leave the courtroom while the court was in session. Finally, in an obvious response to how Judge Edward Blythin had handled Sam Sheppard's original trial, no one other than lawyers and parties were permitted to cross the bar into the well of the courtroom, and no one except attorneys were permitted to handle exhibits.[32]

Within the week, the *Chicago Tribune* filed suit challenging the validity of Judge Paschen's restrictive press order, and its own headline on February 21 read "Tribune Fights Court Gag." Paschen's order was nonetheless upheld by the Illinois Supreme Court on March 1.

Even the process of jury selection concerned the judge and attorneys, eager to seat an unbiased jury. Normally the interview of respective jurors, called voir dire, takes place in a courtroom before groups of prospective jurors, often as many as fifty. The nature of the crime is described and description of the juror's duties given. But the circumstances of this crime were so horrific that description of the events before jurors were seated might upset and inflame entire groups of prospective jurors. To prevent this from happening, the groups of prospective jurors were kept out of the courtroom, with individual jurors brought in one at a time and subject to voir dire. In Speck's case the process of selecting jurors, eventually seven men, five women, and two alternates, which ordinarily might only take a few days, instead took six full weeks and the examination of 609 prospective jurors.

The trial began in earnest on Monday, April 3. Martin's theory was to present witnesses in phases: those who could place Speck in the neighborhood of the nurses' townhouse, those who would present evidence of the crime itself, and finally witnesses who would testify to Speck's movements after the murders, evidencing his consciousness of guilt.

Over the course of eight days of testimony, the prosecution called forty-one witnesses. Martin began with those who had encountered Speck in the South Side Chicago neighborhood in the days preceding the murders, including the owner of the Shipyard Inn, a sailor who had dealt with Speck at the Maritime Union Hall, the Walshes, and Army Sergeant Richard Oliva.

After a series of family witnesses testified to the life and death of the eight victims, Martin called his star witness, Cora Amurao, on April 5. She slipped into the courthouse through a rear entrance while a hired look-alike in dark glasses decoyed members of the media outside the front entrance.[33]

The diminutive young woman was a sensation. After she provided dramatic testimony of the rape and slaughter in the townhouse, Martin asked, "Now, Miss Amurao, if you see that same man in the courtroom today, the man who came to your bedroom door on Wednesday night, July 13, 1966, would you please step down and point him out?" *Time* magazine reported that the words "cast a galvanic spell over the room."[34] Cora slowly descended from the witness box, walked to within a foot of Speck sitting at counsel table, pointed a finger into his pockmarked face, and said, "This is the man."

Martin later described the result of Cora's identification of Speck as "pandemonium."[35] Despite the judge's pretrial order, reporters bolted from the courtroom to fight for the use of the only public phones in the building.[36] When calm again settled over the trial, Getty was unable to shake her on cross-examination, and Martin needed no redirect. The need for secrecy over, Cora exited the courthouse through the front door and into the phalanx of waiting photographers.

Over the remaining four days, Martin presented the testimony of fellow nurses, investigating detectives, and fingerprint experts. The sweat and blood-soaked T-shirts discarded at the townhouse and the matching one cut from Speck's body at the hospital were placed into evidence. The coroner described each victim's injuries. Then Speck's flight from the South Side was recounted. Martin called as witnesses the cab company dispatcher, the cab driver who picked Speck up at the Shipyard Inn and dropped him in Old Town the night after the murders, Raleigh Hotel desk clerk Otha Hullinger, and transient Claude Lunsford who sat drinking with Speck on Friday night discussing with him how to hop an outbound freight. On April 11, the prosecution rested its case in chief.

The capable Getty could now no longer avoid his choice of strategy: either to fight for Speck's innocence using the testimony of South Side witnesses who claimed to have seen Speck elsewhere while the nurses were being systematically slaughtered, or to present an insanity defense. The latter would require Speck to admit to having committed the crimes. Getty chose the former. Challenged afterward for electing this desperate course, he said, "I make it a practice never to judge my clients. You have to represent all comers, and if you judge them, you cannot defend them. Speck told me that he didn't do it, or that if he did, he didn't remember it. I tried to prove that he wasn't at the scene on the night of the crime."[37]

He began with the testimony of Speck's family, solid, God-fearing folk, offered to humanize the defendant. Then Getty called his key witnesses, Murrill Farmer and his wife, Gerdena, proprietors of Kay's Pilot House Bar & Restaurant, who testi-fied with confidence that Speck had been in their establish-ment eating a hamburger at midnight on July 13, and thus not at East 100th Street. Having done what little he could, and gambling that the sowed doubt would be enough to avoid the death penalty, Getty rested his case.

In the closing argument to the jury, the prosecution recounted the deaths of the eight nurses in detail, describing, ordering, summarizing, and occasionally lapsing into rhetoric. Pointing at Speck, the prosecution told the empaneled citizens that "death stalked the hallways that night."[38] Hammering on Speck's attempted suicide as a confession of guilt, Martin urged the jury to give the defendant the penalty that he himself evi-dently believed that he deserved. "He who had that strength to plunge that pocket knife into the heart of Pamela Wilkening," Martin told the jury, "didn't have it when it came to taking his own life. But he knew his own life should be taken." Martin eulogized each nurse in turn, describing how Speck had the strength to stab, strangle, or defile, ending each with the con-demnation "but he didn't have the strength to take his own life." Martin exhorted the jury that they now had to show that they had that strength in their verdict. "Ladies and gentlemen, it is your responsibility to the county and to this sovereign state to say that a man cannot murder eight innocent girls in their beds and expect to spend the rest of his life in a prison cell. . . . Courage is what is required of you. . . ."[39]

Getty, with his enviable record on the line of never yet having lost a defendant to the death penalty, could in closing only attempt to elevate the thirty-minute alibi offered by Murrill and Gerdena Farmer, distracted as they bustled around the busy café, over the four-hour focused nightmare that was

Cora's experience. Exhausted, both Martin and Getty sat back in their chairs as Judge Paschen read the jury their instructions.

It was now noon on April 15, and the jury retired to a sequestered meal and the beginning of their deliberations. Martin and his team walked back to their hotel for lunch and prepared for a long wait after. But before their meals even came, the court clerk called the restaurant. After only forty-nine minutes, the jury had reached a verdict: guilty on all eight counts.[40]

The expected posttrial procedures followed. On May 15, Getty moved for a new trial and was denied. On May 25, Getty was back in court requesting additional medical tests on Speck to determine if he suffered from an alcohol-induced epileptic "furor" on the night of the murders. This motion was similarly denied. On June 2, Getty made a final appeal for mercy, pleading for eight consecutive life sentences. On Monday, June 5, at 11:00 a.m., the lawyers and Speck assembled before Judge Paschen. He asked Speck to rise. "Step up," Getty told his client. Firmly, formally, without excuse, explanation, or doubt, Judge Paschen sentenced Speck to death.[41]

The execution was never carried out. His conviction was affirmed by the Illinois Supreme Court on November 22, 1968, but in June 1971, the US Supreme Court reversed the penalty, citing the systematic exclusion of potential jurors who had expressed reservations against imposition of the death penalty. A year later, the Supreme Court held capital punishment in all states unconstitutional, and in compliance the Illinois Supreme Court voided all death penalties in the state, including that of Speck.

After twenty-five years in jail, Speck died of a heart attack on December 5, 1991, aged forty-nine, one day shy of his fiftieth birthday.

His years of incarceration were not without controversy. The Illinois penal system was then inconsistent and corrupt, and

Speck lived a life behind bars rife with intoxication and sex. He paraded in women's clothing, his former trim figure bloated by prison weight and with enlarged breasts resulting from illicitly obtained hormones. A video surreptitiously shot at Stateville Prison in 1988 shows the prisoners cavorting with drugs and money, and in the middle of it Richard Speck performing oral sex on another prisoner. From behind the camera a prisoner asks Speck why he killed the nurses. Speck shrugs and says, "It just wasn't their night." Asked how he felt, he replies, "If you are asking if I felt sorry, no."[42]

After his death his remains were cremated and his ashes scattered by authorities in an undisclosed location near Joliet, Illinois.

A legacy of Speck's horrific night of crime was a newly found acceptance of mass, motiveless murder. Americans were familiar with killings for passion, for profit, or from madness. Husbands killed wives, and vice versa, and business partners killed each other. Criminals killed unlucky victims, and disgruntled citizens assassinated politicians. But those not insane all had a motive for their actions, stemming from some dark root, tinging each death with shocked acceptance, if not meaning. But never before had Americans experienced the soulless mass slaughter of strangers without reason.

Until Speck. Prosecutor Martin recounts how, a few weeks after that night in the townhouse, while Americans were still coming to grips with this new phenomenon, twenty-five-year-old Charles Whitman climbed to the top of the clock tower at the University of Texas at Austin and with a high-powered rifle killed fourteen people, after killing both his mother and his wife. Thirty-two others were wounded. Martin wonders if the heavily publicized Speck murders and trial factored into Whitman's lashing out against society.[43]

That day was followed by others in the decades to follow, some less shocking, but others much more so. Americans react with sorrow to such slaughters, but are no longer surprised. For prosecutor Martin, as for many, this painful loss of national innocence began with Speck and the murder of eight nurses in Chicago that hot July night in 1966.

CHAPTER 8

1970–1980:
THE TATE-LABIANCA MURDERS AND A MAN NAMED MANSON

The 1970s were a decade of correction and re-examination. The previous decade had birthed the counterculture movement, when the painfully slow-moving fight for civil rights and an unpopular war in Vietnam had led many young people to become disenchanted with the status quo and how the previous generation had run the nation. They questioned the lifestyle and priorities of their elders, rejecting materialism, structured living, the standard nine-to-five working week, and the conventional family unit. Personal freedom was of the upmost importance to them, as were love and acceptance of people of all creeds. These youths, mostly teenagers or twenty-somethings, looked for alternative lifestyles. Disregarding common social conventions, communes sprouted up all over the country, mind-altering drug use increased, and freer sex and open relationships were encouraged. They became known as "hippies."[1]

That final summer of 1969 had been blisteringly hot in Los Angeles, the kind of days that most residents would prefer spending at the beach, lying by the pool, or sitting beneath blasting air-conditioning units. Among those just trying to beat the heat were young Hollywood starlet Sharon Tate, who, clad only in a matching bra and panty set, entertained a few friends at her posh home in the hills above Hollywood, and Leno and

Rosemary LaBianca, a Los Feliz couple returning home from a day spent at Lake Isabella, a popular vacation spot about 150 miles outside the city.

Less concerned with the heat were their killers, who invaded their homes and murdered them in the strangest and most gratuitous of ways. They strung their victims together by rope, masked them with pillowcases, stabbed them dozens of times, and scrawled cryptic words in blood on the walls. This cabal of long-haired, barefooted youths, no older than the local college kids, lived on a ranch not far from the city as members of a cult calling itself the "Family." They had been sent to kill these innocent strangers by their leader, a persuasive, mysterious, and terrifying man by the name of Charles Manson, whose apprehension and trial combined into the milestone event of the 1970s.

The murders they committed sent Los Angeles, indeed the entire country, into a tailspin of shock, fear, and fascination with Manson and everything his "Family" stood for, and the trial that followed was the longest and most costly murder trial in American history. Forty years later, the case remains a topical reference and a subject of cultural significance, even to those too young to have experienced it firsthand. The entire episode has been heralded as one of the most chilling in crime history.[2]

In 1969, Charles Manson, the leader of the Family, was in his midthirties. He was small, only 5'2" and slim, with petite facial features and dark brown hair that he wore long and wild, down to his shoulders. His face would soon become one of the most recognized and feared in America. Born November 12, 1934, in Cincinnati, Ohio, to sixteen-year-old Kathleen Maddox, he never knew his real father; the name Manson was adopted from one of Kathleen's later husbands. Kathleen had trouble with the law, and Manson's early childhood was spent either living with different relatives or, when she was not in prison, moving from motel to motel with his mother and whomever she was dating at the time. When Manson was twelve, Kathleen attempted to place him in foster care and he was sent to a care-taking institution.[3]

Charles Manson arriving at court in handcuffs in Independence, CA.
© Bettmann/Corbis.

He spent the next few years bouncing around different facilities, from which he frequently ran away, and getting in his own legal trouble. At thirteen, he committed armed robbery. At sixteen, he drove a stolen car across state lines, a federal offense, after which he was kept in federal institutions. Sometimes he behaved. Other times, he attacked and sexually assaulted the other boys. He was deemed unstable and "safe only under supervision."[4]

In 1954, at nineteen, Manson was paroled. He worked sporadically as a busboy, service station aid, and parking lot attendant, but he soon resumed boosting cars. He was arrested again in Los Angeles in 1955 and sent to Terminal Island in San Pedro, California. When he was released in 1958, he took up pimping. He was arrested again in 1959 when he attempted to cash a forged check. He was placed on probation, but he quickly violated its terms and returned to prison in 1960.[5]

When he was finally released in the spring of 1967, Manson was thirty-two years old. He had been institutionalized for a total of seventeen years, throughout which he exhibited wild and unpredictable behavior. He had been obsessed at different times with playing guitar, the Beatles, and Scientology, claiming that he had obtained the religion's highest level, that of "theta clear." He had been married twice, once to a seventeen-year-old waitress between his release at age nineteen and his arrest in California, which ended in divorce in 1958, and then to a nineteen-year-old prostitute when he was pimping. In 1963, she, too, divorced him. Each marriage resulted in a son named after him.[6]

Manson had missed the development of the counterculture movement while he was locked up, but he liked what he saw when he was released. He moved north to Berkeley, where he sang, played guitar, and panhandled on the streets of the ultra-liberal college town. There he met Mary Brunner, a twenty-three-year-old college-educated assistant librarian at the university. She was lonely and plain-looking, but he made her feel special. He moved in with her and lived off her income, inviting other young girls he met to do the same.[7]

In April, he began spending the majority of his time in the Haight-Ashbury district of San Francisco, a neighborhood widely known to be a hippie refuge and a place where peace-loving people could find acceptance, cheap rent, and an overabundance of music, drugs, and free love. The neighborhood attracted thousands of young people. It was estimated that during the summer of 1967, when schools across the country closed for summer vacation, 75,000 people took up residence in the area. Many of these arrivals had a real dedication to the hippie philosophies and political goals of peace and acceptance, but many others were simply aimless wanderers or runaway teenagers, naïve and lonely misfits looking to belong. Of the crowds that swarmed the streets, one previous Haight resident remembers "you can't emphasize enough the innocence of most of these starry-eyed kids," that "they were ripe to take advantage of, if anybody wanted to."[8]

And so the area was also full of sidewalk preachers and gurus, people sermonizing their various ideas on life to anyone who would listen. Manson quickly became one of them. His unique brand of thinking combined Beatles lyrics, passages from the Bible, and Scientology, and, being a talented orator, he explained it all in a charismatic and dramatic fashion. Before long, he had attracted many willing followers, both women and men in their late teens and early twenties, and the Family was born.[9] Some of his adherents were from disadvantaged circumstances, others abandoned paying jobs and supportive parents, but all were lonely, unsatisfied, and troubled, eager to believe and belong.

The Haight soon became overcrowded, with hundreds of young people arriving each day, and Manson tired of it. He packed his followers into an old bus and took to the road. For over a year, the group roamed the coastline from Washington State to Mexico, spending much of their time in Los Angeles. They camped, rented, squatted, and stayed with various friends and peripheral acquaintances, including Beach Boy Dennis Wilson, while Manson tried to make it in the music industry. Eventually they settled at Spahn Ranch, a decrepit and isolated ranch outside LA that, in its former days of glory, had been a filming location for movies and television shows. Manson continued to recruit followers along the way, and within months the Family at Spahn numbered at least thirty-five. The ranch's elderly owner, George Spahn, allowed them to stay partially because he was unaware just how many members of the Family were living on his land and partially because Manson assigned one of the young girls to take care of him, physically, emotionally, and sexually.[10]

Life under Manson's rule was bizarrely unconventional. All Family members were expected to turn over their money and personal property to him, but, even so, the group needed more to survive. They scattered into the surrounding area to panhandle, steal, and go on "garbage runs," in which they took unsold food out of supermarket trash cans.[11] As expected, Family members were constantly arrested for loitering, robbery, and grand theft auto. Manson gave everyone new names, sometimes more than one, depending on what he felt fit their personalities.[12] Meals were communal, and no one was served until Manson was seated.[13] Children were separated from their parents and cared for as a group. The Family commonly went on "creepy-crawly" missions, meaning they entered random Los Angeles homes and silently crawled around while the occupants were asleep, moving and rearranging small items.[14] There were countless rules to follow. Wristwatches, calendars, clocks, and glasses were forbidden. Female members were not allowed to carry money. If Manson walked past someone at the ranch, he would make faces and wild gestures, and that person was forced to mimic him until he stopped.[15]

Sex with random partners was encouraged to increase the unity of the group, and it was not uncommon for Manson to assign two people together or forbid a pair from each other. There were orgies that Manson would orchestrate and lead, assigning each person's position and task. Drugs, particularly marijuana and LSD, were free-flowing, although Manson often took less than everyone else when they embarked on communal "trips," enabling him to retain more control over the situation.[16]

Violence was constant. Manson acquired a large cache of guns and knives and threatened anyone who disagreed with him. He killed, or at least ordered killed, several people, including a Spahn ranch hand named Donald "Shorty" Shea, several defecting Family members, and peripheral hangers-on. He shot a drug dealer with whom a deal went awry and left him for dead, though he survived. Manson explained to his followers that fear was beautiful and that the more fear you have, the more awareness you have, thus, the more love you have. He claimed that death was beautiful because people feared death.[17]

The combination of sex, drugs, and fear made Family members not only loyal and submissive to Manson, but somehow made them love and adore him. They admired him and never questioned his authority. For the women, sex with Manson was an honor and a privilege. One Family member, who eventually defected and provided important testimony during the trial, remembered how Manson would lead the orgies, explaining that "he'd set it all up in a beautiful way like he was creating a masterpiece in sculpture."[18] Another member claimed that "Charlie is love, pure love."[19] It was clear to anyone who spoke to a Family member that he or she would go to the ends of the earth for Manson, many believing him to be the second incarnation of Jesus Christ.[20]

Manson preached often and intensely to his avid followers, and his philosophy, while still loosely based on Beatles lyrics and the Bible, had grown and developed over the years. He believed that the world was on the brink of an apocalyptic race war, which he called Helter Skelter. Blacks would win this war, he claimed, and wipe out the white race. But they were not smart enough to adequately run the world they would inherit, so they would naturally ask for help from him and the Family, who would be hiding out in a "bottomless pit" in the desert. They would hand over the reins of power, and Charles Manson would rule the world.[21]

Manson claimed to have found the evidence supporting his theory both in the ninth chapter of Revelation in the New Testament and the White Album released by the Beatles in late 1968. Revelation 9 tells of a bottomless pit in the desert and of five angels, one of which had the key to this bottomless pit. He felt that he was this fifth angel and that the Beatles were the other four. In the White Album, Manson claimed, the Beatles were not only encouraging the start of the race war but were also speaking directly to him. The song "Blackbird," he explained, with its lyrics about a bird learning to fly with broken wings, encouraged blacks to rise up and take over whites. The song "Piggies" was about the rich or anyone belonging to "the establishment." "Revolution 1" and "Revolution 9" (which Manson thought corresponded with Revelation 9) explained how the upcoming revolution would play out. The song "Helter Skelter" told him of the role he would soon play, and when and how to emerge from the bottomless pit in the desert.[22]

The Beatles never supported Manson's interpretation of their lyrics. In September 1970, John Lennon told a member of the press "if I were . . . a praying man, I'd pray to be delivered from people like Charles Manson who claim to know better than I do what my songs are supposed to mean."[23] In an interview he gave to *Rolling Stone* magazine in January 1971 he said, "I don't know what 'Helter Skelter' has to do with knifing somebody." And Manson? "He's cracked all right."[24]

Manson believed that the revolution would start with blacks committing heinous crimes in wealthy white neighborhoods of Los Angeles, but no such crimes were occurring. Manson became anxious, upset by Helter Skelter's slow progress, and decided to get the revolution started himself. The best way for him to do so, he believed, would be to commit a terrible and upsetting murder in a white neighborhood and make it look as if it had been perpetrated by the black community. Such a crime would spark animosity between the races, ignite the revolution, and, as explained by a former Family member, "show blackie how to do it."[25]

On the night of Friday, August 8, 1969, Manson gathered some of his most-loyal followers and instructed them to dress in dark clothing and find their knives. Among those chosen was twenty-one-year-old Susan Atkins, a short brunette Manson called Sadie Mae Glutz and who had been with the Family since November 1967. The product of a troubled home, Atkins dropped out of school at sixteen, worked as a topless dancer, experimented with drugs and satanic worship, and was arrested for armed robbery, all before meeting Manson. Also chosen was twenty-one-year-old Patricia Krenwinkel, called Katie, a dark-haired girl from Los Angeles who left her job as a process clerk for an insurance company to join Manson, and twenty-three-year-old Charles Watson, called Tex, former high school jock, college dropout, and Manson's right-hand man. The final member of the cabal was Linda Kasabian, a twenty-year-old who had been on her own since age sixteen and had spent the past few years living in communes and experimenting with drugs. A relative newcomer to the Family, she had only been living with Manson for about a month but was asked to join the mission because she was the only member of the Family with a valid driver's license.[26]

Manson gave explicit instructions to Tex and told the others to obey his orders.[27] The four set out from Spahn Ranch and drove to a home on Cielo Drive in Benedict Canyon, the area above Hollywood and Beverly Hills. The house belonged to a man named Rudi Altobelli and was being rented by famous movie director Roman Polanski and his beautiful wife, twenty-six-year-old actress Sharon Tate. The Polanskis, however, had spent much of the summer in Europe, so the house was being tended to by their friend, twenty-five-year-old Abigail Folger, heiress to the Folgers Coffee fortune, and her boyfriend, thirty-two-year-old Wojiciech "Voytek" Frykowski. Tate had returned from Europe a few days prior and was staying at the house with Folger and Frykowski until Polanski came home. Manson and Watson had been to this house before. Dennis Wilson had once introduced Manson to the house's previous occupant, Terry Melcher, record producer, son of Doris Day, and boyfriend of Candace Bergen. Melcher had declined to sign a contract with Manson, but Manson chose the house not out of revenge but because he knew it would be isolated.[28]

The group arrived at the house after midnight, cut the telephone lines, climbed the gate, and slaughtered everyone inside. Afterward, they got back in the car, changed clothes, tossed their bloody garments and knives over the side of the canyon, and drove back to Spahn Ranch.

The murders were not discovered until the next morning when the housekeeper, Winifred Chapman, arrived and, upon seeing a body, telephoned the police. The officers arrived sometime around nine in the morning and found themselves at a crime scene unlike any they had seen before. On the front lawn they found the bodies of Frykowski and Folger. Frykowski had been shot twice, hit repeatedly in the head with a blunt object, and stabbed fifty-one times. Folger had been stabbed twenty-eight times, her once-white nightgown completely stained with blood. Inside, they found the body of eight-month pregnant Sharon Tate, stabbed sixteen times. Also inside was the body of Jay Sebring, hairstylist to the stars and Sharon Tate's close friend. He had been shot once and stabbed seven times. Sharon lay in the fetal position, and Jay looked as if he died trying to ward off future blows. In the driveway, slumped in the driver's seat of a white Rambler, was the body of eighteen-year-old Steven Parent, who had been shot four times. Unconnected with Tate or any other of the victims, Parent, a Los Angeles local who had just recently graduated from Arroyo High School, had been visiting William Garretson, a young man Rudi Altobelli had hired to live in the back house and take care of the property while he was away.

If the carnage and savagery of the murders were not enough, the scene itself was bizarre and grotesque. Tate and Sebring had been tied together by a rope that had been strung over a ceiling rafter and looped around their necks. A bloodstained towel had been thrown over Sebring's face. The word "PIG" was written on the front door in blood.[29]

News of the murders spread quickly, and investigations began immediately. But back at Spahn Ranch, Manson was unhappy with how the events of the previous evening had unfolded. He felt that it had been "too messy" and prepared his team to strike again that night. This time, they were joined not only by Manson himself but also by Leslie Van Houten and Steve Grogan. Twenty-year-old Van Houten had gotten hooked on LSD at age fourteen and moved to the Haight. At one point, she finished high school, took a year of secretarial courses, and began training to be a nun, but she dropped out, took up drugs again, and lived on a commune until meeting Manson.[30] Grogan, an eighteen-year-old known to the Family as "Clem," had been arrested countless times and was diagnosed by psychiatrists as "presently insane."[31] Sentenced to a stay at Camarillo State Mental Hospital, he had managed to escape with help from the Family. Together, they drove through Pasadena and east Los Angeles. Manson gave directions and looked for a random home to target, passing over his first few choices because he saw pictures of children in the window and because the houses were too close together.[32]

Eventually, he settled on a home in Los Feliz belonging to Leno and Rosemary LaBianca. Leno, age forty-four, was the president of a local grocery store chain, and his thirty-eight-year-old wife, Rosemary, to whom he had been married for ten years, owned and operated a successful clothing boutique. Rosemary had two children, aged fifteen and twenty-one, from a previous marriage.[33] Manson entered the home alone, tied up the couple, and returned to the car. Watson, Krenwinkel, and Van Houten then entered, murdered the LaBiancas, and hitchhiked back to Spahn Ranch. Manson, on his way home, stopped for milkshakes.[34]

The bodies of the LaBiancas were discovered the following evening by Rosemary's children. The police, upon arrival, found a scene equally if not more shocking than the one at the Tate residence. Leno was in the living room, a pillowcase over his head and a lamp cord wrapped around his neck. His hands had been tied behind his back. He had been stabbed twelve times with a knife and an additional fourteen times with a two-pronged kitchen carving fork, which was left protruding from his abdomen. The word "war" had been carved into his skin. Rosemary's body was found in the bedroom. She had been stabbed forty-one times in the back and legs, and, like her husband, a pillowcase had been placed over her head and a lamp cord wrapped around her neck. The words "DEATH TO PIGS" and "RISE" were written in blood on the living room walls and "HEALTER SKELTER" incorrectly spelled out in blood on the refrigerator door.[35]

The Los Angeles Police Department immediately began their investigations, but it took a long time for them to connect the two murders to the Manson Family, or even to each other. Assigned to separate LAPD investigative teams, the Tate investigation was led by Lieutenant Robert Helder and his team, while the LaBianca case was covered by Lieutenant Paul LePage and an entirely different group of detectives.[36]

Several theories circulated about the Tate murders. Cocaine and marijuana had been found among the victims' possessions, leading some to believe that the murderous rampage had been the result of a drug trip gone wrong or a drug deal turned violent. Another promising theory was that William Garretson, the groundskeeper, was behind the killings. He was found that morning in the guesthouse and claimed to have heard or seen nothing unusual the night before. He was arrested and questioned but was eventually cleared of suspicion.[37] The LaBianca detectives were operating under the suspicion that the murders had been the result of an upset robbery. Two months after the murders, neither team had made much headway.

On October 15, the LaBianca team asked the Los Angeles County Sheriff's Office (LASO) if it was investigating any other murders that might be similar to the LaBianca case. LASO officers told their LAPD colleagues about the murder of Gary Hinman, a thirty-four-year-old music teacher, who had been found dead in a home in Malibu in July. He had been stabbed to death, and the words "POLITICAL PIGGY" were written on the wall in blood. LASO had arrested a suspect, Robert "Bobby" Beausoleil, shortly after. Beausoleil had been in custody since August 6, so he could not have been involved in the LaBianca murder, but prior to his arrest he had been living at Spahn Ranch with Manson.[38] Spahn Ranch had been raided in August, and several Family members had been arrested as suspects in an auto theft ring.[39]

Following the August raid, Manson had moved the Family to Barker Ranch, an extremely remote and isolated homestead near Death Valley. Barker Ranch was raided in early October, and twenty-four Family members, including Manson, were arrested on a wide variety of charges. They were being held in jail in Inyo County, about five hours outside of Los Angeles, still unconnected to the Tate and LaBianca murders.

During the raid, Inyo County law enforcement had come across two young girls attempting to flee the Family. One was seventeen-year-old Kitty Lutesinger, Bobby Beausoleil's girl-friend. Lutesinger remembered hearing that Susan Atkins had also been involved in the Hinman murder. Atkins, arrested in the Barker Ranch raid and being held in Inyo County, was ques-tioned, booked for suspicion of murder, and moved to Sybil Brand Institute, a women's detention center in Los Angeles.[40] There she was placed in a cell with two former call girls, Ronnie Howard, in jail for forging prescriptions, and Virginia Graham, arrested for violating her parole. Atkins was talkative in jail, and she told her cellmates all about life with Manson. She also told them about killing Hinman and, eventually, that she had killed Sharon Tate and her guests, and that her friends had killed the LaBiancas.[41] Howard would remember her saying that it "felt so good the first time I stabbed [Sharon Tate]" and that "the more you [murder], the better you like it." She bragged that she and the Family were responsible for eleven murders that police would never solve and that there would be more to come.[42]

A scared and concerned Howard told on Atkins. Taken out of Sybil Brand for a court appearance on November 17, she telephoned the LAPD, claiming to know who had committed the Tate murders. That evening, two officers came to Sybil Brand and interviewed her, placed her into protective custody, and brought the news back to headquarters. They were convinced that she was telling the truth; Akins had told of several details that were known only by the police and the murderers.[43]

Lutesinger had also told authorities that Manson had attempted to recruit members of the Straight Satans, a motorcycle gang, as bodyguards. On November 12, a member of this gang named Al Springer was picked up and questioned on an unrelated matter, and the LaBianca detectives took the opportunity to interview him about Manson. Springer never joined Manson's Family, but he did remember Manson bragging about killing five people and about writing on a refrigerator in blood.[44]

Springer also directed the police to Danny DeCarlo, a member of the Straight Satans who had spent a great deal of time at the ranch with Manson. DeCarlo confirmed Springer's story. He remembered Clem bragging to him about killing five "piggies." He recalled that Manson had a favorite gun that had disappeared after the weekend of the murders, and, knowledgeable about firearms, he was able to draw a picture of the weapon. Pieces of a broken and bloodstained gun handle had been found at the Tate residence, and DeCarlo's drawing was an exact match to the gun to which these pieces belonged. Finally, he described a certain kind of rope, kept at Spahn Ranch, which matched the rope used to tie up Tate and Sebring.[45]

Having implicated herself, Atkins was charged with the Tate murders, and the case was assigned to Deputy District Attorney Vincent Bugliosi and head of the Trials Division, Aaron Stovitz. Thirty-five-year-old Bugliosi was an experienced and confidant prosecutor who had been practicing with the Los Angeles County District Attorney's Office since 1964. He had tried 104 felony cases and lost only one.[46] Stovitz would be taken off the case for inadvertently violating a gag order shortly after the trial began and replaced by District Attorneys Donald Musich and Steven Kay, but Bugliosi remained the chief prosecutor for the duration of the trial and played an active role in the investigative processes.[47] Richard Caballero, a former district attorney who had gone into private practice, was already representing Atkins in the Hinman case and would now represent her in the Tate case as well.[48]

Slowly but surely, the LAPD identified the remaining murderers. Interviews with other Family members exposed Watson, Krenwinkel, and Kasabian as those present at the Tate residence, and warrants were issued for their arrests. Watson was found in his hometown of McKinney, Texas, Krenwinkel was arrested in Mobile, Alabama, where she had been staying with family, and Kasabian surrendered to law enforcement in Concord, New Hampshire.[49] Interviews with Atkins exposed the involvement of these three, plus Manson and Van Houten in the LaBianca murders.[50]

In light of the evidence, attorney Caballero struck a deal with the district attorney's office on behalf of Atkins that, in exchange for testifying against the other Family members, the DA would not seek the death penalty against Atkins. On December 5, Atkins testified before the grand jury, explaining in detail the events of those two gruesome nights. The jury was shocked not only by her story but also by her frigid, emotionless, and entirely remorseless telling of it. When asked to identify a picture of Steven Parent, the eighteen-year-old found in the white Rambler at the Tate house, she confirmed "that is the thing I saw in the car." Only after being asked by Bugliosi if "when you say 'thing,' you are referring to a human being?" did she respond, "Yes, human being." Her testimony was so chilling that one of the jurors had to ask to be excused for a few minutes.[51] While Manson himself had not personally committed any of the murders, it was clear from the testimony that he was the mastermind behind them and that he had a powerful hold over the minds and motivations of his followers. When the grand jury returned after deliberating for only twenty minutes, they delivered indictments for murder against Watson, Krenwinkel, Atkins, Kasabian, Van Houten, and Manson. Kasabian and Krenwinkel were returned to Los Angeles to stand trial, and Van Houten and Manson were brought down from Inyo County, where they had been jailed since the Barker Ranch raid. Watson fought extradition from Texas and ultimately had to be tried separately at a later date.[52]

As the investigation continued, physical evidence against the Family members began building up. A fingerprint found on the front door of the Tate house was identified as belonging to Tex, and one found on the inside of the French door in Sharon Tate's bedroom was matched to Krenwinkel.[53] A broken gun found months earlier in the backyard of a home below Benedict Canyon was identified as the gun used at the Tate residence. It was covered in blood of the same subtype as Sebring, and the pieces of gun grip discovered in the house fit its broken handle perfectly. Bullets found at Spahn Ranch were also definitively traced to this gun. Rosemary LaBianca's wallet was discovered in a service station restroom, where it had been left by Kasabian, just as Atkins had described. A television crew, attempting to re-enact the events of Friday, August

8, came across Watson's, Kasabian's, Krenwinkel's, and Atkins's bloody clothing where they had pitched it off the road and into the hillside. Finally, interviews with several other past and present associates of Manson brought to light his philosophies on "piggies" and "Helter Skelter," the words written at the two residences.

The date for the trial was set, and it was bound to be a challenging one. The prosecution would have to prove not only that Watson, Kasabian, Krenwinkel, Atkins, and Van Houten had committed the murders but also that Manson, indicted under conspiracy laws, had compelled them to do so. The "vicarious liability" rule of conspiracy states that a conspirator in a crime is responsible for all the crimes perpetrated by his co-conspirators even if he was not present at the scene and did not physically commit them. The prosecution would have to show that Manson had engineered these murders and that he had used his powerful control over his followers to get them to carry them out for him.[54]

All the defendants besides Watson were to be tried together, and their defense team was made up of a rapidly revolving cast of diverse characters. Manson's case was initially assigned to attorney Paul Fitzgerald of the Public Defenders' Office, but on December 17, almost immediately after being indicted, Manson requested permission to act as his own attorney, claiming that "there is no person in the world who could represent me as a person."[55] After an experienced third-party attorney judged him mentally competent, the presiding judge, William Keene, had no choice but to approve Manson's request.

Manson, however, used his newly acquired position not to build a credible defense but instead to make outrageous motions and requests. He asked that copies of every document related to the case be made and delivered to his jail cell. He asked that he be allowed freedom to travel outside of prison. He asked for the names, telephone numbers, and home addresses of every prosecution witness. Finally, in March, when he asked that the prosecuting attorneys be jailed under conditions similar to his own, Judge Keene revoked his privileges, in response to which Manson screamed, "There is no God in this courtroom!"[56]

The judge next assigned Manson's defense to attorney Charles Hollopeter, but, displeased with some of the motions he made, Manson quickly had him replaced with Ronald Hughes.[57] Thirty-five years old, Hughes was often referred to as a "hippie lawyer." Large and burly, he was balding but sported a long, unkempt beard and mismatched suits that he bought for a dollar apiece from the MGM wardrobe department. He was well acquainted with counterculture, enjoyed hiking and the great outdoors, admitted to have experimented with drugs, and lived in a friend's garage. He had never tried a case before.[58]

In April, Manson filed an affidavit of prejudice against Judge Keene, and the case was re-assigned to Judge Charles Older. A former World War II fighter pilot, Older had developed a reputation as a no-nonsense judge since his appointment to the bench three years earlier.[59]

Only two weeks before the trial's opening day, Manson asked Judge Older to re-assign his case yet again. If he could not act as his own attorney, Manson proclaimed, he wanted to be represented by Irving Kanarek. Kanarek was a well-known although not necessarily well-respected Los Angeles attorney. A stocky man with wavy hair, thick eyebrows, and a slightly receding hairline, he was rumored to wear a new suit on the first day of each trial and continue to wear it every day until the trial was over. A notorious obstructionist, Kanarek was widely recognized for his excessive use of unnecessary objections and other delay tactics. On one occasion, he objected to a witness stating his name, because, having originally heard it from his mother, it was hearsay. On another, he managed to delay a trial for so long that a year and a half after its inception a first witness had yet to be called. After two years, the prosecuting attorney chose to retire rather than finish out the trial. Manson was well aware of Kanarek's reputation, and he claimed that, if he could not represent himself, his "second alternative is to cause you as much trouble as possible." Older acquiesced, and Hughes was replaced by Kanarek.[60]

Meanwhile, Manson was using his power to influence the other defendants and their choices of attorneys. Family members constantly visited Atkins in prison and ferried messages back and forth between her and Manson. In late February, feeling the pressure, Atkins claimed that she had changed her mind and refused to testify at the trial. In March, capitalizing on the privileges afforded him by self-representation, Manson arranged an in-person meeting with Atkins. The next day, Atkins fired Caballero and asked that he be replaced by Daye Shinn, an immigration attorney who had visited Manson in prison over forty times, hoping to be put on the defense case.[61] Shinn, forty-years old and of Korean descent, was new to criminal proceedings.[62]

Krenwinkel requested as her attorney Paul Fitzgerald, the very first attorney assigned to Manson. The Public Defender's Office felt that this assignment constituted a conflict of interest, but Fitzgerald was anxious to be a part of the defense team. He resigned from the office and went into private practice, taking Krenwinkel on as his only client.[63] Tall and slim, with dark curly hair, Fitzgerald was a knowledgeable and experienced defense attorney, having represented almost four hundred people with the Public Defender's Office, only one of whom had been sentenced to death.[64]

Van Houten went through what was perhaps the longest sequence of attorneys. Her case was first assigned to Donald Barnett, whom she asked to be dismissed after he ordered that she undergo a psychiatric evaluation. Her case was then passed to Marvin Part, who made the same mistake. Despite his protestations that Van Houten "has no will of her own left" and "doesn't care whether she is tried together and gets the gas chamber, she just wants to be with the Family," Van Houten's case was transferred to Ira Reiner, an attorney who had met with Manson several times and whom Manson suggested Van Houten request. Reiner lasted eight months, until jury selection, when it became clear that he was trying to separate her defense from that of the rest of the Family. Van Houten had him replaced by Ronald Hughes, the former Manson attorney.[65]

Kasabian was represented by Gary Fleischman, who made it clear from the start that his client was willing to cooperate with the prosecution. She had been the driver and claimed that she had not actually killed any of the victims, that she had been told to stand guard outside the Tate house and had never entered the LaBianca house. She had been new to the Family at the time of the murders, and she felt badly about what had happened. While she openly admitted that she loved Manson, she claimed to have only cooperated in the murderous rampage out of fear for the safety of her daughter who was being cared for back at Spahn Ranch. She was clearly different from the other girls, who struck outsiders as either deceitful, naive, or simply insane. Kasabian was polite, truthful, more grounded, and seemed genuinely devastated by what had transpired. When Atkins reneged on her promise to testify in court, the prosecution team dropped its end of the bargain, sought the death penalty for Atkins, and turned to Kasabian, promising to petition the court for immunity if she testified at the trial. Despite threats made to Fleischman by

Family members that "if Linda testifies, thirty people are going to do something about it," Kasabian agreed and became the prosecution's star witness.[66]

The trial of Manson, Atkins, Krenwinkel, and Van Houten began on June 15 at the Hall of Justice in downtown Los Angeles. Jury selection took five weeks. Bugliosi began his opening statement on July 24. In it, he summarized the events that had taken place at the Tate and LaBianca residences, gave a history of the Family and portrayed Manson as its undisputed leader to whom everyone deferred, and briefly described Helter Skelter and Manson's general philosophies on life. He stressed that Manson had ordered the murders but that Atkins, Krenwinkel, and Van Houten had been willing participants in them, as evidenced by the excessive brutality with which they were committed.[67]

The defense opted to give its opening statement after the prosecution had completed its case, so the prosecution began presenting evidence. Over the next twenty-two weeks, Bugliosi called eighty witnesses and introduced 320 exhibits. The true standout was Linda Kasabian. She testified for a total of seventeen days and gave a detailed account of life with the Family at Spahn Ranch. She made it clear that Manson was in charge and dictated much of daily life, claiming at one point that "the girls worshiped him, just would die to do anything for him." She spoke at length about Manson's feelings on race, his belief in Helter Skelter, his obsession with the Beatles, and gave a very detailed account of the two nights of murder. Although it was brought out that Kasabian had at one point thought that Manson "was the Messiah come again" and that she was "controlled by . . . his vibrations," she was a remarkably valuable witness. Her testimony was truthful, detailed, and consistent, and she sobbed openly when describing the murders and when shown pictures of the victims' bodies.[68]

Other witnesses included Family members and neighbors of the victims, the Polanskis' maid who first discovered the carnage, William Garretson, Virginia Graham, Ronnie Howard, representatives from the medical examiner–coroner's office, and various branches of law enforcement. Testimony also came from several people who had at one time known or been part of the Family, including Straight Satan Danny DeCarlo, Dianne Lake, a former Family member who testified that she had previously lied to the grand jury because she was "afraid that [she] would be killed by members of the Family if [she] told the truth," and Barbara Hoyt, a Family member who testified in spite of an attempt by the Family to silence her by feeding her a hamburger laced with LSD. With the help of these witnesses, Bugliosi matched the knives and guns used at the crime scenes to those at Spahn Ranch, connected the bloody clothes found on the hillside to the defendants, verified the fingerprints found at the Tate residence as belonging to Watson and Krenwinkel, and established the whereabouts of the defendants on that fateful August weekend, all of which corroborated Kasabian's testimony. He also elicited the details of Manson's philosophy, linked him to the words written at the crime scenes, established that Manson felt he had to take Helter Skelter into his own hands, and introduced countless examples of his domination over the Family members. Finally, on Monday, November 13, the prosecution rested.[69]

Kanarek had lived up to his reputation as an obstructionist. On the first day of Kasabian's testimony he objected more than one hundred times. Reporters attempting to keep track of his objections quickly gave up the count. In the trial transcript, often ten or more pages separated Bugliosi's question from the witness's answer. Kanarek was held in contempt several times throughout the trial, but it did nothing to stop him from excessively prolonging the proceedings.[70]

To the astonishment of all present, the defense rested immediately, declining to call any witnesses or present any evidence.
Atkins, Krenwinkel, and Van Houten instantly stood, shouting
and insisting that they be allowed to testify. Judge Older called
a conference of the defense attorneys, who informed him they
had rested because they feared that if they called their clients
to the witness stand, they would take full responsibility for the
murders in order to save Manson. Judge Older, however, ruled
that the accused had a right to testify and that the three would
have to be allowed to take the stand. But before they were given
the opportunity, Manson insisted on speaking himself. Older
allowed him to make a statement but removed the jury before
allowing him to do so.

He gave a rambling, incoherent, two-hour speech, highlights
of which included the claims that "these children that come at
you with knives, they are your children. You taught them. I didn't
teach them. I just tried to help them stand up." He also insisted
that he "may have implied on several occasions to several different
people that I may have been Jesus Christ, but I haven't decided
yet what I am or who I am." When asked by Older if he wanted to
repeat his statement in front of the jury, he declined, stating that
he had "relieved all the pressure" he had. Upon returning to the
defense table, he told the girls that they no longer had to testify,
and they immediately stopped clamoring to do so. With that, the
defense again rested.[71] After a brief suspension, the closing arguments, and the jury instruction, the jury left the courtroom to
deliberate on January 15, 1971. After nine days, it returned and
announced that it had found Manson, Atkins, Krenwinkel, and
Van Houten guilty on all counts.[72]

The guilty verdict was followed by the penalty phase of the
trial. After another eight weeks of testimony, the jury deliberated again and re-emerged on March 29 to sentence all four

defendants to death. They were immediately taken to prison to await their fates.[73]

In addition to being one of the longest criminal trials in history, the Manson trial was also one of the strangest. Family members held a vigil outside the courthouse for the duration of the trial, waiting, as one young woman phrased it, for their "father to get out of jail."[74] They passed out flyers and shouted at passersby. Manson behaved bizarrely the entire time. On the first day, he arrived at the courthouse having carved an "X" into his forehead, and his followers outside passed out a flyer in which he explained that he had "X'd himself from your world" (he has since turned the X into a swastika).[75] He constantly interrupted witnesses and made wild outbursts to the judge, jury, and spectators, making proclamations like "you're going to destruction, that's where you're going" and "it's your judgment day, not mine." He also threatened people, claiming that he "had a little system of [his] own" and that someone should cut Older's head off. He once lunged at Older, brandishing a sharpened pencil, and another time he threw paper clips at the judge. As the evidence accumulated and his guilty verdict seemed imminent, he tried to smuggle a hacksaw blade into his cell and attempted to bribe a bailiff to help him escape. Older constantly had him removed from the courtroom and placed in a side room where he could hear but not interrupt the proceedings.

The girls were equally outrageous. They made protestations, and on one occasion stood up together and started chanting in Latin. Atkins once tried to grab a knife off the evidence table. Another time she kicked a deputy in the leg and grabbed notes off the prosecution table, tearing them in half. They also copied Manson's actions. When they saw that he had carved an X on his forehead, they did the same to theirs. During the penalty phase, Manson shaved his head, and the girls followed suit. When he was removed from the courtroom, they often were not far behind.[76]

The antics of Manson and his followers might have been laughable had they not been truly frightening. It was clear to all involved that the Family had no reservations about using violence or following through on the threats they issued, and they made many of the people around them more than a little nervous. Bugliosi began getting hang-up phone calls at home, even after he changed his unlisted phone number, and he was often followed by Family members when he left the court-house. One day during testimony, Manson turned to a bailiff and told him that he was "going to have Bugliosi and the judge killed." In response, Bugliosi had an intercom system installed in his home that would instantly connect him to the nearest police station and had a bodyguard accompany him for the remainder of the trial.[77] Judge Older had a driver-bodyguard and 24-hour security at his home, and, after the day Manson lunged at him with a pencil, he wore a revolver under his robes.[78] Atkins's attorney Daye Shinn reportedly kept a loaded gun in each room of his house.[79]

As it turned out, they were right to take precautions. Ronald Hughes, Van Houten's lawyer, had been particularly opposed to letting her take the stand. She had only been present at the LaBianca residence, so she was only charged with two counts of murder rather than seven and thus had the most to lose if she sacrificed herself for Manson. After the defense rested, Older granted a ten-day recess in which the attorneys were to prepare their closing arguments. Hughes reportedly planned to use this time to go camping and work on his argument from the Sespe Creek in Los Padres National Forest, just outside of Los Angeles. When the trial resumed, Hughes had van-ished. No one could locate him or had seen or heard from him within the past few days. When he failed to appear again the next day, Older assigned Van Houten's defense to another attorney, Maxwell Keith, and granted his request for a three-week extension so that he could familiarize himself with the case before closing arguments began. Many, including attorney Paul Fitzgerald, speculated that Hughes was dead. Weeks later, Hughes's body was found in the Sespe Creek. Unfortunately, determining a cause of death was impossible because the body had been submerged underwater for so long.[80] Since there was no evidence of foul play, no investigation followed. However, one of the Family members allegedly said later that "Hughes was the first of the retaliation murders."[81]

The trial of Manson, Atkins, Krenwinkel, and Van Houten was one of the most ardently followed and highly publicized trials of all time. Not only Angelinos but people nationwide obsessively listened to, read up on, and talked about the case, the victims, the defendants, the attorneys, and the trial proceedings. They couldn't get enough. On the Monday morning after the murders took place, TV programs were interrupted for updates, and people commuting to work tuned their car radios from music to news coverage.[82] Several of Sharon Tate's movies were rereleased in theaters.[83] Susan Atkins, before she rescinded her grand jury testimony, sold her story to the *Los Angeles Times*, and, before the trial even began, it was published in paperback called *The Killing of Sharon Tate*.[84] On the day of Manson's arraignment, the courtroom was so crowded that Bugliosi would later write "you couldn't have squeezed another person in with a shoehorn."[85] On the first day of the trial, spectators began waiting outside the courthouse at 6:00 a.m., just hoping to get a glimpse of Manson.[86] Before a verdict was even reached, filmmakers went to work on a documentary on the trial, which, after completion, was shown at the 1972 Venice

Film Festival and nominated for an Academy Award.[87] To some, Manson even became a cause célèbre. Shops sold T-shirts, posters, and buttons bearing his face, and the Family grew in numbers while he was in prison.[88]

There were several reasons for the widespread interest in the case. First, it fed off the fascination many Americans had with hippie life and counterculture, from the drugs to the communal living to the kinds of people who partook in them. It also allowed those who were antagonistic toward this lifestyle to voice their concerns and apprehension. Although Manson never claimed to be a hippie nor did he espouse much of the hippie creed, which preached peace over violence, many identified him as one. These people felt that the murders were the dark consequence of going against established and mainstream living. As one author explained, the case "highlighted the growing rift between two generations of Americans."[89] Patt Morrison, columnist at the *Los Angeles Times*, wrote that the case showed the "dark side of paradise." She wrote that because of it "people could shake their fingers and say, 'this is where your high-living, rich, hippie, movie-star lifestyle gets you. This is where drug culture gets you.' It's the boomerang effect, the wages of sin."[90]

Second, the case exuded celebrity. At every turn there was a nationally identifiable name. Sharon Tate was a movie star, her husband a famous movie director, her friend a hairstylist to the stars. Any discussion of their home brought up the names Candace Bergen and Doris Day. Manson had spent months living with Beach Boy Dennis Wilson. While imprisoned at Sybil Brand, Atkins had told Virginia Graham that the Family had a "death list" that included Elizabeth Taylor, Richard Burton, Tom Jones, Steve McQueen, and Frank Sinatra.[91]

Finally, the crimes perpetrated by Manson and his followers

were some of the scariest in recent memory, perhaps in the last century. They were truly the stuff of nightmares. The killings were gruesome, and the violence inflicted on the victims was beyond excessive. The victims were killed within the supposed safety of their own homes and chosen at random. Seemingly anyone could be next. The Family members, both those standing trial and those holding vigil out on the street, were odd and creepy. They had vacant expressions, spouted nonsense to passersby, and seemed to have no remorse for what had happened. Atkins, Krenwinkel, and Van Houten often smiled, sang, laughed, and joked with reporters and spectators when led in and out of trial.[92] They were so young and innocent-looking, yet capable of such violence and terror.

On top of everything else, there was Manson, who by himself was a terrifying character and somehow had warped the minds of America's youth and convinced them to kill for him. He constantly made startling statements like, "If I get the death penalty, there's going to be a lot of bloodletting."[93] He was "the bogeyman under the bed, the personification of evil, the freaky one-man horror show."[94] So focused were people on Manson that the case was commonly referred to as "the Manson case" rather than "the Tate case" or "the LaBianca case" or any other victim, as most cases are.

After Sharon Tate's death, celebrities from Frank Sinatra to Tony Bennett to Steve McQueen went into hiding or increased their security measures. Even ordinary Los Angeles residents were frightened and fearful that they could be next. After the murders, a Beverly Hills sporting goods store reportedly sold 200 firearms over a two-day period, when before it had been selling three or four per day. Security companies around the city doubled their personnel. Guard dog breeders and sellers ran out of dogs. Accidental shootings dramatically increased, as did reportings of suspicious persons to police.[95] Even with five defendants imprisoned, there were countless other Family members out on the streets, apparently capable of the same callous, unfeeling violence, and constantly being quoted as saying things like "there's a revolution coming, very soon," and "you are next, all of you."[96] Americans were terrified.

Yet they simply could not look away. The press capitalized on this widespread fascination. The coverage of the Manson case was outrageously excessive. The story was simply everywhere. Coverage surpassed that of all previous murder cases other than the Lindbergh kidnapping and the assassination of President Kennedy, and had begun instantly.[97] Having monitored police scanners, reporters were already gathered outside the Tate residence when the first police cars arrived, shouting questions as officers came and went: "Is Sharon dead?" "Were they murdered?" The first AP story went out before the names of the victims were even known.[98]

The Tate murders made the headlines of the afternoon papers and were breaking news on television broadcasts not only in Los Angeles but nationwide. "Actress, Heiress, 3 Others Slain," read the page-one headline in the *Washington Post*.[99] The *New York Times* carried a similar story, entitled "Actress Is Among 5 Slain At Home in Beverly Hills."[100]

With little concrete information, reporters published stories brimming with rumors and untruths. Some claimed that Sharon Tate's baby had been cut out of her abdomen. Others claimed that the towel thrown over Jay Sebring's face was a Ku Klux Klan hood.[101] One investigator made the mistake of saying to a reporter that the killings "seemed ritualistic," and the story that ran in the *Los Angeles Times* was headlined "Ritualistic Slayings: Sharon Tate, Four Others Murdered."[102] Papers published long, detailed accounts of the victims' lives, noting

Roman Polanski's penchant for violence in his movies.[103] In most cases, the implication was that these celebrities, with their high living and no-consequence attitudes, had brought their deaths upon themselves. "Live freaky, die freaky," was the oft-quoted general consensus. The coverage was so negative that, on August 19, Polanski called a press conference to clear up some of the rumors and scold the most-shameless reporters.[104]

The LaBianca killings got similar coverage, capturing head-lines and television banners on Monday morning. "Second Ritual Killings Here," cried page one of the August 11 *Los Angeles Times*.[105]

The coverage continued even when there were no updates or promising leads, and reporters were forced to grasp at straws. *Life* magazine filled its pages with photos of the crime scene. *The Tonight Show* featured Truman Capote, the noted author of *In Cold Blood*, discussing what he believed had transpired. Tiny details were described as "breakthroughs."[106] When all else failed, reporters blasted law enforcement for not making any progress. "What is going on behind the scenes in the Los Angeles Police investigation (if there is such a thing)?" asked the *Hollywood Citizen News*.[107]

After Manson and his Family were identified as suspects, the press was re-inflamed. The LAPD held a press conference on December 1 to announce the issuance of arrest warrants for Watson, Krenwinkel, and Kasabian, and over two hundred reporters representing publications and news stations from all over the world were in attendance.[108] Afterward, coverage focused mostly on Manson and his strange followers: their customs, their lifestyle, their history. No detail, if strange and shocking enough, was irrelevant. Reporters traveled to Inyo County and filmed the treacherous journey out to Barker Ranch to show how remote the location was.[109] Unincarcerated Family members were interviewed, some so frequently that they were on a first-name basis with the reporters, as were the parents, siblings, and past friends of the defendants.[110] The *New York Times* published a massive article entitled "Charlie Manson: One Man's Family" that spread over several pages and promised readers "a look at its members and their way of life."[111] The district attorney's office received more than one hundred press inquiry calls each day. Over one hundred reporters flooded the hallways on the day Atkins testified before the grand jury, and one publication reportedly offered $10,000 just to look at a copy of the transcript. Her story sold to the *Los Angeles Times* and was reprinted in other publications across the globe.[112] When the prosecution took Kasabian from jail so that she could show them the route she and the others had taken on the first night of the killings, they had to cut the outing short because they were followed by a television news van.[113]

The press was so ubiquitous that it often beat out investigators when trying to get a story. It was a reporter attempting to identify the unknown victim in the white Rambler at the Tate residence who wrote down the car's license plate number, checked it at the DMV, and traced it to Steven Parent. Similarly, it was a news camera crew, trying to recreate the events of that night for its viewers, that found the bloody clothes on the hillside. The gun was found by a young boy, Steven Weiss, in his backyard and was identified when Weiss's father heard about the gun as described in Atkins's *Los Angeles Times* tell-all and realized that it matched the one found by his son.[114]

The coverage was so excessive and pervasive that the first judge assigned to the case, Judge Keene, issued a gag order, forbidding anyone involved in the trial to speak to the press,[115] and denied Manson's request for a change in venue because "even if warranted, [it] would be ineffectual."[116]

Since it seemed that the publicity would continue at this

level throughout the trial, the jury was immediately sequestered and remained so for the duration of the trial. At 225 days, it was longer than any jury had been sequestered before.[117] The case snagged newspaper headlines nationwide on the first day and every day in which there was dramatic or noteworthy testimony. Some stories were accurate; others were rumor-filled. In early August, President Nixon, commenting on the case, declared Manson guilty, and his statement was so widely published that the windows of the bus that shuttled the jury back and forth from the courthouse to their hotel had to be blacked out to keep the jurors from seeing the headlines of papers on display at newsstands and being read on the streets.[118] When the guilty verdict came in, the *Los Angeles Times* covered it in a special early edition released that afternoon.[119]

After being sentenced to death, Charles Manson was sent to the state prison at San Quentin to await execution. Family members attempted to free him, claiming they planned to hijack a commercial airplane and kill a passenger every hour until he was released. They were unsuccessful.[120] But on February 18, 1972, the California Supreme Court outlawed the death penalty in *People v. Anderson*, finding capital punishment "impermissibly cruel." This decision worked retroactively, commuting all upcoming executions to life in prison.[121] Manson was saved.

He was transferred to several different facilities before being sent to Corcoran State Prison in 1989 where he has remained ever since. He has been a consistent disciplinary problem, acting up and threatening staff. He occasionally comes up for parole, but he uses his hearings to preach his strange philosophy to a new crowd. In recent years, he has simply stopped attending them. He likely will never be released.[122] As of 2015, he is eighty-one years old and last reported to be married to a twenty-seven-year-old woman named Star.[123]

The same state supreme court decision that spared Manson spared Atkins, Krenwinkel, and Van Houten. All three were transferred to the California Institute for Women at Frontera, where they remained. Van Houten appealed for and received a new trial in 1976 in light of the midtrial disappearance of her attorney, Ronald Hughes, but was convicted again. All three women have renounced Manson and expressed deep remorse over what they have done. They were exemplary prisoners at Frontera, and they took their hearings seriously, but none of them received parole.[124] Atkins died of brain cancer in 2009 at age 61.[125] Krenwinkel and Van Houten are still alive.

After being granted immunity, Kasabian returned to New Hampshire where she attempted to live a normal life. However, the media attention on her was so overwhelming that she took on an assumed name and disappeared. She spent twenty years living in hiding until a documentary film crew found her in 2009 living in a poverty-stricken trailer park.[126]

Tex Watson was finally extradited and tried separately. He was convicted of all counts on October 12, 1971, and sentenced to death, but, like the others, his sentence was commuted to life in prison.[127] He is serving out his sentence at Mule Creek State Prison, where he has been ordained as a minister, claiming to have experienced a religious awakening.[128]

Vincent Bugliosi remained in the legal profession but spent the majority of his time writing nonfiction until his death in 2015 at age eighty. His book on the Manson case became a best seller.[129] Irving Kanarek suffered a psychiatric breakdown in 1989 and spent several years recuperating, during which he lost his law practice and the State Bar of California was forced to pay $40,500 to former clients waging claims against him. He retired from the bar and has not practiced since.[130] Paul Fitzgerald remained in private practice in Los Angeles as a prominent and well-respected criminal defense attorney until he died of heart problems in 2001 at age sixty-four.[131] Daye Shinn was disbarred in 1992 for misappropriating client funds.[132]

While Manson still sometimes attracts twisted admirers, the Family has dissipated.

Yet even as the Manson saga came to an end, America's obsession with it did not. There is something about the case that continues to captivate. Bugliosi's book on the trial is the best-selling true crime book in US history, selling seven million copies, and was dramatized for television in both 1976 and 2004.[133] When it aired, the 1976 version was similarly the most watched made-for-television movie in history. A 1994 ABC special on the case received the highest ratings ever garnered for a network magazine show debut.[134]

Manson receives more mail than any other jailed individual in history,[135] and he is continually sought out for interviews by the press. A wax figurine of him stands in Madame Tussauds in London. An opera titled *The Manson Family* premiered at Lincoln Center in New York in 1990.[136] The popular television series *South Park* produced an episode called "Merry Christmas, Charlie Manson!" complete with Manson as an animated character.[137] More than any other criminal, Charles Manson has become part of our cultural consciousness, a reference that everyone recognizes and understands whether or not he or she was alive to experience his trial. As one journalist writing on the fortieth anniversary of the murders phrased it, Manson "remains a household name synonymous with evil, hatred, even the devil."[138]

It is most likely a combination of the gruesome nature of the killings and the pure evil represented by Manson that keeps people intrigued. It is almost as if we still cannot believe that it actually happened. Bugliosi would later describe the events as too unbelievable for a novel and too over-the-top for a horror movie. Manson's bizarre nature and his untempered malevolence continue to scare us to this day. We are constantly reminded of the horror he was capable of inflicting. He still gives interviews that shock and frighten. In 1988, he told journalist Geraldo Rivera, "I'm going to kill as many of you as I can. I'm going to pile you up to the sky." In 2011, he told another reporter, "I don't play, I shoot people . . . I'm everything bad." In 2013, he asked another, "What's violent about pulling your finger across a trigger? There's no violence. It's just a person there and you move your finger and they're gone."[139] He is as outrageous today as he was at his trial. He never apologizes nor shows remorse. Laurie Levenson, professor at Loyola Law School, aptly said, "I think Manson will haunt us forever."[140]

CHAPTER 9

1980–1990:
JEAN HARRIS AND THE DIET DOCTOR

The 1960s ushered in a new phase of feminism commonly referred to as the second wave of feminism. The century's first wave of feminism had focused on legal gender inequalities, such as suffrage and property rights, but this new movement, which gained momentum in the 1970s, revolved more around social and cultural inequalities. The women involved in this movement fought against what they deemed to be sexist attitudes and imbalances of power between men and women in daily life and customs. They protested beauty pageants and the sexist portrayal of women in ads and magazines. The US Supreme Court ruled in *Roe v. Wade* that overly restrictive laws prohibiting abortions were unconstitutional. Several states passed marital rape laws. Military academies and other historically male colleges were opened to women. Women's liberation groups became popular, and Helen Reddy's song "I am Woman" became a rallying anthem.

In the wake of this progress came the *Complete Scarsdale Medical Diet*, which swept the nation when it debuted in 1978. Quickly climbing to the top of the diet trend pyramid, the popular weight-loss plan could, according to its creator Dr. Herman Tarnower, make a person lose twenty pounds in fourteen days and keep them off. His book, which featured a smiling, encouraging Tarnower with a white coat and stethoscope, spent forty-nine weeks on the *New York Times* best-seller list. It sold over 700,000 copies in hardback and an additional two million in paperback.[1]

But the highly structured and unforgiving low-carbohydrate, low-fat, low-calorie regimen was essentially a starvation diet, and it had hundreds of thousands of hungry adherents, dissatisfied with their breakfasts of half a grapefruit, a slice of toast, and black coffee, wishing that someone would kill Dr. Herman Tarnower. Much to their surprise, on March 10, 1980, somebody did.

The culprit was no disgruntled dieter but Mrs. Jean Harris, elite prep school headmistress and Tarnower's longtime girlfriend. His murder and her lengthy trial triggered a maelstrom of press coverage, and the story, which involved a celebrity victim, a vicious love triangle, and a break with propriety and decorum by members of society's upper echelons, captivated a nation and spurred an outpouring of social commentary.

Herman Tarnower first met Jean Harris in 1966 at a dinner party held by mutual friends in New York City.[2] Harris, in her early forties and quite pretty with fair hair, light blue eyes, delicate features, and a high, rounded forehead, was then serving as director of the Springside School in Philadelphia. But her roots were in the Midwest. Born Jean Struven in 1923 to a family of Christian Scientists, she grew up in a fashionable suburb of Cleveland and attended the prestigious Laurel School, followed by Smith College where she graduated magna cum laude with a degree in economics. After college, she returned to the Midwest and married James Harris, a well-bred—but by no means wealthy—executive at Holley Carburetor. They lived in the Detroit suburb of Grosse Point, and to supplement the family income she taught at the highly revered Grosse Pointe Country Day School, which later became the Grosse Point University School. The Harrises had two sons, David and James, born in 1950 and 1952 respectively, but divorced in early 1965.

After the divorce Jean and the boys moved to Chestnut Hill in Philadelphia, where she accepted the position at Springside. Even in her early years, she was described as being ambitious, smart yet sensible, and the utmost example of good manners and restraint, a perfect lady.[3]

Jean Harris. © Bookstaver/AP/AP/Corbis.

Herman Tarnower, called "Hi" by those close to him, was in many respects Harris's opposite. A self-made man, he was the son of Jewish immigrants from Warsaw, Poland, and was born and raised in Brooklyn, where he attended James Madison High School. He completed his undergraduate and medical studies at Syracuse University, graduating in 1933. He then worked as a resident at Bellevue Hospital and attended at White Plains Hospital before serving as a lieutenant colonel in the Casualty Survey Commission in Japan during World War II. After the war, he resumed working as a cardiologist in White Plains for several years before he founded the Scarsdale Medical Group, a successful practice in the suburbs of Manhattan with a following of wealthy patients. A lifelong bachelor, he never married but had an extensive dating history. Tall and tan with light brown eyes and prominent features, he was in his midfifties when he met Harris in 1966. He had a cool, confident, self-controlled manner and was intelligent and well-traveled with a penchant for golfing, hunting, and fine dining. While some friends remembered him as lively and humorous, he was more often described as austere and forbidding.[4] Different in so many ways, Harris would later write that "right from the start [she] was something of a misfit in old Herm's life, and he was certainly a misfit in [hers], but that was part of the attraction."[5]

Shortly after meeting, Harris and Tarnower began dating, embarking upon what would become a fourteen-year-long relationship. They went to social functions with Tarnower's well-heeled friends and traveled the world together, everything from short beach vacations to around-the-world excursions. Harris spent countless weekends at Tarnower's enormous six-acre estate in the town of Purchase in Westchester County, New York, and he would occasionally accompany her to her school functions. In 1972, Harris accepted the position of headmistress at the Thomas School in Rowayton, Connecticut, and bought a home in Mahopac, New York, seemingly to be closer to Tarnower. The Thomas School merged with another school in 1975, and Harris briefly took a position at the Allied Maintenance Corporation in New York City before becoming the headmistress of the very prestigious and high-profile Madeira School in Virginia.[6] Their relationship continued despite her move to Virginia. Harris often drove the five hours to Purchase to spend weekends with Tarnower. He even threw her son David a wedding party when he married in the spring of 1980.

It was during this time that Tarnower published his famed *Complete Scarsdale Medical Diet*. He had been distributing the weight-loss regimen as a mimeographed sheet to patients for years, but after it was mentioned in the *New York Times* in 1978 he agreed to write a full-length book, which he did with the help of diet book author Samm Sinclair Baker. Harris assisted with the research and was included in the acknowledgments. The book made Tarnower abundantly wealthy and turned him into a household name nationwide.

The fourteen years Harris and Tarnower spent together were anything but blissful. Tarnower emotionally tormented Harris. He proposed marriage within two months of meeting her but rescinded his offer shortly thereafter, saying he simply couldn't go through with the wedding.[7] He told her she could keep the diamond engagement ring and offered to store it in his safe for protection but then sold it without telling her.[8] He was emotionally distant and would often say to her, "I don't love anyone, and I don't need anyone."[9]

He also continued to see other women throughout their relationship, the most visible of which was Lynne Tryforos, an attractive divorcee more than thirty years his junior. Tall, slender, and blond, Tryforos, an assistant at the Scarsdale

Medical Practice, began seeing Tarnower romantically sometime around 1974.[10] Tryforos accompanied Tarnower to parties
and public events, traveled with him as frequently as Harris
did, and stayed overnight at his home, sometimes on the night
before he was to see Harris. The women certainly knew about
each other, and Harris was confronted with constant reminders
of Tryforos. They each kept makeup, jewelry, and clothing at
Tarnower's home, and Tryforos often sent letters to him when
he was traveling with Harris. Harris exploded with fury on a trip
to Paris when she spotted an engraving on Tarnower's cufflinks
that read "All my love, Lynne."[11] During their Christmas vacation of 1979, which Tarnower and Harris spent with friends in
Florida, Harris noticed an advertisement on the front page of
the *New York Times* that read "Happy New Year Hi T. Love Always
Lynne," to which she responded, "Why don't you suggest she
use the Goodyear Blimp next year? I think it's available."[12] Tryforos even appeared at the house one day to paint the patio
furniture while Harris was lounging by the pool. Friends and
observers remember that Tarnower would play them off each
other, disparaging each to the other woman, encouraging Tryforos to think of Harris as old and annoying and Harris to think
of Tryforos as promiscuous and frivolous.[13]

The relationship between the two women soon became
violent. Harris began receiving vicious anonymous phone calls
and, assuming Tryforos was the one behind them, called Tryforos every night in the middle of the night.[14] When she and
Tarnower returned from a trip to the Bahamas in the spring
of 1979, Harris found all the clothes she had left in his home
slashed and torn.[15]

Yet it seemed that nothing could shake Harris's love for Tarnower, not his cruelest actions nor the fact that she was steadily
losing her position to a younger (and, in her opinion, inferior)

woman. She never discussed the shredded clothing with him for fear of ruining the weekend she was planning on spending with him.[16] She was reduced to groveling for his affections. When he canceled a weekend with her, she wrote him a letter, decrying the cancelation as the kind of punishment she had not earned and begging him not to punish her anymore. "What I am most grateful for for all my life," she wrote, "is the time I have with you."[17] After she helped with his book, Tarnower gave her a check for $4,000, and, in response, she wrote him a distraught letter telling him that the money made her feel like a prostitute and that all she needed was a thank-you. She only hoped, she went on, that, if the book was successful, he would "decide on another trip, somewhere, anywhere, together."[18] He was critical of her, but she liked when he spoke down to her, claiming it was just what she needed.[19] Years later, she wrote that she "had long since had every reason to be disillusioned with [Hi], his obsession with self, his insensitivity" but that she "would never love anyone else" because "too many lovely memories had woven a knot that no one would ever unravel."[20] After she moved to Virginia, she saw Tarnower less as Tryforos saw him more. She recognized that they were drifting apart but was too devoted to him to leave.

The weekend of March 8, 1980, was a breaking point for Harris. She was working at Madeira while Tryforos was spending the weekend with Tarnower. Harris felt she desperately needed to speak with Tarnower and called him several times but each time was told that he was unavailable. Unable to reach him by telephone, she composed an eleven-page letter, known afterward as the "Scarsdale letter," and sent it to him via registered mail.[21]

She finally spoke with him by telephone at his office on the morning of Monday, March 10, although, according to phone records the call only lasted a few minutes. She tried to go about her business for the rest of the day, but she tired and told her secretary to cancel the rest of her appointments. She called Tarnower again at five o'clock that evening and begged him to let her come up to Purchase that night. Reluctantly, he agreed. Setting out for New York, she left in plain view on her desk several documents that she had hastily composed and took with her a .32 caliber handgun that she had purchased a year and a half earlier.[22]

Tarnower spent the evening having dinner at his home with Tryforos and his niece Debbie Raizes, who was married to another doctor at the Scarsdale Medical Group. The dinner ended early, and he went to sleep at about 8:30 p.m.

It was nearly eleven when Harris arrived and let herself in through the garage entrance, as she had done many times before, and made her way up to Tarnower's bedroom. Not long after, Suzanne van der Vreken, Tarnower's long-time house-keeper and cook, heard the sound of the buzzer that accompanied the intercom that linked Tarnower's bedroom and the kitchen. When she answered the phone, she heard chaos on the other line: shouting, banging, a voice that she recognized as Harris's, and the sound of a gun being fired. She woke up her husband, Henri, Tarnower's chauffeur, and called the police before running upstairs. She found Tarnower on the bedroom floor, bleeding profusely. He had been shot four times: in the right shoulder, right upper arm, right back, and through the palm of his right hand. There were smears of blood around the room and personal items belonging to Tryforos thrown about.[23]

Harris left the house and drove away but only made it down the road before she decided to turn back. She was seen making a U-turn by the police officer that had been called to the scene, and he trailed her back to the house. Several other detectives followed shortly, as did an ambulance, and Tarnower was taken to St. Agnes Hospital in White Plains. He was pronounced dead at 11:58 p.m.[24] Harris fainted when she saw him carried out on a stretcher. She waived her rights to an attorney, confessed openly to having shot Tarnower with her own gun, and showed the detectives to her car, where the gun was lying on the front seat. She was arrested and taken to the county jail in Valhalla, from which she was released on bail put up by her brother, Captain Robert Struven of the United States Navy.[25]

The legal proceedings commenced immediately. Harris hired attorney Joel Aurnou, a smart and seasoned forty-nine-year-old defense attorney who had also briefly served as county judge. Described as "badger shaped," he was a courthouse regular. He first consulted with Harris in the early-morning hours of March 11 while she was being held in Valhalla.

Assistant District Attorney George Bolen led the prosecution team. Though only thirty-four, he had extensive prosecutorial experience, having worked for years under famed District Attorney Frank Hogan in Manhattan. Since moving to Westchester, he had tried between twenty and thirty cases, winning most of them. He was tall and slim with dark hair, glasses, and a serious look about him.[26]

Preliminary hearings began in a small courtroom in Harrison, New York, on March 14, and Harris was indicted for second-degree murder on March 25. However, just what had really happened in Tarnower's bedroom on March 10 was anything but clear. Harris had certainly shot Tarnower, but the lingering question to be settled at the trial was why. The prosecution initially believed that Harris, filled with jealousy and rage, had planned to kill Tarnower all along. However, this idea was swiftly dispatched in favor of a different theory when, during hearings, a police officer testified that Harris had gone to Purchase that night to get Tarnower to kill her but instead had killed him when a struggle ensued. The officer's testimony centered on several comments Harris made at the scene, including how ironic it was that Tarnower should get to die when she wanted to die and he wanted to live, and that she loved him very much but that he slept with every woman he could and she had had it. Harris claimed that she did not remember making any such comments.[27]

After the indictment, Aurnou held a press conference and alleged that these reports were based on a misunderstanding. Harris, he claimed, had been planning to commit suicide and had simply wanted to see and talk to her longtime companion one last time. The shooting had been an accident. She had never had any intent to kill Tarnower, and the prosecution could not prove that she did. She was innocent of second-degree murder, he stressed, and he was "going for broke" and would not seek lesser charges. On March 26, Harris was arraigned and pled not guilty.[28]

The press pounced on the story immediately. With Tarnower's household fame and Harris's high-stature job, the case made national headlines. "'Scarsdale Diet' Doctor Slain; Headmistress Charged," blasted a special edition to the *New York Times* published on March 12.[29] The front page of the *Los Angeles Times* on March 11 bore a picture of Harris accompanied by the headline "Scarsdale Diet Author Slain; Headmistress Held."[30] The *Washington Post* ran an extensive piece entitled "Madeira School Headmistress Held: Madeira Headmistress Charged in Slaying of Diet Book Author" that started on the front page and went on to include an excerpt from the acknowledgments page of Tarnower's book and a dramatic picture of a phone lying off its cradle, supposedly in Harris's home.[31]

And the story remained in the news for months, throughout indictment, arraignment, and pretrial preparations. During preliminary hearings, press photographers strained to take pictures of the courtroom from behind the judge's chair and through cracks in doorways. Publications of all kinds covered the murder, from major newspapers to women's magazines and university rags like the *Harvard Lampoon*.[32] Harris's face was everywhere; photos from her college days were dug up and published in major papers. There was even a filmed re-enactment of the shooting that ran on television as an advertisement for a series about Harris soon to appear in newspapers.[33]

Nearly all of the press played up the romantic aspects of the case, outlining Tarnower's relationships with both Harris and Tryforos and portraying his death as the consequence of a wild love triangle. One piece, published on the first page of the *Washington Post*, ran under the title "Romance Cited in Diet Author's Death" and quoted a neighbor who called the situation between Tarnower, Harris, and Tryforos "the eternal triangle."[34] Other headlines included "Harris Told Police She'd 'Been Through Hell' Over Tarnower"[35] and "'Scarsdale' Trial: Passion and Mystery."[36] The media also focused heavily on the "Scarsdale letter," the letter Harris had mailed to Tarnower before she drove to Purchase. The letter had arrived at his office on March 12 and had been picked up by the defense attorney before the prosecution had a chance to get a federal warrant for it. No one knew what the mysterious letter contained.[37]

The country was fixated with the case. Tarnower's book, which had been hibernating in the number three slot on the *New York Times* best-seller list, reclaimed its position as number one. Bantam Press ordered another 200,000 copies as people scrambled to get their hands on it.[38]

But it was really Harris who got all the attention, and she had thousands of women rallying to her cause. In light of the pervasiveness of the second wave of feminism, it is not surprising that many women sympathized with her, believing her a victim of the male-dominated society and larger social problems.

They identified with her and perhaps even admired her ability to break free from her façade of respectability and decorum to take matters into her own hands. One female author who closely followed the case wrote that Harris "was a symbol of our capacity for hurt and rage" and compared her to Anna Karenina and Emma Bovary. Another author, who attended every day of her trial, wrote "I saw her first on TV, stepping out of a police car and thought—she reminds me of me."[39] Harris got hundreds of sympathy cards and letters from total strangers.[40] The feminist *Ms. Magazine*, established just eight years earlier in 1972, featured an interview with defense attorney Aurnou.[41] The case was, as *Time* magazine billed it, "the old battle of the sexes, fraught with newer, feminist tonalities."[42]

Not all women felt this way, of course, but people everywhere could not help but be enthralled by the literature-like aspects of the case. *Time* claimed the shooting of Tarnower had "all the elements of an Agatha Christie mystery" and that the background story was "the stuff of soap operas."[43] One columnist writing for the *Chicago Tribune* put it best when she wrote that the case had "all the elements of a juicy potboiler—whiffs of veiled passion, a cast that includes the doctor's pretty medical assistant, talk of suicide, a newly revised will, and a mysterious bulky letter" and that people were "frankly salivating in anticipation of the drama."[44]

Pretrial hearings began on October 6, 1980, presided over by Judge Russell Leggett, a forty-nine-year-old Bronx native who had been a county judge for over a decade.[45] Among several other motions, Aurnou moved for the press to be excluded from the hearings in light of the widespread media coverage, claiming it negatively impacted his client, but Leggett denied his request.[46]

After a painstaking jury selection, the trial began on November

21 with Bolen's opening statement. He took the jury through a chronology of March 10 and promised to prove that Harris was guilty of murder. Aurnou countered Bolen's statement by claiming that the shooting of Tarnower was no more than a tragic accident that occurred when Harris and Tarnower were struggling over the gun. Harris had planned to kill herself because of "her own feelings, her own emotions, independent of a man" and for reasons that were "in Virginia, not in New York." He counted concerns about aging, her stressful job, and the end of her role as an active mother. She had gone to New York, he argued, to say goodbye to the love of her life, and, after he was shot, Tarnower and Harris rang the buzzer for Suzanne together before she left to go get help.[47] He claimed the case would be an illustration of the meaning and importance of reasonable doubt.[48]

There was some truth to Aurnou's arguments, truths that had, for the most part, been kept out of the press and the public's knowledge. Harris was undoubtedly depressed. After her release from Valhalla County Jail, she spent ten days in the psychiatric ward of United Hospital in Port Chester, where she was diagnosed with acute suicidal depression with transient psychotic features. In June, insurance physicians diagnosed her with major affective disorder with symptoms of severe depression, insomnia, and agitation.[49] Since 1971, she had been dependent on the drug Desoxyn, a fast-acting methamphetamine stimulant that Tarnower continuously prescribed for her ever-increasing fatigue. In fact, she had run out of her supply of Desoxyn only a few days before killing Tarnower, and the withdrawal from the stimulant may have exaggerated her feelings of depression and helplessness.[50]

She also certainly was having trouble at work. The job of headmistress was incredibly demanding and, in her case, quite thankless. The board of Madeira had very little confidence in her, and the decision to hire her had been far from unanimous. In 1979, the board hired a group of consultants from Russell R. Browning Associates to evaluate the school. Many of the comments made by directors and parents during the investigation were extremely critical of Harris, and the report issued by the consultants recommended that Madeira fire Harris immediately. The board kept her on and subsequently renewed her contract, but the damage had been done. Harris's own confidence and enthusiasm for her job were gone.[51] Additionally, just days before Tarnower's death, she had the unfortunate responsibility of expelling four popular and well-respected seniors for possession of marijuana, and dealt with the subsequent backlash from their parents and other students.[52]

Prosecutor Bolen presented a parade of witnesses, starting with the correctional officers who had been on duty at Valhalla County jail the night Harris was brought in. They testified as to her appearance and demeanor when she was arrested and the clothes she had been wearing were placed into evidence. The officers were followed by salesmen from Irving's Sports Shop, where Harris bought her gun in October 1978, who testified that she was clearly very unfamiliar with firearms when she made her purchase. Next came the superintendent of buildings and grounds at Madeira who confirmed what time Harris left Madeira on March 10.[53]

The next witness was housekeeper Suzanne van der Vreken, whose testimony lasted several days. She established the floor plan of Tarnower's house and spoke about the nature of his relationship with both Harris and Tryforos, remembering that Harris spent less time at the Purchase estate after moving to Virginia. She also testified about the relationship between the two women, claiming that Harris "used some words—not very nice—about that lady." Bolen then led Van der Vreken through the events of March 10, from Harris's many phone calls to the housekeeper hearing the buzzer, discovering the bleeding Tarnower, and calling the police, all of which established the timeline for the crime. She described the state of Tarnower's room and bathroom when she found him, recalling the location of bloodstains and that many of Tryforos's belongings, including jewelry and hair curlers, had been strewn about the room. Pictures of the scene were entered into evidence. She also remembered seeing Harris reach down, touch Tarnower's face, and say, "Oh Hi, why didn't you kill me?"[54]

Other than brief appearances by Tarnower's grief-stricken niece Debbie Raizes and chauffeur Henri van der Vreken, the balance of the remaining prosecution testimony was highly technical and came from a variety of police officials, forensic serologists, and ballistics experts. These witnesses testified primarily about what happened when they arrived at the scene that evening and in the subsequent few days. Among other things, they confirmed that they adequately informed Harris of her rights before asking her if she shot Tarnower and testified about the trail of blood and shell casings in the bedroom and bathroom.[55]

Several of these witnesses were particularly important for the prosecution's case. Dr. Harold Roth, the police surgeon who had been on call on March 10 and examined Tarnower, testified about the dire condition in which he was found. He also described a hand wound in which a bullet usually enters the palm and exits the top of the hand, as in Tarnower's case, as a classic defense wound, obtained when a victim is reaching out to ward off a gun.[56] He was followed to the stand by Tarnower's ophthalmologist, who demonstrated using a chart how poor the doctor's vision was and testified that it would be difficult for him to do anything without his glasses. It was already established that Tarnower's glasses had been found on a shelf above his bed and that he was not wearing them that night, which gave further credibility to the theory that the shooting had been a surprise attack.[57] Deputy Medical Examiner Dr. Louis Roh, who had performed the autopsy on Tarnower, confirmed that the cause of Tarnower's death had been hemorrhaging from the bullet wounds he sustained. He also claimed that the wounds to Tarnower's right hand and right shoulder had been caused by the same bullet. Tarnower had likely tried to shield himself with his hand, the doctor explained, and the bullet had pierced both hand and shoulder when they were aligned. In Roh's opinion, the wounds that Tarnower sustained were simply not compatible with a struggle over a gun between a left-handed woman with a height of 5'4" and a weight of 110 pounds and a right-handed man of 5'10" stature and 175 pounds.[58] Aurnou's cross-examination of these witnesses elicited little of substance.

When the prosecution was finished, Aurnou launched into his own stream of witnesses. He started with several character witnesses who testified as to Harris's upstanding character both professionally and personally. Next followed an ophthalmologist who claimed that a person with Tarnower's vision would not be wholly dependent on glasses, although when it was revealed that the witness was an acquaintance of Aurnou's, his credibility was shattered.[59] Next on the stand were Nancy Baxter Skallerup, a former president and teacher at Madeira, and Alice Watson Faulkner, the Madeira board chairman, both of whom told of going to Harris's campus home early in the morning of March 11 and finding the documents she left behind; these were subsequently entered into evidence. Among the papers were a letter to her sister and a notarized will that stated "I want to be immediately cremated and thrown away." Another of the documents, a short letter addressed to Faulkner, read,

I'm sorry. Please for Christ's sake don't open the place again until you have adults and policemen and keepers on every floor. God knows what they're doing.

And next time choose a head the board wants and supports. Don't let some poor fool work like hell for two years before she knows she wasn't ever wanted in the first place. There are so many enemies and so few friends. I was a person and nobody ever knew.[60]

These two women were followed by forensic scientist and professor Herbert Leon MacDonnell who had analyzed the blood-splatter patterns and a bullet hole in the glass door of Tarnower's bedroom. He concluded that they were consistent with Harris's story of what had happened, only possible if Harris and Tarnower had been standing precisely where she claimed they were when the gun went off. He also analyzed the blood on the sheets and Tarnower's pajamas and testified that the stains were not consistent with the wounds described in Roh's testimony. While convincing, his testimony was entirely overshadowed when Bolen countered with eight different skin pathologists who contradicted MacDonnell's conclusions.[61]

The final witness for the defense was Jean Harris herself. On the stand for eight days, she began by recounting her relationship with Tarnower from start to finish: meeting him, spending the weekends with him, his proposal, their travels, her knowledge of his relations with other women, their happy times together as well as his callous treatment of her. Aurnou took her through her experiences at Madeira and the stress that her job had placed on her. He questioned her about her psychological state. She had been going through an identity crisis, she explained, and "wasn't sure who [she] was and it didn't seem to matter." For many years she had been mentally and physically exhausted, she claimed, routinely taking Desoxyn.[62]

Her testimony then turned to the events of March 10. She discussed the stressful situation at Madeira that had occurred over the weekend and the writing and mailing of her mysterious Scarsdale letter, which she described as a "wail." She had instantly regretted sending it, she claimed, and, when she finally spoke to Tarnower on the phone, she begged him not to read it and to dispose of it immediately. She had decided to kill herself because she "couldn't function as a human—as a useful person anymore," and she wanted to see Tarnower one last time before she did it. At about 5:15 that evening she called him and asked if she could come up to Purchase. He responded, "Suit yourself." She had practiced firing her gun on the terrace of her home and then gotten in her car to drive to New York.[63]

Finally, Aurnou led her through what had happened in Tarnower's bedroom. She had entered and found him sleeping, she claimed. She woke him up and tried to start a conversation with him, imploring him to talk to her for just a short while, but he continually refused, telling her that they would talk in the morning. Frustrated that the evening was not going according to her plan, she had gone into the bathroom and seen a negligee and set of hair curlers belonging to Tryforos. She had thrown them on the floor of the bedroom and smashed a mirror in the bathroom, in response to which Tarnower had slapped her. She asked him to hit her again, and when he wouldn't she took the gun from her purse and placed it to her head. Just as she pulled the trigger, Tarnower snatched it away from her and the bullet went through his hand.

Tarnower then went into the bathroom to examine his hand, she explained, and she reclaimed the gun. When he saw her with it again, he fought her for it, finally making her drop it. He sat on the bed with the gun in his lap and pressed the buzzer and picked up the phone to speak with Van der Vreken.

She had been desperate to be dead before help arrived, and she tried to take back the gun. They struggled again, and, at one point, the gun was in her hand, and, thinking she felt the muzzle in her stomach, she pulled the trigger. Tarnower fell to his knees. She stood up and tried, once again, to shoot herself, but the gun misfired. She pulled the trigger again, but it was now out of bullets. She took the extra bullets she had brought from her coat pocket into the bathroom but did not know how to reload the gun. She banged it against the bathtub in an attempt to open it, but the gun broke.

Resigned, she had gone back into the bedroom and seen Tarnower on the floor. She helped him onto the bed and then, thinking the phone in the bedroom was broken, had gone downstairs to drive to the local community center where she knew there was a telephone, one she had used before when Tarnower's had been out of order. On her way there, she had seen the lights of the approaching police car and had turned around so it could follow her back to the house. She swore that she only remembered firing those three shots, and the only wound she recalled seeing was the one in Tarnower's hand. She had not known that there was an independent phone line elsewhere in the house. She maintained that Tarnower had nothing to do with her wanting to commit suicide. She had never wanted, as the rumors had claimed, for Tarnower to kill her nor had she ever planned to kill Tarnower. And she insisted that her feelings on Tryforos had no bearing on her going to Purchase that night.[64]

Bolen spent several days cross-examining Harris, and the responses he elicited from her would completely and irreparably destroy her case. She did stick to her story, explaining that she had been depressed for many years and was just coming to realize it and that all she hoped when she went to Tarnower's that night was that "he would sit up and say 'come on in and sit down and talk a while.'" However, the impression she left upon the jury was one of intense bitterness and snobbery. Bolen asked her extensively about her knowledge of the relationship between Tarnower and Tryforos. She knew all about their relationship, she explained, but she was not upset about it nor was she jealous. She did feel, however, that Tryforos, whom she found "rather tasteless," certainly "denigrated" Tarnower and "gave [her] a great deal of trouble with [her] own integrity." It was not like her, Harris stated, to "rub up against people like Lynne Tryforos."[65]

Bolen also managed to enter into evidence the Scarsdale letter because it provided honest insight into Harris's mental state just hours before the shooting took place. The letter, a lengthy and chilling diatribe in which Harris aired all her grievances against Tarnower and Tryforos, was clearly the follow-up to a recent conversation she had with Tarnower. In it, she recounted a list of what she called "fourteen years of broken promises," chief among them replacing her with Tryforos as beneficiary in his will. She wrote that she had "grown poor" loving him while Tryforos had grown rich and accused him of making her feel so "like a piece of old discarded garbage" that she "seriously consider[ed] borrowing $5,000 just before [she] left New York and telling a doctor to make [her] young again." She mentioned all the ways in which Tryforos had lashed out at her in the past, lamenting that the "very things your whore does openly and obviously . . . you now have the cruelty to accuse me of." She further called Tryforos a "vicious, adulterous psychotic" and a "self-serving ignorant slut." Yet throughout the letter, she showed her unalterable dependence on Tarnower, stating that he was "the most important thing in [her] life, the most important human being in [her] life, and that will never change." Knowing she would see him again, she wrote, "was something in life to look forward to" but now he was "taking that away from [her] too and [she was] unable to cope." After pages upon pages of harshly worded criticism, she begged him to let her spend the month of April with him.[66]

Bolen ended the cross-examination with a series of questions, mostly about the telephone conversation Harris had with Tarnower on the morning of March 10. He asked Harris if Tarnower had told her that he was proposing to Tryforos, that he preferred Tryforos to her, that Harris had lied, that she had cheated, that she was set to inherit $240,000 regardless, and that he wanted her to stop bothering him, all of which she adamantly denied. After asking her one final time if she hadn't intended all along to kill Tarnower because, if she couldn't have him, then no one could, Bolen rested. Aurnou asked a few clarifying questions before Harris left the stand and then concluded the defense's case.[67]

The prosecution called several rebuttal witnesses, each of whom helped to eviscerate the defense's argument. The first witness was a patient of Tarnower's named Juanita Edwards. Edwards had been in an appointment with Tarnower on the morning of March 10 when the phone rang. Tarnower answered and excused himself to take the call in another room but failed to fully hang up the receiver in the exam room, thus allowing Edwards to hear parts of his conversation. She testified to hearing Tarnower's voice loudly and angrily arguing with what sounded like a female caller. She claimed she heard him say "you've lied and you've cheated" and "you're going to inherit $240,000" and that he cried "goddamnit, Jean, I want you to stop bothering me."[68] This testimony, coming immediately after Harris had denied that such things happened, was incredibly damning.

Edwards was followed by a return to the stand by Dr. Roh, who testified that he could now confirm that three microscopic tissue samples found in Tarnower's shoulder wound were either from the soles of his feet or the palms of his hand, adding more weight to the defensive wound theory. Aurnou countered with his own expert, but the result was only further confusion for the jury members. With that, after over two months of testimony, both sides rested, gave their closing statements, and the jury was charged. The jury deliberated for eight days and returned with a verdict of guilty on all accounts: murder in the second degree and criminal possession of a weapon in the second and third degrees. Harris was sentenced to fifteen years to life in prison without the possibility of parole for fifteen years.[69] After the trial, jury members reported that it was her own testimony that convicted her. They had re-enacted her account and simply did not find it plausible, feeling that too many shots had been fired for it to truly have been an attempted suicide gone wrong. They also wondered how, if they had truly fought over the gun, only Tarnower had been injured.[70] Yet, at her sentencing, Harris stayed true to her position, maintaining that she was innocent and that "no one in the world" felt the loss of Tarnower more than she did.[71]

The press blasted the guilty verdict from every media platform. Reporters had been as enthusiastic about the trial as they had been about the shooting, even more so after Harris's testimony and the reading of the Scarsdale letter. News from the courthouse was published in print or broadcast on television or radio almost daily. More than one hundred reporters from all over the country chronicled the case, and the courthouse lobby was constantly overrun with news photographers and television crewmembers, who were not allowed above the first floor.[72] The trial was even attended by representatives from the

American Association of Retired Persons who filed reports to be read by shut-ins.[73] One author described the trial as "carnival time in medialand," claiming that it elicited "miles of film" and "oceans of ink."[74] Early in the trial, Judge Leggett even issued a gag order, barring the attorneys from speaking to the press about the case because even small trivial details in the case were being so sensationalized.[75]

The trial attracted dedicated followers, and hundreds of spectators came to court to watch the proceedings. One author, writing after Harris's death, remembers herself and her friends as being "Jean Harris groupies" and waking up at dawn to drive to the courthouse to see her testify.[76] Another author, an expert on female murderers, described the public sentiment aptly when she wrote the following in a piece published after the trial:

> What I hadn't counted on is how much all of us would be fascinated by the thing itself, how much all of us seemed to want to hear about the helpless passion of this particular woman who seemed outwardly so self-possessed. First the journalists were drawn into the case, and through their efforts the rest of us, until it became impossible to avoid. People I scarcely knew began inviting me to dinner in the hope that as an authority on homicide I would have something new to contribute to conversation that, as the trial dragged on, grew repetitive. Otherwise serious and sensitive people took straw polls at parties to determine the guilt or innocence of Jean Harris.[77]

But, as the trial wore on, contempt for the celebrity defendant began to grow even among her most ardent supporters. Many felt misled by all that they had read about her in the papers and heard about her on the news. Her behavior during the trial was erratic. She spoke candidly to reporters, having to be corralled by her lawyers, and she was prone to angry outbursts during sessions when she was displeased with testimony.[78] While on the stand, she had an aura of hysteria, unable to control herself, and she spoke directly to the judge when under cross-examination, forcing Leggett to remind her that she had a lawyer to make objections for her.[79] Her testimony, particularly the Scarsdale letter, showed her to be not the battered woman with the stiff upper lip, the proper lady victimized by a cruel male-dominated world that many of her sympathizers believed her to be, but actually a spiteful woman capable of wild and unpredictable behavior. Few still thought of Harris as a victim and heroine, but was she simply, as one author put it, a pathetic masochist? Or was she something in between? The trial triggered a torrent of social commentary as people pondered what her story said about their social norms and the society they lived in. The same author who confessed to being a Harris groupie called the trial "a flash point for that particular cultural moment."[80]

Harris attempted both state and federal appeals on the grounds that, by not presenting any form of psychiatric or insanity defense, her attorney had been ineffective and had violated her constitutional right to a fair trial. She was denied each time.[81] She served her sentence at the Bedford Hills Correctional Facility for Women in Westchester County, where she was active in the children's center and taught mothering skills to expectant inmates. In 1992, she was granted clemency by Governor Mario Cuomo in light of her failing health; she had recently suffered two heart attacks and was scheduled for quadruple bypass surgery. After her release she remained involved in inmate rights advocacy and established Children of Bedford, a nonprofit organization that provided educational opportunities and scholarships to the children of female prisoners. She died in December 2012 at the age of eighty-nine.[82]

Thirty years after the death of Dr. Tarnower, the story of

Jean Harris still captivates people. It has inspired several films, including 1981's *The People vs. Jean Harris* starring actress Ellen Burstyn as Harris. Another film, made in 2006 for HBO, featured Annette Bening and Ben Kingsley as Harris and Tarnower, both of whom received Emmy and Golden Globe nominations for their performances.[83] Mentions of Harris and Tarnower abound in entertainment and popular culture. Even the popular television comedy series *Seinfeld* featured a reference in an episode that first aired in May 1997, in which one character mistakenly receives a Tony award for working on *Scarsdale Surprise,* a fictional musical about the killing of Tarnower.[84] Between the household celebrity, the upper classes of modern society, the twisted love triangle, and the woman scorned, when Jean Harris pulled a trigger and shot Herman Tarnower she turned a story straight from literature into one from the real world. She was not the first woman to kill a lover, and she won't be the last, but she was one who made the world take notice.

CHAPTER 10

1990–2000:
O. J. SIMPSON AND THE BLOODY GLOVE

If you are old enough to be reading this, you likely experienced firsthand the trial of O. J. Simpson for the murder of his ex-wife, Nicole Brown Simpson, and her friend Ronald Lyle Goldman. The final trial of the century was covered to saturation by both the electronic and print press, and avidly followed by consumers of spectacle, both in America and abroad. No trial before or since has captured the minds and passions of so many Americans, or sparked so much media attention.

That is partially because O. J. Simpson was the most famous American celebrity to be charged with murder in three generations. Celebrity victims, certainly, and even notorious criminals, but not since the trial of Roscoe "Fatty" Arbuckle for the murder of actress Virginia Rappe in 1921 had an American of Simpson's popularity and stature been charged with murder. Also contributing to the coverage was the fear and fascination Americans have with race relations, as the trial was that of an African American for the murder of his Caucasian ex-wife and her Jewish friend, surrounded by the aura of potentially racist white policemen allegedly driven to frame him for a murder he didn't commit, with guilt determined by a predominantly female black jury. But overriding all was the fact that television reporting had come of age in the 1990s, matured from its grainy youth of the 1960s. More than one station carried every moment of the nine-month trial from gavel to gavel, and every other television network, newspaper, and newsmagazine covered the story on a daily basis.

Simpson was born on July 9, 1947, in San Francisco, the son of working-class parents who separated when he was five. He grew up in the housing projects of the Potrero Hill neighborhood, where as a teenager he ran with a fast crowd and was briefly incarcerated at the San Francisco Youth Guidance Center. After recovering from rickets, which caused him to wear braces on his legs as a youth, Simpson excelled in athletics in high school and at City College of San Francisco and was eventually awarded an athletics scholarship to the University of Southern California, where he played running back for the Trojans in 1967 and 1968. He set rushing records and won numerous awards, including college football's most prestigious honor, the Heisman Trophy.[1]

He was drafted by the Buffalo Bills in the first round in 1969. He struggled early with the poorly performing Bills, but eventually had breakout years from 1972 to 1976, winning the NFL rushing title four times. He played in six Pro Bowls and is the only player in NFL history to rush for over 2,000 yards in a fourteen-game season. He was elected to the NFL Hall of Fame in 1985, his first year of eligibility.

Injuries ended his career with the Bills, and he played his final two seasons with the San Francisco 49ers. As his professional football career wound down, Simpson smoothly moved to a career in acting in the late 1970s, starring in several major films, including *The Towering Inferno* in 1974, *Capricorn One* in 1978, and *The Naked Gun* trilogy between 1988 and 1994. He appeared as a commentator for Monday Night Football, and his fame and popularity led to numerous endorsements, including that of spokesman for the Hertz rental car company, in whose commercials he sprinted through airports like a running back, dodging obstacles and leaping suitcases. He was more than a popular football player; he was a personality. At 6'1", 210 pounds, and classically handsome, he was "O. J.," and instantly recognized wherever he went. He thrived on the attention, stopping to sign autographs for all who asked.[2]

O. J. Simpson. © Bill Nation/Sygma/Corbis.

Simpson met the blond and beautiful Nicole Brown in 1977 at a Beverly Hills nightclub where she worked as a waitress. She was then eighteen and just three weeks out of high school. Born May 19, 1959, in West Germany, Nicole had moved as a toddler with her German mother and correspondent father, Juditha and Lou Brown respectively, to Southern California, where she was raised with three sisters.[3]

That their relationship would be stormy was immediately evident. When Nicole came home from her first date with Simpson, her roommate expressed shock to see her jeans ripped open, the result of Simpson's impatience to make love. "No, wait," Nicole explained. "I like him."[4]

Simpson was still then married to his first wife, Marguerite, and the father of two children, Arnelle and Jason. Marguerite was pregnant with a third child, Aaren, born September 24, 1977. In August 1979, Aaren drowned in the family's swimming pool. Their marriage already troubled, Simpson and Marguerite were divorced that same year.

After many years of dating, Simpson and Nicole were married in February 1985. Their first child, Sydney, was born in October, followed by a second child, Justin, born in August 1988. But Simpson's marriage to Nicole was no easier than his first. Physical and mercurial, Simpson was unquestionably abusive to Nicole, and police were called at least nine times to break up domestic disputes.[5] He beat her and threw her into walls. He once grabbed her crotch in public, proclaiming, "This belongs to me."[6] She filed for divorce on February 25, 1992, after seven years of marriage.

Shortly after 10:00 p.m. on June 12, 1994, Nicole Brown Simpson and Ron Goldman were murdered outside Nicole's condo on Bundy Drive in the affluent Brentwood neighborhood of Los Angeles, just a few blocks from Simpson's Rockingham Avenue estate. Hollywood could not have devised a crime scene with greater drama, or a killing more savage. They were not coolly gunned down from a distance as hundreds are every year in gang-torn parts of Los Angeles, but butchered: furiously slashed and stabbed multiple times. A veteran LAPD detective, one of the first officers to arrive at the scene, said, "It was the bloodiest crime scene I have ever seen."[7] Nicole and Ron were found in pools of blood. Barefoot and wearing a loose shift, Nicole lay curled up at the foot of the stairs outside her front door, stabbed seven times in her neck and head. She was apparently facedown when the murderer put a foot in her back, pulled her head up by her hair, and nearly decapitated her with a fatal slash from left to right across her neck that severed her carotid arteries and left jugular vein and nicked her spine. Ron was stabbed thirty times all over his body. Both victims had defensive wounds to their hands, incurred trying to ward off the assault.

The evidence against Simpson was initially overwhelming. His long history of physical violence against Nicole included a conviction in 1989 for spousal abuse.[8] Photographs surfaced of a bruised and battered Nicole from prior altercations with Simpson. Police had responded to her 911 calls, and she had warned them that she feared Simpson would kill her. At the crime scene, five drops of blood led away from the bodies, four of which were on the left side of bloody size twelve shoe prints, indicating that the assailant was injured on the left side of his body.[9] Simpson wore size twelve shoes, and the next day police observed him wearing a bandage over a deep cut to the middle finger of his left hand. Preliminary tests on all five blood drops at the crime scene matched Simpson, and Nicole's and Ron's blood was found in Simpson's car, and more of his blood on the driveway of his home.[10]

And while he could account for most of his time that day, he had no alibi for the hour in which the murders took place. Twenty-four-year-old limo driver Allan Park was waiting outside Simpson's gated Rockingham residence at 10:22 p.m. that night to take him to the airport for a planned flight to Chicago, but no one answered several rings at the gate. At 11:00 p.m. Park saw a figure matching Simpson arrive at the residence and enter the front door. Park rang again, and this time Simpson answered, telling him that he had overslept and just gotten out of the shower. "I'll be down in a minute," Simpson told the driver.[11]

Shortly thereafter, Simpson's luggage was loaded into the limo and Park drove him to the airport for an 11:45 p.m. flight to Chicago.

Alerted by her barking dogs, neighbors discovered the bodies of Nicole and Ron just after midnight, and a small army of police converged on the crime scene, stringing bright yellow tape and conducting an examination of the condo and its grounds. Photos were taken, measurements made, and various items packaged and marked for evidence.[12]

The first investigators on the scene were Los Angeles Police Department detectives from the West LA Division, Ron Phillips and Mark Fuhrman, who arrived together at 2:10 a.m. Patrol officer Robert Riske met them and reported his findings, then walked them along the perimeters of the scene and through the garage into the condo, where they could survey the bodies from the top of the three steps at the open door of Nicole's residence. Fuhrman later testified that he could see the bodies, bloody heel prints leading away from them, and a discarded knit cap and a leather glove. Shortly thereafter, Phillips and Fuhrman were advised that the case was being taken over by the elite Robbery/Homicide Division, and told to take no further action.[13]

The Robbery/Homicide detective in charge was Philip "Dutch" Vannatter, a veteran of twenty-five years with the Los Angeles Police Department and an experienced and well-respected homicide investigator. Silver-haired, fit, and tough talking, Vannatter was known among his colleagues as a "super cop." His prior cases included the arrest in 1977 of film director Roman Polanski, husband of Manson victim Sharon Tate, on charges of unlawful sex with Samantha Geimer, the model of a fashion shoot and then just thirteen years old. Vannatter arrived at the Bundy condo at 4:00 a.m., followed by his partner, Tom Lange, a few minutes later. After inspecting the scene and collecting information, including Simpson's prior history of battery against Nicole, he drove to Simpson's nearby Rockingham residence, arriving at approximately 5:00 a.m. With him went Detectives Lange and Phillips. Fuhrman, still on the scene two and a half hours after being told at 2:30 a.m. that he was no longer on the case, volunteered to drive. Vannatter later testified that Simpson was not then a suspect and that they only went to advise him of the death of his ex-wife.[14]

Simpson's white Bronco was parked outside the gated drive, but the detectives were unable to reach anyone inside the house by intercom or telephone. After Fuhrman told the other detectives that he had seen blood on the door of the Bronco, but without a warrant, Vannatter instructed Fuhrman to scale the wall and open the gate.

Vannatter and his fellow detectives knocked on the front door without response, then walked around the north side of the house to a row of guest quarters. In the first they roused houseguest Brian Kaelin, who told them that Simpson was not home but that his daughter Arnelle was staying in the adjoining guest residence. Fuhrman stayed with Kaelin while the other three detectives went to wake Arnelle. With her they gained admission to the main house and were able to contact Simpson in Chicago by phone.

Brian "Kato" Kaelin was a thirty-five-year-old bit actor and radio show host from Wisconsin. Fuhrman interviewed Kaelin, who in response to questioning told Fuhrman that the white Bronco belonged to Simpson, who had left the night before by limousine. Asked if anything unusual had happened during the night, Kaelin described how at about 10:45 he had heard three loud bangs against the outside wall of his guesthouse, an area that formed a narrow space between the back of the row of guesthouses and the perimeter wall of the property. A "cracking" he called it and thought it might have been an earthquake.[15] Fuhrman went to investigate. A few minutes later he returned to inform his fellow detectives that he had discovered in the small space a right-hand leather glove still wet and sticky with blood. It was the match of the left-hand glove found at the Bundy Drive murder scene.

The sky now lightening, Vannatter and the detectives observed drops of blood in the driveway that led from the parked Bronco to the front door of the main residence, and more drops inside the main house. Vannatter declared the Rockingham residence an extension of the crime scene and left to get a search warrant.

Contacted in Chicago early that Monday morning after the murders, Simpson immediately returned to Los Angeles. Accompanied by his attorney, Howard Weitzman, Simpson was interviewed by Detectives Vannatter and Lange at Parker Center, the downtown headquarters of the Los Angeles Police Department. He was read his Miranda rights and briefly handcuffed, but not arrested. In the thirty-minute taped interview, Simpson did not confess to the murders but was vague about his whereabouts the evening before, and he could not recall how he had cut his hand. "I have no idea, man," he told the detectives.[16] He allowed his blood to be taken for sampling and his injured left hand to be photographed, and he was then released.

Late on Thursday, June 16, initial tests on the blood drops found at the murder scene proved a match to Simpson, and the next day the LAPD notified lawyer Robert Shapiro, who had taken over the representation of Simpson, that they were ready to charge and arrest his client. Shapiro negotiated a delay until 11:00 a.m. for Simpson to voluntarily turn himself in. That morning Simpson was at the home of friend and lawyer Robert Kardashian where he had stayed since his return from Chicago. With him was Al Cowlings, who had known Simpson since their high school days in San Francisco and had played football with him for USC and the Buffalo Bills. The two friends left the Kardashian residence in the late morning in Cowlings's matching white Ford Bronco, but when Simpson did not appear at Parker Center where more than a thousand reporters waited, police announced an all-points bulletin that lasted the day.

Six hours later, Simpson and Cowlings were located by police tracking their cell phone use to a freeway some eighty miles south in Orange County, near the cemetery where Nicole had been buried just the day before. What followed was the now-famous two-hour slow speed chase at thirty-five miles per hour along Los Angeles freeways back to Simpson's home in Brentwood, a media event watched by millions of people both in the United States and abroad. Television coverage of the event shows spectators pulled over on the freeway and out of their cars to watch and wave as the procession went by, and thousands of others lining overpasses to witness the spectacle of Cowlings's Bronco trailed by a string of squad cars. Some held up crudely lettered signs in support of the football legend. More than a dozen helicopters followed overhead.[17]

There is some question whether this behavior suggested suicide or flight. With Simpson in Cowlings's car was approximately $9,000 in cash, a gun, his passport, and all the makings of a disguise, including a fake goatee, moustache, glue, and remover. Receipts found with the items show them to have been purchased in Burbank, California, on May 27, 1994, some two weeks before the murders of Ron and Nicole.[18] But Cowlings told pursuing police that Simpson was threatening suicide, and photos taken at the time show Simpson in the car with the gun to his head. In telephone calls from the fleeing Bronco to police, friends, and family, Simpson said that he had been trying to get to Nicole's grave to kill himself and that he had already said goodbye to his children.

That morning he left with Kardashian a letter begun earlier but finished that day, with farewell sentiments to his family and friends, containing all the hallmarks of a suicide note:

> I can't go on. No matter what the outcome, people will look and point. I can't take that. I can't subject my children to that. This way, they can move on and go on with their lives. . . . Don't feel sorry for me, I've had a great life, great friends. Please think of the real O. J. and not this lost person. Thanks for making my life special. I hope I helped yours. Peace and love, O. J.[19]

Back at the Rockingham estate, Simpson was allowed to call his mother, drink a glass of orange juice, and was then taken into custody.

The weeks following the double murder were a bonanza for the media. The *Los Angeles Times*, the premier newspaper in Southern California and ideally positioned to report on the sensational crime directly centered in its community, dedicated an extraordinarily large group of reporters to the coverage.

For the fourteen days that followed the Sunday night on which Nicole and Ron were murdered, forty-nine different reporters were named as contributors to articles covering their deaths and Simpson's arrest, with a total of ninety articles published in the *Times*, a rate of more than six per day.[20] This was only the start of the massive coverage by the *Times*. Five reporters covered the case full-time for more than a year, and the *Times* published nearly a thousand case-related news articles between the discoveries of the bodies and the trial verdict, including 398 front-page articles.[21]

The *Times* was not alone in its extraordinary coverage. News organizations from print to radio to television quickly joined the effort, producing stories that were voraciously consumed. In the United States alone, 95,000,000 viewers watched the slow speed chase on June 17 as Simpson and Cowlings made their way back to the Rockingham Avenue residence.[22] Many more watched in foreign countries, from Toronto to Tel Aviv.

Prosecutors were convinced of Simpson's guilt. Held without bail, Simpson was arraigned on June 20, and the assistant district attorney assigned to the case, Marcia Clark, standing with District Attorney Gil Garcetti, declared in a press conference afterward that Simpson was the sole murderer. The press conference capped a week of timed police "leaks" of information to the media that strongly implicated Simpson. His attorneys responded in kind, constantly defending their client in the days following the murders.[23]

The first legal sparring came with the grand jury, where a prosecution sets out its case in secret without defense lawyers present. Simpson's lawyers instead forced this presentation before the public in a preliminary hearing, allowing for their cross-examination of witnesses who are typically less thoroughly prepared than they would be for trial, at the disadvantage of having the community and the potential jury pool poisoned by the mostly negative testimony.[24] Accordingly, the grand jury was recused on the defense's motion on June 24 and the open preliminary hearing convened a few days later. On July 8, after six days of hearing testimony, Judge Kathleen Kennedy-Powell declared that there was "ample evidence" to try Simpson on two counts of first-degree murder. On July 22, Simpson pled, "Absolutely one hundred percent not guilty," and the trial was assigned to Judge Lance A. Ito.[25]

Because the murders were committed in the upscale West Los Angeles neighborhood of Brentwood, the district attorney's office would have been within its rights, indeed would have kept with practice, by filing the charges in the Santa Monica judicial district where the crimes occurred. Instead, District Attorney Garcetti filed the case in the central district downtown, where the percentage of potential black jurors was much higher, allegedly for the convenience of attorneys and court staff. It was a tactical decision later criticized as a "monumental blunder."[26]

That was evident when jury selection got underway on September 24. Present that day were 250 potential jurors, attorneys Robert Shapiro and Johnnie Cochran for Simpson, and Marcia Clark and Bill Hodgman for the prosecution. Both sides were accompanied by jury consultants. The ultimately chosen jury of ten women and two men consisted of eight African Americans, two Hispanics, one Caucasian/Native American, and one Caucasian female. Two were college graduates, nine were high school graduates, and one a high school dropout. In voir dire, each of the twelve told attorneys that he or she never read the newspaper, although most regularly watched tabloid TV shows. All were Democrats, and at least five reported that either they or another family member had had a negative experience with police. The racial composition of the jury differed dramatically from that of the community, and even from the pool of prospective jurors, which had initially been 40% white, 28% black, 17% Hispanic, and 15% Asian.[27]

The jury selection process consumed more than two months. Because of the presumed length of the trial, fifteen alternates were then selected over the next few weeks. On December 4, the assembled jurors were instructed by Judge Ito and told that they would be sequestered for the duration of the trial, expected to last seven months.

Simpson quickly assembled for himself a powerful team of lawyers. Lead attorney Howard Weitzman gave way that first week to Robert Shapiro, perhaps as a consequence of Weitzman's questionable early decision to allow Simpson to be interviewed under oath by Vannatter and Lange at Parker Center the day after the murders without counsel present. Though well respected, Shapiro had not yet tried a murder case.[28] He was soon joined by Johnnie Cochran, an experienced criminal defense attorney best known for his unsuccessful defense of Black Panther member Elmer "Geronimo" Pratt some twenty years earlier, and the more recent acquittal of Michael Jackson on child molestation charges. Next to come aboard was F. Lee Bailey, long past his youth but famous for the defenses of Sam Sheppard and Patty Hearst. Two New York lawyers, Barry Scheck and Peter Neufeld, were hired to handle the blood evidence, and nationally known Harvard law professor Alan Dershowitz was retained to manage appellate issues. Arguably the best lawyers money could buy, they were quickly dubbed by the media the "Dream Team."[29]

Arrayed against them was the entire weight of the prosecutor's office, marshaled under lead trial attorneys Marcia Clark and Christopher Darden. Clark was a prosecutor with fifteen years of experience, notable for having successfully prosecuted troubled fan Robert John Bardo for the murder of actress Rebecca Schaeffer in 1989. Darden, then thirty-eight, had gained a reputation for prosecuting police misconduct, and as an African American he was thought to defuse the perception of racial bias on the part of prosecutors. They were joined by a small army of consultants, experts, investigators, and attorneys. All told, twenty-five prosecuting attorneys were assigned to the case, thirteen full-time and twelve part-time.[30]

After nearly two months of pretrial motions, opening statements came on January 23, 1995. Over the following months, until jury deliberations began on October 2, 1995, the prosecution and defense together presented 150 witnesses, alternating by turns from sensational to mind-numbingly tedious. The jury chafed at the length of the proceedings, but the media reveled in it. Two hundred fifty new phone lines had to be installed in the court's pressroom to handle the needs of more than 1,150 journalists credentialed to cover the trial.[31] Of the fifty-eight seats in the courtroom, twenty-four were set aside for the press, five permanently for the *LA Times* and four other mainstream news organizations, two for book authors, including Dominick Dunne, and the remaining seats rotated between the other credentialed observers. Those reporters not seated inside roamed the corridors, interviewing anyone with any connection to the trial, and some without.

And of course the proceedings were televised. CNN, Court TV, and local station KTLA covered the trial live every day. Every other news organization summarized the daily proceedings, often with commentators, "talking heads," of varying quality. On CNBC, attorney-turned-journalist Geraldo Rivera hosted a nightly roundup of each day's testimony.[32]

The live broadcast of criminal trials was then, and remains

today, controversial. Judges, lawyers, and witnesses cannot resist performing for a television audience, and the interests of the criminal defendant suffers. The number of objections by attorneys multiply exponentially as they perform for the cameras—in the Simpson trial an astonishing 16,000 times—and juries grow weary as trials lengthen.[33] Measured against these disadvantages are the rights of citizens to witness a free and open courtroom dispensing justice in the manner the law requires. Of perhaps greater concern to the city of Los Angeles were the still-raw memories of the riots two years earlier following the acquittal by a suburban white jury of the four police officers who beat black motorist Rodney King. In that frightening and bitter week, fifty-three citizens died and more than three thousand buildings were torched. Garcetti's decision to allow Simpson to be tried downtown by a black jury on television speaks to the strength of his certainty that the evidence against Simpson was overwhelming, and that conviction was inevitable.[34]

After opening statements by both sides, the first prosecution witness, Los Angeles Police Department 911 dispatcher Sharyn Gilbert, took the stand at the end of January 1995. She was followed by more than seventy witnesses over ninety-nine full trial days in a detailed and complex presentation by Los Angeles prosecutors. These witnesses were grouped into what attorneys Clark and Darden believed was a coherent system designed to prove the guilt of Simpson beyond a reasonable doubt, but the sheer number of witnesses and the length of the prosecution was daunting. The first group of witnesses included relatives and friends of both Simpson and Nicole whose testimony was intended to evidence Simpson's former brutal treatment of Nicole and his documented history of abuse. They included Nicole's sister Denise, Nicole's friend Candace Garvey, wife of former Los Angeles Dodgers star Steve

Garvey, and numerous friends, acquaintances, and neighbors. Simpson's friend Ron Shipp testified that Simpson had confided on the night of the murder a dream of murdering Nicole. Police investigator Michael Stevens testified to drilling open Nicole's deposit box to find letters from Simpson and photographs of Nicole's bruised and battered face, placed there by her as insurance against future abuse from her ex-husband. Police dispatchers and investigators testified to prior incidents of violence between the two, including the frantic call from Nicole that led to Simpson's pleading of no contest in 1989 to spousal abuse. Various neighbors of Nicole testified to the behavior of the defendant and victim, including Carl Colby, son of former CIA director William Colby, who testified that he once called 911 after observing Simpson in front of Nicole's condo peeping through her windows. This corroborated grand jury testimony that Simpson spied on Nicole as she had sex with other men, and intimidated them after. "I'm O. J. Simpson and she's still my wife," he told one of Nicole's lovers. Various staff members of Mezzaluna, the trendy West Side restaurant where Nicole and her family had dinner the night of the murder, testified to her last evening. It was because Nicole's mother accidentally left her sunglasses at the restaurant that waiter Ronald Goldman was sent to return them to Nicole's condo, an errand that cost him his life. Nicole's sister, Denise Brown, a near twin in looks but with darker hair, testified that at Sydney's dance recital the afternoon of the murder Simpson looked "frightening" and "spooky."[35]

The second set of witnesses presented by the prosecution was offered to prove that Simpson had the time and opportunity to commit the murders, which the prosecution contended took place at approximately 10:15 that Sunday evening. Limo driver Allan Park described the difficulties he had finding

Simpson when he arrived the night of the murders to take him to the airport, and that when Simpson entered the limo he carried a small black bag, which Simpson would not let him touch. The bag was never seen again, suggesting how the murderer's missing bloody clothes and murder weapon were disposed of. His testimony was followed the next day by that of James Williams, a skycap at the Los Angeles International Airport, who testified that he saw Simpson near a trash bin that night and that he had only three of the four bags that Park had said he started with.[36]

One of the trial's most talked about witnesses, houseguest Kato Kaelin, was able to establish Simpson's timeline before and after the murders took place. The two had gone for a hamburger at McDonald's, returning to Rockingham at 9:35 p.m. After that, Kaelin couldn't account for Simpson's whereabouts until after 11:00 p.m. when he helped O. J. load his luggage into the limousine. He testified to having heard the loud thumps on the wall of his guesthouse at 10:45, and he asked the limo driver Allan Park if there had been an earthquake. Marcia Clark inquired about Simpson's demeanor as he loaded his things into the limo. "Well, that's one of the first times I have seen him like late for something like a flight," responded Kaelin. "So I can't compare to. But yeah, he was in a hurry and it was—it was frazzled to get in the car." An instant celebrity to viewers with his bleach-blond hair and surfer mannerism, Kaelin, during his testimony in the criminal trial, rambled and was at times unclear. Deferential to Simpson, Kaelin denied noticing wounds or cuts on the defendant's hands. Prosecutors struck back by declaring him a hostile witness, allowing more aggressive examination, but Kaelin's testimony was not decisive for either side.[37]

Contradicting Simpson's expected testimony that he did not leave his house between 9:30 and 11:00 that night, the prosecution produced telephone records that showed Simpson used his automobile cell phone at 10:03 p.m. to call his girlfriend, Vogue model Paula Barbieri.

The final witnesses in the prosecution's case in chief were those intended to tie Simpson directly to the murders. Detectives Phillips, Lange, Fuhrman, and Vannatter, along with Lieutenant Frank Spangler, detailed the circumstances of the murder, the investigations into the victims' wounds, the visit to Simpson's residence at 5:00 a.m. the next morning, and the eventual arrest of the defendant. What followed was long and technical testimony regarding the results of tests on blood, fibers, hair, and footprints from the crime scene and Simpson's residence.

The blood evidence was the most telling. Forty-one blood samples were harvested from the Bundy condo, Simpson's Bronco, the Rockingham Avenue driveway, and from his bathroom floor. Most but not all were subjected to DNA tests. PCR[38] tests are less precise but can be conducted on quite small blood samples. RFLP[39] tests are more accurate but require larger samples. Police investigators conducted PCR tests on four of the five blood drops at the Bundy crime scene that led away from the bodies, and three of the four showed DNA markers that only one out of every 240,000 people have, including Simpson. The fourth blood drop had markers that only one out of every 5,200 people have, again including Simpson. The fifth blood drop was large enough for a RFLP test, and that showed markers carried by only one out of every 170,000,000 people, the equivalent of only forty-one people on earth, including Simpson. The blood drop on the rear gate at Bundy was most definitive, with markers that only one out of 57 billion had, only one person on earth could have, and that one person was Simpson. A second RFLP test on blood found on two black socks in O. J.'s bedroom tested positive for Nicole's blood, with odds of one out of 6 billion having the same blood markers. This long and technical testimony, difficult for even lawyers to follow, occupied nearly twelve weeks of trial, beginning on April 3, 1995, with the testimony of Dennis Fung, the Los Angeles Police Department criminologist who collected the blood samples after the murder, and ending with FBI special agent Douglas Deedrick on July 6.

But in the midst of this testimony came what many saw as the turning point in the trial: the prosecution's instruction to Simpson to try on the bloody gloves. They were unusual and uncommon gloves, with only a few hundred made, and the prosecution offered evidence both of Simpson's purchase of identical gloves and photos of him wearing them. There was no doubt that Simpson owned these gloves, or ones exactly like them.[40] Yet still it was a reckless miscalculation by prosecutors so convinced of Simpson's guilt that they chanced a demonstration without knowing with certainty that the gloves would fit.

It was a disaster. To all appearances struggling to pull the battered gloves on over latex under-gloves, Simpson said loud enough for the jurors to hear, "They don't fit." The latex gloves may have inhibited the fit, or the leather gloves may have shrunk from wetness, exposure, or nonuse, but it was a setback from which the prosecution never recovered.[41]

On July 10, Simpson's lawyers began their defense in chief. They had scored numerous small victories in their cross-examination of the prosecution's witnesses. Countering the testimony of Denise Brown and Cindy Garvey that Simpson looked angry and threatening at the dance recital on the afternoon before the murder, they presented a private video of the event that showed Simpson cheerful and jocular. They elicited evidence that Cellmark, the lab that conducted most of the DNA testing for the prosecution, had failed proficiency tests in the 1980s.

They spent eight days cross-examining the coroner, forcing admissions that the office had committed errors in Nicole's autopsy and in prior autopsies.

Now they went on the offensive. Their argument was two-fold: first that the blood evidence was collected and tested in such a way that it was corrupted and thus unreliable, and second that Simpson was framed by the investigating officers, primarily Mark Fuhrman and Phillip Vannatter, who the defense contended had dripped Simpson's uncorrupted blood on the back gate of the crime scene, his driveway, and his home, and had intentionally removed a bloody glove from the Bundy crime scene and planted it behind Kaelin's guesthouse.

They began with an attack on the reliability of police testing procedures. Defense attorney Barry Scheck elicited from Collin Yamaguchi, the police criminologist who conducted the initial DNA tests, that in opening the vial of Simpson's reference blood a small amount had spilled onto his latex gloves. While Yamaguchi testified that he then changed his gloves, the defense argued that the evidence samples could have been contaminated. The defense next proved that the blood samples from the five blood drops at the Bundy condo were left after collection in the crime scene truck through the hot summer day following the murder, suggesting that it had degraded. The evidence was so complicated that defense attorney and Harvard law professor Alan Dershowitz, arguably one of the smartest lawyers of his generation, later wrote that although he had been teaching law and science for a quarter of a century, much of the expert testimony was incomprehensible to him.[42] In the face of that complexity, the prosecution failed to point out, and the jury obviously failed to comprehend, that while degradation of blood evidence might cause analysis to fail to identify a defendant or a victim, no amount of degradation or mishandling could cause numerous samples to all point to Simpson.[43] Crowning the defense presentation on blood evidence was forensic expert Henry Lee, whose excellent credentials and friendly demeanor provided the jury with generous grounds for doubt. His simple conclusion about the DNA testing by the prosecution's experts was that "Something's wrong," which became a catchphrase in the defense's presentation.[44]

As the defense presentation unfolded, the claim that Simpson had been framed resonated ever more clearly. The arguments for a police frame-up were based on circumstantial evidence but played well to the minority jury. The defense questioned the warrantless invasion of Simpson's Rockingham residence early that following morning, challenging Vannatter's testimony that he went simply to notify Simpson the death of his ex-wife, that it took four detectives to do so, and that they only entered the property without a warrant when they became fearful that other victims might be inside. With Simpson in Chicago, the defense argued, a racist Mark Fuhrman took the opportunity to plant the bloody glove that he had allegedly brought from Bundy Drive.

The defense next discredited the police department's chain of possession of the reference blood drawn from Simpson at Parker Center the day after the murder. Nurse Thano Peratis initially testified that he had collected 8 cc of blood from Simpson. Phillip Vannatter admitted to taking possession of the vial of blood to turn it over to criminologist Fung then at the Rockingham residence, rather than immediately checking it into the evidence room at Parker Center. When evidence was presented that there was only 6.5 cc of blood in the vial, the defense argued persuasively that Vannatter had no valid reason to have been walking around for three hours on the day after the murders with a vial of Simpson's blood in his pocket. His credibility ruined by his implied untruthfulness in entering the Rockingham estate without a warrant, it was only a short jump to the accusation that Vannatter had sprinkled the missing blood at Simpson's residence. Peratis later testified that he was mistaken in his earlier estimation of how much blood was withdrawn from Simpson, but the damage was done.[45]

There was also surprising testimony about the bloody glove found behind the Kaelin guesthouse at the Simpson residence. It was still wet and sticky at 5:00 a.m., when independent tests showed that blood exposed to the air for some seven hours should have dried. There was also no evidence of blood on the ground or leaves around it, although there was also no testimony that the police criminologists had searched for any. How Fuhrman could have spirited the glove from a crime scene bustling with fourteen patrol officers, none of whom had seen a second glove, was never explained, but in a courtroom charged with racism and conspiracy, no explanation was necessary.

Finally, there were the socks allegedly found on the floor of Simpson's bedroom. Police investigators claimed to have found a pair of the defendant's socks marked with both his blood and that of Nicole's. But they didn't appear on an inventory videotape initially taken by the LAPD to protect them from later claims of theft from the property, and Simpson's blood allegedly contained traces of a preservative added to his reference blood taken for sampling. Most tellingly, the socks had splatter patterns on both sides, suggesting that the blood had soaked into the socks when there was no foot in them.[46]

But the most electrifying testimony came from Detective Mark Fuhrman. Questioned by F. Lee Bailey whether he had ever used the N-word in the past ten years, he responded that he had not. Yet in the possession of the defense were thirteen hours of taped interviews that Detective Fuhrman had given to a professor and aspiring screenwriter from North Carolina, Laura Hart McKinney. In those tapes, recorded between 1985 and 1994, he used the epithet some forty times, along with racially tinged statements against blacks, Jews, and other minorities. "I used to go to work and practice movements," he could be heard saying on the tapes. "Niggers. They're easy. I used to practice my kicks."[47]

With the jury absent on September 6, 1995, Fuhrman was asked by defense attorney Gerald Uelmen whether he had ever falsified a police report, planted or manufactured evidence in the Simpson case, and whether his testimony given at the preliminary hearing was completely truthful. To each question, Fuhrman asserted his Fifth Amendment privilege not to incriminate himself. When the testimony ended, Simpson sat at the defense table, his face buried in his hands and crying.[48]

Simpson never testified in his own defense.

Final summation by both sides occupied four days in the last week of September 1995. Prosecutors Clark and Darden were nearly apologetic in tone. "Nobody," Darden told the jury, "wants to do anything to this man." They were uncentered, almost fatalistic. They made no attempt to explain, defend, or rehabilitate Fuhrman, and devoted little effort to point out the unlikelihood or even the practical absurdity of an entire police department impulsively conspiring to frame an innocent man.[49]

By contrast, the defense came out swinging. Recognizing the weakness and complexity of their blood arguments, they devoted almost all of their energy to convincing the jury that Simpson had been framed for the murders by racist white officers. Cochran talked of almost nothing else. "Mark Fuhrman," he told the jurors, "is a lying, perjuring, genocidal racist." He compared him to Hitler. On September 27, he finally addressed the bloody glove. Rising above the almost indisputable evidence that the gloves belonged to Simpson, Cochran locked eyes with the jury and told them, "If it doesn't fit, you must acquit."[50]

The jury retired for deliberations shortly after 9:00 a.m. on October 2, but in only four hours they notified Judge Ito that they had reached a verdict. The court adjourned with instructions that the verdict would be read at 10:00 the following morning, October 3.

The entire country came to a halt to hear the verdict that morning. Ninety-one percent of all televisions in operation in America were turned to the coverage, only the first US moon landing and the funeral of John F. Kennedy attracting a larger share of the audience.[51] The LAPD went to full alert, arrayed against a repeat of the Rodney King riots. President Bill Clinton was briefed on national security measures, then left the Oval Office to watch with staffers, one of an estimated 140,000,000 Americans tuned in. Larry King, host of CNN's *Larry King Live*, told his viewers, "If we had God booked, and O. J. was available, we'd move God."[52] *Time* magazine described it as the single most successful moment in television history.

To the surprise of most of America, the jury found Simpson not guilty.

The mostly black jury, and most of black America, saw the case as primarily about race. Even those who rejoiced at Simpson's acquittal did not believe him to be innocent. He benefited from the anger blacks felt at mistreatment by white law enforcement in general, and the oppressive LAPD in particular. And ironically, in many ways Simpson the individual had transcended race. He was famous, rich, and popular, welcome at any restaurant, hotel, or club in any state in the nation. While not completely unsupportive, he was no champion of blacks in America, nor a spokesman for black causes. He was largely perceived as having abandoned his black roots to move in a socially white world.[53]

But skin color can never be erased, never forgotten, and Johnnie Cochran knew that. Black himself, he preached to the jury. In his now-famous sing-song cadence, he cited Cicero, Frederick Douglas, and the Bible. He was escorted to the courthouse by bodyguards supplied by the Nation of Islam, resplendent in their perfectly pressed dark suits and trademark bowties. He reportedly invited civil rights icon Rosa Parks to come sit in the courtroom and listen to closing arguments, but she refused. By positioning his client to a predominantly black jury as a victim of framing by racist white policemen, he attained for Simpson a not guilty verdict without the necessity of proving his innocence.

Vincent Bugliosi, the successful prosecutor of Charles Manson two decades earlier, was harshly critical of Garcetti, Clark, Darden, and indeed the entire prosecution team. "The prosecution of O. J. Simpson was the most incompetent criminal prosecution I have ever seen," he wrote. "By far. There have undoubtedly been worse. It's just that I'm not aware of any."[54] Decisions to move the trial downtown, seat a nearly all-black jury, and present a bloated and overly complex slate of witnesses put prosecutors at a critical disadvantage. They neglected to offer as evidence Simpson's suicide note, his incoherent and incriminating statements under oath at Parker Center the day after the murders, or evidence of his flight with Cowlings. These missteps, coupled with the prosecution's failure to recognize the fundamental weakness of their case, that one or more overzealous LAPD officers may have enhanced the evidence, not to frame a man they believed to be innocent but to ensure the conviction of a man they were convinced was guilty, ensured Simpson's acquittal.

Released after fifteen months in jail, Simpson along with his lawyers and friends celebrated that night at Rockingham,

Simpson holding a Bible.[55] "When things have settled down a bit," he said, "I will pursue as my primary goal in life the killer or killers who slaughtered Nicole and Mr. Goldman." He gave interviews and released a mail-order video declaring his innocence, but no one has ever seriously suggested another suspect in the double murder.

The camaraderie between Simpson's lawyers was short-lived. Disgusted with Cochran's tactics, cocounsel Shapiro accused him the next day of playing the race card, echoing an opinion piece published six weeks earlier in the *LA Times* in which Joseph Wambaugh, former LAPD officer and best-selling author of *The Onion Field*, wrote,

> The bottom line is this: although the crimes perpetrated in the King and Simpson cases had nothing to do with racism, the aftermath of those events had everything to do with racism. Johnnie Cochran has not only played the race card, he's dealt it from the bottom of the deck.[56]

Cochran fired back that Shapiro was suffering from a bruised ego, the result of his being supplanted as Simpson's lead counsel. Bailey agreed with Cochran, and Shapiro replied that he'd never work with either lawyer again.[57]

Two years later, after several months of trial in which Simpson was compelled to testify, a civil jury in Santa Monica found Simpson liable for the wrongful deaths of Ron and Nicole, ordering Simpson to pay $33,500,000 in damages. Little of that judgment was ever recovered. "I'm not going to go and work and give my money to Fred Goldman,"[58] Simpson told CNN. In 1999, his Heisman trophy was auctioned off along with various other memorabilia. Valued as high as $4,000,000, it sold for only $230,000. Other items fetched another $100,000. One bidder paid $16,000 for various items including two jerseys with Simpson's iconic number 32, and then burned them in protest on the steps of the Los Angeles courthouse.[59] Simpson's Rockingham residence, lost to foreclosure in 1997, was bulldozed by new owners in July 1998. This time police officers were present just to control traffic, not to investigate. His pension protected by law from creditors, Simpson continued to live his lavish lifestyle.

But miscellaneous civil, tax, and criminal problems continued to dog him, and he appeared in the news frequently in one scrape after another. Finally, in September 2007, he led a group of armed men into a hotel room at the Palace Station Casino in Las Vegas to recover sports memorabilia allegedly stolen from him. Arrested two days later, he was charged with multiple felonies including conspiracy, kidnapping, assault, robbery, and the use of a deadly weapon. Three codefendants accepted plea deals in return for their testimony, and Simpson and codefendant Clarence Stewart were convicted on all charges. On December 5, 2008, Simpson was sentenced to thirty-three years in prison and incarcerated at the minimum security correctional center in Lovelock, Nevada, where he remains.[60]

As the publicity surrounding the trial faded, so did the public's interest in the other players in the Simpson drama. Marcia Clark and Christopher Darden both left the district attorney's office after the trial and published books on the experience. Los Angeles district attorney Gil Garcetti survived the loss and was re-elected in 1996. His second term was consumed by the controversy surrounding allegations of extreme police misconduct in the city's Rampart Division, including the alleged framing of suspects, and he lost his bid for a third term. Claims against his department by one of his deputies led to the controversial US Supreme Court decision in *Garcetti v. Ceballos*, which on a narrow 5–4 ruling failed to uphold alleged constitutional rights of workplace whistle-blowers.[61] Garcetti went on to serve on the City's Ethics Commission, and his son Eric was elected mayor of Los Angeles in 2013.[62]

Johnnie Cochran continued to handle high-profile cases and to make frequent appearances as a commentator on television. He is mentioned in numerous television shows, movies, and even a Broadway play, and famously parodied in several episodes of *Seinfeld* in the character of Jackie Chiles.[63] His boyhood middle school in Los Angeles was renamed for him. He died in 2005 from a brain tumor, aged sixty-seven. Among many other celebrities, Simpson attended his funeral in Inglewood, California.[64]

F. Lee Bailey, one of the most-famous lawyers of the second half of the twentieth century, endured a tumultuous fall from grace. Ordered to turn over assets in another case, he was jailed in 2000 for forty-four days for contempt and eventually disbarred.[65]

Defense attorney Robert Shapiro also went on to other high-profile cases and controversy. In widely publicized cases he sued former outfielder Daryl Strawberry for unpaid fees, and was sued by record producer Phil Spector for the return of $1,000,000 in unearned fees.[66] He is the public face for LegalZoom.com, an online document preparation service for non-lawyers.

Friend and lawyer Robert Kardashian, who sat at Simpson's side throughout the trial, died of cancer in 2003 at the age of fifty-nine. After the acquittal he expressed misgivings about the jury's decision. "I have doubts," he told an ABC interviewer. "The blood evidence is the biggest thorn in my side; that causes me the greatest problems."[67] His children went on to fame as stars of the reality television show *Keeping up with the Kardashians*.

Tough-talking Philip Vannatter died of cancer in January 2012. His partner, Tom Lange, retired from the LAPD shortly after the acquittal, wrote a book with Vannatter, and became involved in other entertainment projects. Ron Phillips stayed on with the LAPD for at least another decade before his retirement.

On July 5, 1996, the Los Angeles prosecutor's office announced the filing of perjury charges against Mark Fuhrman. In October of that year, he accepted a plea deal and pleaded no contest, stating that it was in the best interests of his family.[68] Sentenced to probation and fined two hundred dollars, Fuhrman's is the only conviction achieved following the brutal murder of Nicole Brown Simpson and Ron Goldman. Fuhrman retired from the LAPD, moved to Idaho, and has written extensively on the Simpson murders and other cases.

That the Simpson case was ultimately about race was understood by the media immediately. It is tempting to believe that by 1995 a post–civil rights America had shrugged off its legacy of prejudice, but the reality is different. Most white Americans polled opine that the laws and institutions in America are color-blind, and this lets them rationalize the abolition of affirmative action and a judicial system that incarcerates a much greater percentage of black males. In their turn, black Americans feel abandoned by the loss of preferences that only sought to make up for the centuries-old head start that white Americans enjoy. Consistent with their beliefs, white Americans polled before the verdict predominantly believed Simpson to be guilty, while black Americans believed the opposite. Those beliefs did not change with Simpson's acquittal.

In fact, that acquittal only fed those divergent beliefs. Black Americans felt vindicated in the face of a biased police establishment, while white Americans were convinced that a black jury ignored the evidence to free a clearly guilty black celebrity.

Defense counsel Alan Dershowitz is more nuanced. While not asserting Simpson's innocence, he believes that the prosecution intentionally put on a case it knew to be partially false, in order to prove what it honestly believed to be Simpson's guilt. Such conduct being improper under the law, he contends Simpson to have been properly acquitted.[69] Dershowitz wrote,

> Only time will tell whether the O. J. Simpson trial was a great case that made bad law, or merely another media event that brought fleeting fame to all who participated in it. One observation that will not be disputed is that it was a case for the 1990s, involving as it did the most controversial and divisive issues of this decade; spousal abuse, racial politics, economic inequalities, scientific innovations, criticism of lawyers, and instant communication.[70]

EPILOGUE

CASEY ANTHONY AND THE TRIALS FOR A NEW CENTURY

Over the course of a century, little has changed in the appetite of the American public for sensation, and the willingness of the media to provide it. But an explosive increase in technology, literacy, and leisure over that period has resulted in a vastly greater capability to provide the information at a level of saturation few early–twentieth century editors could have predicted.

When the call came in to 911 in Orlando, Florida, on July 15, 2008, that a two-year-old was missing, the toddler was but one of 800,000 children to be reported missing in America each year.[1] What made the call unusual was the content of the report. The caller to the emergency line was the child's grandmother, who told the operator that her car, her daughter, and her granddaughter had disappeared a month before, that the daughter had now returned without the infant, and that the car had just been reclaimed from impound smelling as if a dead body had been stored in the trunk. She asked that someone come to the home and arrest her daughter, Casey Anthony.

In the coming months, the following headline appeared on the website of HLTV, an affiliate of CNN: "Casey Anthony: Trial of the Century." Appearing more than a hundred years after the media furor following Henry Thaw's murder of Stanford White that fateful evening in 1906, it is a stark reminder that the framers of the news neither feel the need to acknowledge the past, nor a responsibility to consider the future. Never mind that the century was only eight years old. For a reporter, only today exists. Enthralling and repulsive by turns as the Anthony trial was, if there is a single thing that we have gleaned from an examination of the twentieth century, it is that the coming decades of the twenty-first century will provide innumerable trials of equal drama. Yet the Anthony trial is illustrative of how dramatic has been the change in the delivery of news over that century.

No one had seen two-year-old Caylee in more than a month, not since June 15, 2008, Father's Day, when Casey Anthony had taken her daughter and left the house. Over the next thirty days, Casey visited with friends, telling various stories about where her daughter was. Caylee was at the beach, she would say, or at Sea World, always with a nanny.[2]

Freed of child-care, Casey went dancing and got "Bella Vida" ("beautiful life") tattooed on her shoulder while chatting happily on her cell phone.[3] She went shopping at various stores, purchasing nothing suitable for a toddler, and paid with checks that she stole from a vacationing friend. She steadfastly refused to allow her parents, Cindy and George Anthony, to see Caylee. She was too busy with work, she told them. Having trouble reaching her daughter, Cindy opened a Myspace account on July 6 to communicate with Casey, and the next day her daughter responded, "What is given can be taken away. Everyone lies. Everyone dies."[4]

On July 15, after receiving notice by certified mail, Cindy and George retrieved the missing car from impound, and the stench coming from the trunk was unmistakable. Cindy finally located Casey and the call to 911 followed.

When police arrived they found no body. What they found instead was Casey Anthony, an unapologetic twenty-two-year-old party girl and compulsive liar.[5] Little Caylee was alive, Casey told the officers, but she now claimed that her daughter had been kidnapped by the nanny, to whom she gave the unusual name of Zenaida Fernandez-Gonzalez. Zanny the nanny. Police escorted Casey to the apartment where she said the nanny lived, but there was no response to their knock. They interviewed the building manager, who told them that no one had lived in that apartment for some six months.[6]

Police asked Casey if she had told anyone about the kidnapping, and she said that she had talked about it at her job at Orlando Universal Studios.[7] She gave them the names of coworkers and supervisors. Did she have their phone numbers? Not on her, but she had the numbers in her cell phone. Did she have that with her? No, she had left it at work.[8]

Taken by the investigating officers to Universal, Casey led them on a random tour before she stopped suddenly, put her hands in her back pockets, and turned to face them with a shy grin. "Okay," she confessed, "I don't really work here."[9] It turned out that she had been fired more than two years before, but had kept up the pretense of a job for her friends and family, and to explain her long hours away. The coworkers and supervisors? All invented.

Her fabricated world collapsing, and unable to produce Caylee, Casey was arrested and charged with child neglect and lying to investigators.

The arrest of Casey Anthony on July 16 became instant news. By July 18, a reporter from *People* magazine was camped in the office lobby of Casey's newly retained attorney, Jose Baez, and *20/20*, *Dateline*, and the *CBS Morning Show* had all called. *Fox News* sent former LAPD detective Mark Fuhrman, a central figure in the O. J. Simpson trial, to take Baez to lunch.[10] What had started as an odd local story in the Orlando newspapers quickly caught the attention of the nation, fascinated by a missing child and revolted by a mother who couldn't be troubled for more than a month to report the alleged kidnapping of her two-year-old daughter. Caught up in the human drama, Cindy and George Anthony appeared to be concerned grandparents, heartbroken over their missing grandchild. On July 25, they started a website for the missing Caylee, and on August 1 appeared on *Larry King Live.*

Casey was charged with only a third-degree felony but suspected of foul play, and her bond was set at $500,000. Casey's parents had neither the money nor the desire to post bail. Following her arrest, the always frosty relationship between Casey and her parents deteriorated. She refused numerous requests to visit by her parents or her brother Lee. As a result, Casey languished in jail until August 31, when Leonard Padilla, an ex-con and media-savvy California bounty hunter feeding on the rising celebrity of the case, arranged to post her bail.[11] Released, she was confined to her parents' home, while outside increasingly violent protests continued day after day. Signs read "You killed Caylee" and "I hope you die." The Anthonys turned the hose on them. On September 18, rock-throwing protesters attempted to drag George Anthony into the street.

Casey would be rearrested, released, arrested yet again, and eventually charged with a capital crime on October 15, the case against her resting on evidence no stronger than her lack of character until December 11, when the scattered bones of a small child were reported by a utility meter reader in a wooded area only a quarter of a mile from the Anthony home. The remains were identified a week later as those of little Caylee. The meter reader, Ray Kronk, told *Good Morning America* that he had notified authorities of the dumped body numerous times as early as the previous August, but that the investigating sheriffs had ignored his tips because the area was wet and snake-infested.[12]

Over the next twenty-four months, the prosecution team, led by Linda Drane Burdick, painstakingly built their case on the slimmest of circumstantial evidence and Casey's trail of lies. A strand of hair from the car trunk was microscopically similar to hair taken from Caylee's hairbrush. Experts found traces of chloroform in the trunk, and the computer to which Casey had access showed Internet searches for chloroform, neck-breaking, and suffocation. Duct tape on the child's skull included residue of an incongruous heart-shaped sticker, and a Winnie-the-Pooh blanket found at the crime scene matched Caylee's bedding.[13]

Casey's defense team was captained, from the day after her arrest, by Jose Baez, a forty-year-old local lawyer from Puerto Rico by way of the Bronx, who had dropped out of high school in the ninth grade, went back to obtain an equivalency degree, served in the navy, and after discharge earned degrees from Florida State and St. Thomas University School of Law in Miami Gardens. A practicing lawyer only three years at the time of his retention by Casey Anthony, he was derided by the prosecution and the press for his limited experience and troubled background.[14] Nevertheless, Baez set about constructing a defense strategy based on the refutation of each and every piece of prosecution evidence. With no confession, no witnesses, and no provable cause of death, Baez believed that he could demonstrate reasonable doubt. Short of money for attorneys and experts, Casey sold pictures of Caylee to ABC for $200,000.[15]

But long before jury selection began on May 9, 2011, the media had pronounced Casey guilty, championed by self-proclaimed victims' rights TV advocate Nancy Grace, host of cable's HLN. A former prosecutor and political commentator, Grace had started her media career with TruTV, successor to CourtTV, which had come into its own covering first the trial of Lyle and Erik Menendez for the murder of their parents and then the O. J. Simpson case. By the time of Caylee's death, Nancy Grace had been on television more than twelve years. One of the first to report on Caylee's disappearance, over the course of the investigation and trial, she devoted hundreds of segments of her show to the Anthonys, reporting under the banner of "Justice for Caylee" and derisively calling Casey the "Tot Mom."[16]

By the time the trial commenced before Judge Belvin Perry in May 2011, media attention in Orange County, Florida, was so pervasive that jurors had to be brought in from neighboring Pinellas County. On the first day of jury selection, an entire panel of fifty potential jurors had to be dismissed as tainted. With jury selection lagging and the initial trial date lost, Judge Perry lectured the attorneys that he would not tolerate further delays in the start of the trial, which he set for May 23, scheduled to be held six days a week, Sundays excepted, until completed. The jury was sequestered throughout.

The defense turned the case inside out on the first day. "This is not a murder case," attorney Baez told the jury in his opening statement. "It is a sad, tragic accident."[17] Young Caylee accidentally drowned in the family swimming pool on June 16, 2008, he explained. She was found by Casey's father, George, who hid the body in the woods near the house. Threatened by George that she would go to jail for child neglect, Baez argued, Casey failed to report the death and went on with her life. Acknowledging her pattern of lies, he told the jury that Casey was cowed by a lifetime of sexual abuse. George had been abusing her since she was eight, he told them, as did her older brother Lee. Baez told the jury that the FBI had conducted genetic testing to see if Lee was in fact Caylee's father.

Disgusted and enthralled, Americans couldn't turn away. "It's been a day of bombshells," reported the *Orlando Sentinel*.[18]

Opening statements concluded, the prosecution presented fifty-nine witnesses over the next three weeks, beginning with George Anthony, who denied both the drowning and the sexual abuse. Forensic experts testified to the condition of the remains and the duct tape on the skull, casting doubt on an accidental death. "There is no child that should have duct tape on its face when it dies," chief medical examiner Jan Garavaglia testified.[19] A computer expert described how someone had searched for "chloroform" eighty-four times on the desktop computer in the Anthony home. Other experts opined on the manner of death, the presence of chloroform, and the smell of decomposition of human flesh. Friends and acquaintances were called to illustrate Casey's dissolute lifestyle during the thirty-one days that Caylee went unreported, and photos were admitted into evidence of her during this period shopping at numerous stores and dancing at the Fusion nightclub in a hot body contest.

The defense responded with forty-seven witnesses over two weeks of testimony. Experts challenged the evidence of duct tape on Caylee's skull, and Cindy Anthony testified that they had in the past buried family pets in the woods, wrapped in blankets and sealed with duct tape. The medical autopsy testimony was challenged and contradicted. The computer expert was forced to admit that a flaw existed in his software and that "chloroform" had only been searched for once on the Anthony computer, not eighty-four times.[20] In the end, Casey Anthony did not testify.

The media's assurance of Casey's guilt was only strengthened by the testimony as it was elicited. Highly regarded outlets such as the *New York Times* and *Time* magazine reported that most trial watchers were convinced she was guilty of, or at least involved in, young Caylee's death.[21] Accordingly, Nancy Grace was not the only reporter shocked when on July 5 the jury returned not guilty verdicts on all major charges, convicting Casey only on charges of lying to authorities. On that night's segment, a stern-faced Grace called the verdict a stunning blow to justice and told 5,200,000 viewers, "The devil is dancing tonight."[22]

The day the verdict was announced, Baez had his choice of interviewers, and he asked for, and got, Barbara Walters. He flew that night to New York to tape her show.[23]

When Casey was released from jail ten days later, the delay caused by her need to serve out the rest of her sentence on unrelated check forgery charges, hundreds of reporters, protestors, and spectators milled outside the building, many with signs vilifying her. A plane flew overhead towing a banner that read "She's Guilty And She Should Die."[24] SWAT officers escorted Casey, with Baez at her side, to an idling SUV, which drove off with reporters following. After a short drive the SUV pulled into a nearby parking structure where four different cars with papered windows waited. Baez and Casey got into one, and the four cars drove off, one each heading east, west, north, and south in an effort to throw off pursuit. Overhead, the hovering helicopters split up, one following each car. Others circled the local executive airport where a private jet was rumored to await the lawyer and his now-freed client. The two waited hours under the cover of trees until the helicopters had to refuel, then sped to the hanger, boarded the jet, and escaped.[25]

The story of the Casey Anthony trial and public reaction is remarkably similar to the other landmark trials of the twentieth century, but it differs in the way in which information about it spread. The advent of the Internet has fundamentally changed how we consume news. A study by the Pew Research Center has found that 61% of Americans get at least some of their news online as opposed to only 54% who get news from the radio and 50% who get news from print newspapers. What's more, a whopping 75% of Americans claim they get news from e-mails or from posts on social media.[26]

The Casey Anthony trial, which *Time* called the "social media trial of the century," clearly illustrates this evolving shift. When the verdict was read, CNN's website received one million live-video users, a number thirty times higher than its average over the past weeks.[27] ABCNews.com had five times as many visitors than its average, and its video of the verdict was viewed 1.2 million times just in the hours following the announcement.[28]

News also poured from nonconventional outlets, such as Facebook and Twitter. The *Orlando Sentinel* operated a twitter account entirely devoted to the case named OSCaseyAnthony. The Ninth Judicial Circuit Court of Florida itself, tweeting from the account name NinthCircuitFL, was one of the most-reliable sources for updates.[29] One reporter noted that many news outlets were updating their Facebook pages before they updated their official home pages.[30]

This new and widespread use of social media made it not only possible for people to obtain instantaneous, real-time updates about the case but also allowed followers to immediately voice their opinions. For a century, what people had to wait to talk about around the dinner table or the office water-cooler, they could now share instantly with their social media friends and followers. And they did. Facebook pages devoted to justice for Caylee or Casey's guilt were filled with hundreds of comments within just minutes of the verdict. Twitter was flooded with tweets, including one from Kim Kardashian, celebrity and daughter of Simpson trial lawyer Robert Kardashian, who posted *"WHAT!!!!???!!!! CASEY ANTHONY FOUND NOT*

GUILTY!!!! I am speechless!!!"[31] As one reporter poignantly observed,

> If you looked at O. J. Simpson in 1995 and saw a cold-blooded killer trying to get away with it, you could only scream at the television. But if you see murder in Casey Anthony's big brown eyes during a live feed of her trial, you can tell all the world how delectable you will find her execution.[32]

This use of new social media surrounding the Anthony trial created, as one media analyst called it, a "collective echo chamber [that was] unprecedented."[33] And this echo chamber is likely to expand as time passes, with both more users and broader content. As of 2015, the top news websites get more hits on their sites for mobile phones than their sites for computers, meaning that Americans take news, and the opinions of their acquaintances regarding it, wherever they go.[34]

The trial of the century. The more things change, the more they stay the same.

Acknowledgments

The authors wish to express their thanks to the many people who assisted them in this endeavor, particularly Ellie Herman, David Levinson, and Andrea Grossman who each read portions of the manuscript and gave wonderful advice and encouragement, Claire Norman who contributed her research skills while a journalism student at Madill, Premini Scandurra who typed and retyped initial chapters, Sharon Wu who gave expert advice and support, and friends and family who endured with patience and good humor the long process that goes into writing a book of this kind.

NOTES

INTRODUCTION

1. Keith Hopkins, "The Colosseum: Emblem of Rome," http://www.bbc.co.uk/history/ancient/romans/colosseum_01.shtml (accessed April 6, 2016); "Water Battles at the Colosseum," http://www.tribunesandtriumphs.org/colosseum/water-battles-at-the-colosseum.htm (accessed April 6, 2016); "Wild Animals at the Colosseum," http://www.tribunesandtriumphs.org/colosseum/wild-animals-at-the-colosseum.htm (accessed April 6, 2016).

2. Marisa Linton, "The Terror in the French Revolution" (PDF) (for the number of victims); http://www.theguillotine.info/articles/reignofterror.php (for vendors selling programs and spectators bringing children) (accessed April 6, 2016).

3. "Facts About the Newgate Calendar," http://www.bl.uk/learning/histcitizen/21cc/crime/media1/calendar1/facts1/facts.html (accessed April 6, 2016); Catherine Curzon, "The Newgate Calendar, or, Malefactor's Bloody Register," http://englishhistoryauthors.blogspot.com/2014/09/the-newgate-calendar-or-malefactors.html (accessed April 6, 2016).

4. "Paper for the People, Dime Novels and Early Mass Market Publishing," https://exhibits.library.villanova.edu/dime-novels/the-basics (accessed April 6, 2016); "Dime Novel," *Wikipedia,* https://en.wikipedia.org/wiki/Dime_novel (accessed April 6, 2016); David E. Sumner, *The Magazine Century: American Magazines Since 1900* (New York: Peter Lang Publishing, Inc., 2010), p. 23.

5. "Newspaper Circulation Figures 1880–1910," *Coursehero.com,* https://www.coursehero.com/file/p5rnbr/Newspaper-Circulation-Figures-1880-1910-1880-850-pubs-circ-31-mill1900-1967/ (accessed April 6, 2016).

6. Douglas O. Linder, "State v. John Scopes ('The Monkey Trial')," http://law2.umkc.edu/faculty/projects/ftrials/scopes/evolut.htm (accessed April 6, 2016).

7. Jim Crogan, "The LA 53," http://www.lafire.com/famous_fires/1992-0429_LA-Riots/LAWEEKLY-2002-0426/2002-0426_laweekly_The LA 53

_Crogan.htm (for number of deaths) (accessed April 6, 2016); Robert Reinhold, "Riots in Los Angeles: The Overview; Cleanup Begins in Los Angeles; Troops Enforce Surreal Calm," *New York Times*, May 3, 1992, http:// www.nytimes.com/1992/05/03/us/riot-los-angles-overview-cleanup-begins -los-angeles-troops-enforce-surreal-calm.html?pagewanted=all (for buildings burned).

CHAPTER 1.   1900–1910: "HE DESERVED IT"–
THE CASE OF HARRY KENDALL THAW

1. Sven Beckert, "High Society in New York: That Other Gilded Age," *The Economist*, May 31, 2001, http://www.economist.com/node/638697; "Gilded Age," *American Experience*, 2009, http://www.pbs.org/wgbh/amex/ carnegie/gildedage.html (accessed January 22, 2014).

2. "Gilded Age," *American Experience*.

3. Susannah Lessard, *The Architect of Desire: Beauty and Danger in the Stanford White Family* (New York: Dial, 1996), p. 240.

4. Michael Macdonald Mooney, *Evelyn Nesbit and Stanford White: Love and Death in the Gilded Age* (New York: William Morrow, 1976), pp. 22–31.

5. Ibid.

6. Ibid., p. 36.

7. Lessard, *Architect of Desire*, pp. 76–89.

8. Mooney, *Evelyn Nesbit and Stanford White*, pp. 44–48.

9. Evelyn Nesbit, *Prodigal Days: The Untold Story*, ed. Deborah D. Paul (New York: Lulu.com, 2005), pp. 37–38.

10. Mooney, *Evelyn Nesbit and Stanford White*, pp. 55–60.

11. Cecilia Rasmussen, "Girl in Red Velvet Swing Longed to Flee Her Past," *Los Angeles Times*, December 11, 2005, http://articles.latimes .com/2005/dec/11/local/me-then11.

12. Ibid.

13. Mooney, *Evelyn Nesbit and Stanford White*, pp. 60–86.

14. Ibid., pp. 76–78.

15. Nesbit, *Prodigal Days*, p. 46.

16. Mooney, *Evelyn Nesbit and Stanford White*, pp. 89–90.

17. Ibid., pp. 98–108.

18. Ibid.

19. Ibid., pp. 90–98.

20. Ibid., p. 76.

21. Ibid., p. 200.

22. Nesbit, *Prodigal Days*, p. 107.

23. Mooney, *Evelyn Nesbit and Stanford White*, p. 109.

24. Ibid., p. 201.

25. Ibid., p. 205.

26. Lessard, *Architect of Desire*, p. 218.

27. Nesbit, *Prodigal Days*, p. 118.

28. Mooney, *Evelyn Nesbit and Stanford White*, p. 225.

29. Ibid., p. 226.

30. Harry K. Thaw, *The Traitor* (New York: Dorrance, 1926), p. 11.

31. "Murderers' Row Gets Harry Thaw," *New York Times*, June 27, 1906, p. 1.

32. "The Brainstorm and the Barrister's Barley," *Rengstorff House*, 2013, http://www.r-house.org/barristers-barley.html (accessed January 22, 2014).

33. Lessard, *Architect of Desire*, pp. 249–50.

34. Mooney, *Evelyn Nesbit and Stanford White*, pp. 252–59.

35. "Testimony of Evelyn Nesbit Thaw," *University of Missouri—Kansas City School of Law*, 2009, http://law2.umkc.edu/faculty/projects/ftrials/thaw/evelynthawtestimony.html (accessed January 28, 2013).

36. "Summation of Delphin Delmas for the Defense," *University of Missouri—Kansas City School of Law*, 2009, http://law2.umkc.edu/faculty/projects/ftrials/thaw/delmassummation.html (accessed January 28, 2013).

37. Mooney, *Evelyn Nesbit and Stanford White*, p. 264; Lessard, *Architect of Desire*, p. 253.

38. Mooney, *Evelyn Nesbit and Stanford White*, pp. 270–71.

39. Lessard, *Architect of Desire*, p. 198.

40. Mooney, *Evelyn Nesbit and Stanford White*, p. 247.

41. Ibid., p. 240.

42. Ibid., p. 231.

43. Ibid., p. 236.

44. Lessard, *Architect of Desire*, p. 248.

45. Ibid., p. 199.

46. "Comstock Wants to Tell About White and Others," *New York Times*, June 29, 1906, p. 2.

47. Lessard, *Architect of Desire*, p. 242.

48. "Harry Thaw, in Jealous Frenzy, Shoots Stanford White to Death," *Washington Post*, June 26, 1906, p. 1.

49. "Harry K. Thaw Murders Enemy in Gotham Show," *Chicago Daily Tribune*, June 26, 1906, p. 1.

50. "Murder: Harry Thaw for a Woman Kills White," *Atlanta Constitution*, June 26, 1906, p. 1.

51. "For a Woman, Thaw Kills Most Noted Architect," *Los Angeles Times*, June 26, 1906, p. 1.

52. Mooney, *Evelyn Nesbit and Stanford White*, p. 247.

53. Lessard, *Architect of Desire*, p. 245.

54. "When Little Harry Thaw Was Terror," *Atlanta Constitution*, January 23, 1908, p. 1.

55. Mooney, *Evelyn Nesbit and Stanford White*, p. 244.

56. Lessard, *Architect of Desire*, p. 249.

57. Ibid., p. 250; Mooney, *Evelyn Nesbit and Stanford White*, p. 247.

58. Lessard, *Architect of Desire*, p. 247.

59. Mooney, *Evelyn Nesbit and Stanford White*, p. 270.

60. Ibid., p. 241.

61. "Can Thank His Wife: If Harry Thaw Escapes the Penalty for the Murder," *Spokane Daily Chronicle*, March 8, 1907, p. 8.

62. Mooney, *Evelyn Nesbit and Stanford White*, p. 249.

63. Ibid., pp. 272–74.

64. Ibid., pp. 274–75.

65. Rasmussen, "Girl in Red Velvet Swing."

66. Lessard, *Architect of Desire*, pp. 302–303.

67. Mooney, *Evelyn Nesbit and Stanford White*, p. 291.

68. Rasmussen, "Girl in Red Velvet Swing."

69. Bosley Crowther, "Screen: Musty Scandal; 'Girl in Red Velvet Swing' Is at Roxy," *New York Times*, October 20, 1955, http://www.nytimes.com/movie/review?res=9402E6DD133DEF34BC4851DFB667838E649EDE; Rasmussen, "Girl in Red Velvet Swing."

70. E. L. Doctorow, *Ragtime* (New York: Random House, 1975).

71. "Ragtime," *IMDB*, 2013, http://www.imdb.com/title/tt0082970/ (accessed January 28, 2013).

72. "Crime of the Century," *Ragtime the Musical*, RCA Victor, 1996.

73. "Evelyn Nesbit," *Smithsonian*, 2013, http://americanhistory.si.edu/collections/search/object/nmah_1276018 (accessed January 28, 2013).

74. "Interview with Gretchen Mol," *HBO.com*, 2012, http://www.hbo .com/boardwalk-empire/cast-and-crew/gillian/interview/interview-with -gretchen-mol.html# (accessed January 28, 2013).

75. Irvin S. Cobb as quoted in *University of Missouri – Kansas City School of Law*, 2009, http://law2.umkc.edu/faculty/projects/ftrials/thaw/ thawhome.html (accessed January 28, 2013).

CHAPTER 2. 1910–1920: THE DEATH OF MARY PHAGAN— THE TRIAL OF LEO MAX FRANK

1. Marshall Cavendish, *Murder Casebook* 5, no. 64 (1991): 2272.

2. Steve Oney, *And the Dead Shall Rise: The Murder of Mary Phagan and the Lynching of Leo Frank* (New York: Pantheon Books, 2003), p. 4. Oney has written the definitive modern telling of the trial and death of Leo Frank.

3. Coroner's Inquest, *Atlanta Constitution*, May 1913.

4. Cavendish, *Murder Casebook*, p. 2273.

5. Oney, *And the Dead Shall Rise*, p. 20.

6. Ibid., p. 21.

7. Ibid., pp. 20–21.

8. Cavendish, *Murder Casebook*, p. 2273.

9. Charles Pou, "The Leo Frank Case," http://georgiainfo.galileo .usg.edu/topics/history/article/progressive-era-world-war-ii-1901-1945/the -leo-frank-case (accessed April 5, 2016).

10. Cavendish, *Murder Casebook*, p. 2275.

11. Oney, *And the Dead Shall Rise*, pp. 35, 39–40, 52.

12. John Davison Lawson, ed., *American State Trials Volume X* (St. Louis: F. H. Thomas Law Book, 1918), p. 211.

13. *Atlanta Constitution*, May 1, 1913, p. 1.

14. Pou, "The Leo Frank Case."

15. Cavendish, *Murder Casebook*, p. 2279.

16. Oney, *And the Dead Shall Rise*, p. 119.

17. Ibid., p. 131.

18. Ibid., p. 136.

19. Ibid., p. 140.

20. Cavendish, *Murder Casebook*, p. 2280.

21. Oney, *And the Dead Shall Rise*, p. 239.

22. Ibid., p. 241.

23. Cavendish, *Murder Casebook*, p. 2287.

24. Oney, *And the Dead Shall Rise*, p. 249.

25. Ibid., p. 255.

26. Ibid., p. 259.

27. Ibid., p. 275.

28. Ibid., p. 305.

29. Ibid., p. 324.

30. Ibid., p. 327.

31. Ibid., p. 335.

32. Ibid., pp. 338–39; Cavendish, *Murder Casebook*, p. 2289.

33. *New York Times*, December 14, 1914.

34. Cavendish, *Murder Casebook*, p. 2289.

35. Ibid.

36. *Atlanta Constitution*, August 26, 1913; Oney, *And the Dead Shall Rise*, p. 341.

37. Oney, *And the Dead Shall Rise*, p. 451.

38. *Jeffersonian*, March 19, 1914.

39. *Jeffersonian*, December 3, 1914.

40. *Jeffersonian*, February 4, 1915.

41. Cavendish, *Murder Casebook*, p. 2294; Oney, *And the Dead Shall Rise*, p. 364.

42. Oney, *And the Dead Shall Rise*, p. 149.

43. Frank v. Mangum, 237 U.S. 309 (1915).

44. Oney, *And the Dead Shall Rise*, p. 372.

45. *Jeffersonian*, March 25, 1915.

46. *Jeffersonian*, May 6, 1915.

47. Oney, *And the Dead Shall Rise*, p. 477.

48. Ibid., p. 483.

49. Ibid., pp. 469–70.

50. Ibid., p. 491.

51. Ibid., pp. 498–99.

52. Cavendish, *Murder Casebook*, p. 2294; Oney, *And the Dead Shall Rise*, p. 489.

53. Oney, *And the Dead Shall Rise*, p. 503.

54. Ibid., p. 504.

55. Cavendish, *Murder Casebook*, p. 2293.

56. Ibid., p. 2295.

57. Oney, *And the Dead Shall Rise*, pp. 549–50.

58. Cavendish, *Murder Casebook*, p. 2299; Oney, *And the Dead Shall Rise*, p. 565.

59. Oney, *And the Dead Shall Rise*, p. 565.

60. Ibid., pp. 566–68.

61. Ibid., p. 571.

62. Ibid., p. 574.

63. Ibid., p. 589.

64. Athan G. Theoharris and John Stuart Cox, *The Boss: J. Edgar Hoover and the Great American Inquisition* (Philadelphia, PA: Temple University Press, 1988), p. 45.

65. Oney, *And the Dead Shall Rise*, pp. 610–11.

66. Ibid., p. 647.

67. Ibid., p. 649.

CHAPTER 3. 1920–1930: "FATTY" ARBUCKLE AND THE DEAD ACTRESS

1. Andy Edmonds, *Frame Up!; The Untold Story of Roscoe "Fatty" Arbuckle* (New York: William Morrow, 1991), p. 16. Infamous as a womanizer and a philanderer, Conkling was notorious for an affair with Kate Chase Sprague, daughter of Treasury Secretary Salmon P. Chase and wife of William Sprague, US senator and governor of Rhode Island. According to popular rumor, in 1879 Sprague had surprised the couple and chased Conkling off his Narragansett estate with a shotgun.

2. Ibid., p. 21.

3. Ibid., p. 26.

4. Ibid., p. 32.

5. Aloof, difficult, and considered by some to be ruthless, Pantages was in his turn charged in the rape of a young actress, vilified in the newspapers of William Randolph Hearst, and eventually acquitted only to face financial and social ruin.

6. Edmonds, *Frame Up*, pp. 36–37.

7. Ibid., p. 50.

8. Ibid., p. 51.

9. Ibid., p. 64.

10. Ibid., p. 136; Benjamin Welton, "No More Laughs for the Fat Man:

The Case of Fatty Arbuckle," *Crime Magazine*, March 24, 2014, http://www.CrimeMagazine.com/node/1575 (accessed April 5, 2016); Jennifer Rosenberg, "Fatty Arbuckle Scandal," *About.com*, http://history1900s.about.com/od/famouscrimesscandals/a/fattyarbuckle.htm (accessed April 5, 2016); Gilbert King, "The Skinny on the Fatty Arbuckle Trial," *Smithsonian.com*, http://www.smithsonian.com/history/the-skinny-on-the-fatty-arbuckle-trial-131228859/?no-ist (accessed April 5, 2016); Elizabeth Fischer, "The Fatty Arbuckle Trial: The Injustice of the Century," *Constructing the Past* 5, no. 1 (2004): Article 5.

11. Edmonds, *Frame Up*, p. 88.

12. Ibid., p. 84.

13. Ibid., pp. 79–80. Within days of her release from the hospital, Normand attempted to drown herself, then spiraled into a life of drug addiction and abusive behavior. In 1922 she was implicated as a prime suspect in the murder of director William Desmond Taylor, one of the great scandals of its day. She contracted tuberculosis, her health rapidly declined, and she died ruined and unhappy at the age of thirty-five.

14. Ibid., pp. 102–103.

15. Ibid., p. 137.

16. Ibid.

17. Ibid., p. 149.

18. Ibid., p. 154.

19. Ibid.

20. Ibid., p. 158.

21. Ibid., p. 155.

22. Denise Noe, "Fatty Arbuckle and the Death of Virginia Rappe," *TruTV.com*, http:// www.TruTV.com/library/crime/notorious_murders/classics/Fatty_Arbuckle (accessed April 5, 2016).

23. Edmonds, *Frame Up*, p. 156.

24. Ibid.; Noe, "Fatty Arbuckle and the Death of Virginia Rappe," *TruTV.com*.

25. Edmonds, *Frame Up*, p. 148.

26. Ibid., p. 155.

27. Ibid., p. 252.

28. Ibid., p. 162.

29. Ibid.

30. Ibid., pp. 171, 252.

31. Ibid., p. 171.

32. Ibid., p. 173.

33. Ibid., pp. 174–76.

34. Ibid., p. 206.

35. Fischer, "Fatty Arbuckle Trial," Article 5.

36. *Washington Times*, September 14, 1921.

37. *Washington Times*, September 15, 1921.

38. *Washington Times*, September 16, 1921.

39. *Tulsa Daily World*, September 13, 1921, p. 1.

40. King, "Skinny on the Fatty Arbuckle Trial," *Smithsonian.com.*

41. *Washington Times*, September 13, 1921, p. 3.

42. Ibid.

43. *Washington Times*, September 14, 1921.

44. *Washington Times*, September 16, 1921.

45. Edmonds, *Frame Up*, p. 219.

46. Ibid., p. 186.

47. Ibid., p. 220.

48. Ibid., p. 221.

49. Ibid., p. 223.

50. Ibid., pp. 222–24.

51. Ibid., pp. 225–26.

52. Ibid., pp. 230–36.

53. Ibid., p. 239.

54. Ibid., p. 240.

55. Minta Durfee Arbuckle, "The True Story About My Husband," *Movie Weekly*, December 24, 1921, http://www.public.asu.edu/~ialong/Taylor28.txt (accessed April 7, 2016).

56. Edmonds, *Frame Up*, p. 246.

57. Ibid., pp. 247–48.

58. Ibid., p. 209; King, "Skinny on the Fatty Arbuckle Trial," *Smithsonian .com.*

59. King, "Skinny on the Fatty Arbuckle Trial," *Smithsonian.com.*

60. Arbuckle, "True Story About My Husband."

61. *San Francisco Bulletin*, February 2, 1922.

62. Edmonds, *Frame Up*, p. 254.

63. Ibid., p. 259.

64. Ibid., pp. 261–62, 265–67.

65. Ibid., pp. 163, 271.

66. Ibid., p. 274.

67. King, "Skinny on the Fatty Arbuckle Trial," *Smithsonian.com*; Rosenberg, "Fatty Arbuckle Scandal," *About.com*.

68. Edmonds, *Frame Up*, p. 257.

CHAPTER 4. 1930-1940: BRUNO HAUPTMANN AND THE LINDBERGH BABY

1. "Automobiles," http://www.history.com/topics/automobiles (accessed March 26, 2016).

2. "Kidnapper-Murderer Twice Defeated Death in N.J. Chair," *Washington Post*, April 4, 1936, p. 6.

3. Jim Fisher, *The Lindbergh Case* (New Brunswick: Rutgers University Press, 1994), pp. 8–10; "Charles Lindbergh," *Bio.com*, 2013, http://www.biography.com/people/charles-lindbergh-9382609 (accessed April 23, 2013).

4. Fisher, *Lindbergh Case*, pp. 9–10.

5. Ibid., p. 8.

6. Susan Hertog, *Anne Morrow Lindbergh* (New York: Doubleday, 1999), p. 143.

7. Ibid., p. 134.

8. Fisher, *Lindbergh Case*, p. 10.

9. Hertog, *Anne Morrow Lindbergh*, p. 157.

10. Fisher, *Lindbergh Case*, p. 10.

11. Hertog, *Anne Morrow Lindbergh*, p. 162.

12. Ibid., p. 163.

13. Ibid., pp. 164–65.

14. Fisher, *Lindbergh Case*, p. 12.

15. Ibid., p. 18.

16. Hertog, *Anne Morrow Lindbergh*, p. 168.

17. Ibid., pp. 169–70.

18. Ibid., p. 168.

19. Ibid., p. 176.

20. Ibid., p. 172.

21. Fisher, *Lindbergh Case*, p. 17.

22. Ibid., p. 21.

23. George Waller, *Kidnap: The Story of the Lindbergh Case* (New York: Dial, 1961), p. 17.

24. Waller, *Kidnap*, p. 19; Hertog, *Anne Morrow Lindbergh*, p. 181.

25. Fisher, *Lindbergh Case*, p. 21.

26. Ibid., p. 20.

27. Ibid., p. 21.

28. Ibid., p. 46.

29. Hertog, *Anne Morrow Lindbergh*, pp. 178, 210.

30. Fisher, *Lindbergh Case*, p. 32.

31. Hertog, *Anne Morrow Lindbergh*, pp. 175–179.

32. Ibid., p. 172.

33. Fisher, *Lindbergh Case*, pp. 33–35.

34. Hertog, *Anne Morrow Lindbergh*, p. 171.

35. Fisher, *Lindbergh Case*, p. 21.

36. "Authorities Clear Nurse of Suspicion: Declare Miss Gow Blameless in Kidnapping of the Baby After Questioning Her," *New York Times*, March 7, 1932, p. 7.

37. "Kidnapers Puzzle to Psychiatrists: One Group of Criminals That Experts Are Unable to Classify," *Washington Post*, March 4, 1932, p. 2.

38. "Baby Expected Back Today: Lindbergh in Night Vigil; Secrecy is Used As Help," *Chicago Daily Tribune*, March 3, 1932, p. 1.

39. Hertog, *Anne Morrow Lindbergh*, p. 176.

40. *Time: The Weekly Newsmagazine*, Nov. 1932.

41. Hertog, *Anne Morrow Lindbergh*, p. 179.

42. "Prayers for Safe Return of Kidnapped Baby Offered in Churches of Many Faiths: 500 Orphans Pray for Lindbergh Baby; Seek Child Daily on Steps of Jersey Home," *New York Times*, March 7, 1932, p. 11.

43. Hertog, *Anne Morrow Lindbergh*, p. 183; "Kidnapping is Topic at Cabinet Session," *Washington Post*, March 5, 1932, p. 3.

44. Fisher, *Lindbergh Case*, p. 14.

45. Ibid., pp. 40–42.

46. Ibid., p. 45.

47. Ibid., pp. 50–61.

48. Hertog, *Anne Morrow Lindbergh*, p. 187.

49. Fisher, *Lindbergh Case*, p. 77.

50. Hertog, *Anne Morrow Lindbergh*, pp. 191–98.

51. Fisher, *Lindbergh Case*, p. 107.

52. Ibid., pp. 113–14.

53. Hertog, *Anne Morrow Lindbergh*, p. 203.

54. Ibid., p. 205.

55. Fisher, *Lindbergh Case*, p. 119.

56. Hertog, *Anne Morrow Lindbergh*, p. 251.

57. Fisher, *Lindbergh Case*, p. 184.

58. Hertog, *Anne Morrow Lindbergh*, pp. 248–50.

59. Fisher, *Lindbergh Case*, p. 199.

60. Hertog, *Anne Morrow Lindbergh*, p. 252.

61. Fisher, *Lindbergh Case*, pp. 186–228.

62. Ibid., p. 203.

63. Ibid., pp. 257–63.

64. Waller, *Kidnap*, pp. 257–58.

65. Ibid., p. 276.

66. Fisher, *Lindbergh Case*, p. 269.

67. Ibid., pp. 272–273.

68. Hertog, *Anne Morrow Lindbergh*, p. 25.

69. Fisher, *Lindbergh Case*, pp. 279–322.

70. Ibid., pp. 324–26.

71. Ibid., pp. 337–40.

72. Ibid., pp. 359–60.

73. Ibid., pp. 362–73.

74. "The Trial of the Century: Examining the Lindbergh Kidnapping and the Growth of a New Kind of American Journalism," *Morristown & Morris Township Library*, http://www.jfpl.org/polCalendarEvent.cfm?Event_Id=1512 (accessed April 4, 2016).

75. Waller, *Kidnap*, p. 251.

76. Fisher, *Lindbergh Case*, p. 270.

77. Ibid., p. 285.

78. John F. Keenan, "The Lindbergh Kidnapping Revisited," *Michigan Law Review* 84.4/5 (1986): 823.

79. Waller, *Kidnap*, p. 252.

80. Keenan, "Lindbergh Kidnapping Revisited," p. 823.

81. Waller, *Kidnap*, pp. 253–54, 283.

82. Fisher, *Lindbergh Case*, pp. 298, 345.

83. Hertog, *Anne Morrow Lindbergh*, p. 257.

84. Waller, *Kidnap*, p. 378.

85. Fisher, *Lindbergh Case*, p. 285.

86. Waller, *Kidnap*, p. 403.

87. Fisher, *Lindbergh Case*, p. 364.

88. Julie Gilbert, *Ferber: Edna Ferber and Her Circle* (New York: Applause Books, 1999), pp. 324–26.

89. Fisher, *Lindbergh Case*, p. 374.

90. Waller, *Kidnap*, pp. 494–98.

91. Fisher, *Lindbergh Case*, pp. 380–82.

92. Ibid., pp. 385–429.

93. "Trial of the Century," *Morristown & Morris Township Library.*

94. Fisher, *Lindbergh Case*, p. 429.

95. Ibid., pp. 391–92.

96. "Charles Lindbergh," *Bio.com.*

97. "Lindbergh Kidnapping," *Wikipedia,* http://en.wikipedia.org/wiki/Lindbergh_kidnapping#The_Lindbergh_kidnapping_represented_in_the_arts (last modified April 1, 2016).

98. Waller, *Kidnap*, pp. 497–98.

99. Keenan, "Lindbergh Kidnapping Revisited," p. 821.

100. "Who Killed Lindbergh's Baby?" *NOVA*, PBS, Washington, DC, January 30, 2013.

101. Dan Aubrey, "The Lindbergh Kidnapping: The 1932 Crime Still Serving Time," *U.S. 1* 21 (November 2012): 20–21.

102. "Presentation: 12 Theories of Who Kidnapped the Lindbergh Baby," *Hunterdon County Democrat,* April 6, 2013, http://www.nj.com/hunterdon-county-democrat/index.ssf/2013/04/presentation_12_theories_of_wh.html.

103. Fisher, *Lindbergh Case*, p. 274.

104. Waller, *Kidnap*, p. 490.

CHAPTER 5. 1940–1950: WAYNE LONERGAN
AND THE BLUDGEONED HEIRESS

1. William Darby Perry, *A Chair for Wayne Lonergan* (New York: Macmillan, 1972), p. 5.

2. James Devlin, "Lonergan Slew Wife Over Baby, Says Confession," *Atlanta Constitution,* October 29, 1943, p. 1.

3. Albin Krebs, "Wayne Lonergan, 67, Killer of Heiress Wife," *New York Times,* January 3, 1986, http://www.nytimes.com/1986/01/03/obituaries/wayne-lonergan-67-killer-of-heiress-wife.html.

4. Mel Heimer, *The Girl in Murder Flat* (New York: Gold Medal Books, 1955), pp. 9–10.

5. Perry, *Chair for Wayne Lonergan,* pp. 4–5.

6. Dominick Dunne, *Justice: Crimes, Trials, and Punishments* (New York: Crown Publishers, 2001), p. 274.

7. Heimer, *Girl in Murder Flat,* p. 11.

8. Perry, *Chair for Wayne Lonergan,* pp. 6–8.

9. Ibid., p. 8; Heimer, *Girl in Murder Flat,* p. 11.

10. Dunne, *Justice,* pp. 275–76.

11. Perry, *Chair for Wayne Lonergan,* p. 19.

12. Dunne, *Justice,* pp. 273–74.

13. Perry, *Chair for Wayne Lonergan,* pp. 11–13.

14. Ibid., p. 14.

15. Dunne, *Justice,* p. 277.

16. Heimer, *Girl in Murder Flat,* p. 11.

17. Perry, *Chair for Wayne Lonergan,* p. 21.

18. Ibid., pp. 22–24.

19. Heimer, *Girl in Murder Flat,* p. 9.

20. Perry, *Chair for Wayne Lonergan,* p. 22.

21. Dunne, *Justice,* p. 272.

22. Ibid., p. 278.

23. Heimer, *Girl in Murder Flat,* p. 12.

24. Perry, *Chair for Wayne Lonergan,* pp. 35–37.

25. Dunne, *Justice,* p. 280.

26. Perry, *Chair for Wayne Lonergan,* pp. 39–41.

27. Ibid., pp. 50–51.

28. Ibid., pp. 42–44.

29. Ibid., pp. 154–57.

30. Heimer, *Girl in Murder Flat,* p. 6.

31. Dunne, *Justice,* p. 283.

32. Heimer, *Girl in Murder Flat,* p. 5.

33. Ibid., pp. 14–17.

34. Perry, *Chair for Wayne Lonergan*, pp. 43–44.

35. Ibid., p. 53.

36. Heimer, *Girl in Murder Flat*, p. 19.

37. Ibid., pp. 18–19.

38. Dunne, *Justice*, p. 282.

39. Perry, *Chair for Wayne Lonergan*, p. 61.

40. Dunne, *Justice*, p. 284.

41. Ibid., p. 285.

42. Heimer, *Girl in Murder Flat*, p. 19.

43. Perry, *Chair for Wayne Lonergan*, p. 66.

44. Heimer, *Girl in Murder Flat*, pp. 22–23.

45. Ibid., pp. 93–97.

46. Ibid., pp. 97–102.

47. Ibid., p. 24.

48. Ibid., pp. 24–25.

49. Ibid., p. 27.

50. Perry, *Chair for Wayne Lonergan*, pp. 87–92.

51. Ibid., p. 88.

52. Ibid., p. 90.

53. Heimer, *Girl in Murder Flat*, pp. 30–31.

54. Perry, *Chair for Wayne Lonergan*, p. 105.

55. Ibid., pp. 113–23.

56. Heimer, *Girl in Murder Flat*, p. 45.

57. Ibid., pp. 34–35, 49–54.

58. Ibid., pp. 52–53.

59. Ibid., p. 53.

60. Ibid., p. 54.

61. Perry, *Chair for Wayne Lonergan*, pp. 144–46.

62. Ibid., p. 152.

63. Ibid., pp. 153–155.

64. Heimer, *Girl in Murder Flat*, pp. 70–72.

65. Perry, *Chair for Wayne Lonergan*, p. 159.

66. Heimer, *Girl in Murder Flat*, pp. 85–92.

67. Perry, *Chair for Wayne Lonergan*, p. 178.

68. Ibid., pp. 181–82.

69. Heimer, *Girl in Murder Flat*, pp. 111, 118.

70. Perry, *Chair for Wayne Lonergan*, pp. 186–93.

71. Ibid., pp. 199–200.

72. Ibid., pp. 203–209.

73. "RCAF Cadet's Wife Slain in Home Here," *New York Times*, October 25, 1943, p. 1.

74. "Husband is Held for Questioning in Heiress Murder," *New York Times*, October 26, 1943, p. 1.

75. Perry, *Chair for Wayne Lonergan*, p. 62.

76. Meyer Berger, "Lonergan Here, Questioned Again; Fingerprint Found in Bathroom," *New York Times*, October 28, 1943, p. 1.

77. Perry, *Chair for Wayne Lonergan*, p. 84.

78. Ibid., pp. 78–85.

79. Ibid., p. 141; Heimer, *Girl in Murder Flat*, p. 28.

80. Heimer, *Girl in Murder Flat*, p. 36.

81. Perry, *Chair for Wayne Lonergan*, p. 119.

82. Ibid., pp. 116–21.

83. Heimer, *Girl in Murder Flat*, p. 57.

84. Dunne, *Justice*, p. 283.

85. Ibid., p. 286.

86. "35 Years to Life Given to Lonergan," *New York Times*, April 18, 1944, p. 1.

87. Quoted in Perry, *Chair for Wayne Lonergan*, p. 139.

88. Ibid., p. 63.

89. Ibid., p. 140.

90. Ibid., p. 139.

91. Heimer, *Girl in Murder Flat*, p. 58.

92. Ibid., p. 56.

93. "Wife Slayer Calm in Cell," *Atlanta Constitution*, October 31, 1943, p. 10B.

94. Perry, *Chair for Wayne Lonergan*, pp. 117–19.

95. Ibid., p. 84.

96. Nancy Hendricks, "Painstaking Police Work Solves Lonergan Murder: Slayer Made One Slip, Cops Capitalized on It," *Sunday Herald* [Bridgeport], November 5, 1950, p. 56.

97. "McNabb-Mallory Rule," *Legal Information Institute*, August 19, 2010, Cornell University Law School, http://www.law.cornell.edu/wex/mcnabb-mallory_rule (accessed February 15, 2013).

98. Perry, *Chair for Wayne Lonergan*, pp. 216–19.

99. Ibid., pp. 282–83.

100. Dunne, *Justice*, p. 289.

101. Perry, *Chair for Wayne Lonergan*, pp. 71–72.

102. Ibid., pp. 64–66, 77.

103. Ibid., p. 224.

104. Dunne, *Justice*, pp. 292–94.

105. Krebs, "Wayne Lonergan."

106. Dunne, *Justice*, p. 284.

107. Perry, *Chair for Wayne Lonergan*, pp. 211–23.

108. Ibid., p. 223; "$6,800,000 Surprise: 'Orphan' Boy Learns 3 Astonishing Facts," *Miami News*, February 6, 1954, p. 4B.

109. Perry, *Chair for Wayne Lonergan*, p. 225.

110. Heimer, *Girl in Murder Flat*, p. 139.

111. Ibid., p. 20.

CHAPTER 6. 1950-1960: WHO KILLED MARILYN?—
THE SAM SHEPPARD CASE

1. Sheppard v. Maxwell, 384 U.S. 358 (1966).

2. "Famous Trials, Dr. Sam Sheppard Trial," http://law2.umkc.edu/faculty/projects/ftrials/sheppard/samsheppardtrial.html (accessed April 4, 2016).

3. Jack P. DeSario and William D. Mason, *Dr. Sam Sheppard on Trial* (Kent, Ohio: Kent State University Press, 2003), p. 15. DeSario teaches political science and has a law degree. Mason successfully defended the State of Ohio against the suit brought by Sam Reese Sheppard to clear his father's name.

4. Cynthia L. Cooper and Sam Reese Sheppard, *Mockery of Justice* (New York: Onyx, 1997), p. 68.

5. DeSario and Mason, *Sheppard on Trial*, pp. 19, 78.

6. Cooper and Sheppard, *Mockery of Justice*, p. 26.

7. DeSario and Mason, *Sheppard on Trial*, p. 20.

8. Sheppard v. Maxwell, 231 F. Supp. 37 (SD Ohio 1964)

9. Statement of Sheppard dated July 10, 1954, p. 3; DeSario and Mason, *Sheppard on Trial*, p. 345.

10. *Sheppard*, 384 U.S. at 336–37.

11. Ibid. at 337.

12. Ibid.

13. Cooper and Sheppard, *Mockery of Justice*, p. 61.

14. Ibid., p. 19.

15. *Sheppard*, 384 U.S. at 338.

16. Ibid. at 399.

17. *Sheppard*, 231 F. Supp. at 48.

18. Ibid. at 49.

19. For this and the following paragraphs see *Sheppard*, 384 U.S. at 339–40.

20. *Cleveland Plain Dealer*, July 27, 1954.

21. *Sheppard*, 384 U.S. at 340; Cooper and Sheppard, *Mockery of Justice*, p. 86; *Cleveland Press*, July 21, 1954, p. 1.

22. Cooper and Sheppard, *Mockery of Justice*, p. 93.

23. *Sheppard*, 231 F. Supp. at 51.

24. Ibid. at 53.

25. *Sheppard*, 384 U.S. at 341.

26. Cooper and Sheppard, *Mockery of Justice*, p. 93.

27. *Sheppard*, 384 U.S. at 342.

28. Ibid. at 343.

29. Ibid.

30. *Sheppard*, 231 F. Supp. at 54–56.

31. DeSario and Mason, *Sheppard on Trial*, p. 5.

32. For this and the testimony in the next several paragraphs see DeSario and Mason, *Sheppard on Trial*, p. 203; Cooper and Sheppard, *Mockery of Justice*, pp. 98–110.

33. Cooper and Sheppard, *Mockery of Justice*, p. 107.

34. Ibid., pp. 98–105.

35. Ibid., p. 108.

36. Ibid., pp. 106–10.

37. For this and the newspaper articles that follow see *Sheppard*, 231 F. Supp. 37.

38. *Sheppard*, 384 U.S. at 359.

39. Cooper and Sheppard, *Mockery of Justice*, p. 46.

40. Ibid., p. 69.

41. Ibid., p. 114, 116.

42. *Editor & Publisher Magazine*, January 8, 1955.

43. Cooper and Sheppard, *Mockery of Justice*, p. 114.

44. Ohio v. Sheppard, 135 N.E. 2d 340 (1956); *Sheppard*, 231 F. Supp. 37.

45. DeSario and Mason, *Sheppard on Trial*, p. 58; Cooper and Sheppard, *Mockery of Justice*, p. 150.

46. *Sheppard*, 384 U.S. 333.

47. Ibid. at 362.

48. Cooper and Sheppard, *Mockery of Justice*, pp. 151–54.

49. DeSario and Mason, *Sheppard on Trial*, p. 78; Cooper and Sheppard, *Mockery of Justice*, pp. 156–57.

50. DeSario and Mason, *Sheppard on Trial*, p. 79.

51. Ibid. for this and the following paragraph.

52. Cooper and Sheppard, *Mockery of Justice*, p. 30.

53. "The Fugitive," *IMDB*, http://www.imdb.com/title/tt0106977/ (accessed April 4, 2016).

54. DeSario and Mason, *Sheppard on Trial*, p. 7.

55. Cooper and Sheppard, *Mockery of Justice*, pp. 203–12.

56. Ibid., pp. 155–58 for this and the following paragraph.

57. For this and the following paragraphs see James Neff, *Wrong Man* (New York: Random House, 2001), pp. 295–98; DeSario and Mason, *Sheppard on Trial*, pp. 147–49; Cooper and Sheppard, *Mockery of Justice*, pp. 313–14.

58. Neff, *Wrong Man*, pp. 295–98.

59. DeSario and Mason, *Sheppard on Trial*, pp. 313–24.

60. Murray v. State, Cuyahoga App. No. 78374, 2002 Ohio 664 (Feb. 22, 2002); Murray v. State, Ohio S. Ct. No. 2002-0626 (2002).

61. DeSario and Mason, *Sheppard on Trial*, pp. 3, 51.

62. State v. Sheppard, 165 Ohio St. 293 (1956).

CHAPTER 7. 1960–1970: EIGHT DEAD STUDENT NURSES
AND THE TEXAS DRIFTER

1. Dennis L. Breo and William J. Martin, *Crime of the Century* (New York: Bantam Books, 1993) pp. 36–41. The description of this meeting, and many of the details that follow, are found in the excellent and very thorough exploration of Speck's night of crime in July 1966 and the resulting trial. Breo was a newspaper reporter in Chicago and Martin the lead prosecuting attorney in Speck's trial.

2. "Crime: 24 Years to Page One," *Time*, July 29, 1966, http://content.time.com/time/magazine/article/0,9171,899278,00.html.

3. Breo and Martin, *Crime of the Century*, p. 11.

4. For this and subsequent paragraphs see "Crime: One by One," *Time*, July 22, 1966, http://content.time.com/time/magazine/article/0,9171,836066,00.html.

5. Breo and Martin, *Crime of the Century*, pp. 56–57.

6. Ibid., pp. 63–64; "Crime: One by One"; "Trials: Masakit in Peoria," *Time*, April 14, 1967, http://content.time.com/time/magazine/article/0,9171,836939,00.html.

7. "Crime: One by One."

8. Breo and Martin, *Crime of the Century*, p. 65.

9. Ibid., pp. 68–73.

10. Ibid., p. 85.

11. Ibid., p. 84.

12. Ibid., pp. 92–98.

13. Ibid., p. 102.

14. Ibid., p. 105.

15. Ibid., pp. 108–109.

16. Austin C. Wehrwein, "Survivor Sees Speck in Room in Hospital," *New York Times*, July 19, 1966, p. 1; "Richard Speck," *Bio.com*, http://www.biography.com/people/richard-speck-11730438 (accessed April 4, 2016).

17. Breo and Martin, *Crime of the Century*, pp. 115–20; "Crime: 24 Years to Page One"; "Crime: One by One."

18. Breo and Martin, *Crime of the Century*, p. 124.

19. Ibid., p. 174; "Crime: 24 Years to Page One."

20. Miranda v. Arizona, 384 U.S. 436 (1966).

21. Breo and Martin, *Crime of the Century*, p. 221.

22. Ibid., pp. 253–54.

23. Ibid., p. 115.

24. "Slaying Suspect-Man on the Run," *Chicago Tribune*, July 17, 1966, pp. 1–2.

25. Ibid.

26. William Conway, "Seaman Sought as Slayer of Eight Student Nurses," *Washington Post*, July 16, 1966, p. 1.

27. "News Summary and Index," *New York Times*, July 17, 1966, p. 71.

28. Wehrwein, "Survivor Sees Speck in Room in Hospital," p. 1.

29. "Will Publicity Hinder Fair Trial?" *Boston Globe*, July 18, 1966, p. 4.

30. Breo and Martin, *Crime of the Century*, pp. 160–61, 186.

31. Ibid., pp. 275–82.

32. For this and the next paragraph see "Trials: The Press and Richard Speck," *Time*, March 3, 1967, http://content.time.com/time/magazine/article/0,9171,843499,00.html; Breo and Martin, *Crime of the Century*, pp. 302–305.

33. For this and subsequent paragraphs see Breo and Martin, *Crime of the Century*, pp. 370–73.

34. For this and the next paragraph see "Trials: Masakit in Peoria."

35. Breo and Martin, *Crime of the Century*, p. 373.

36. Ibid.

37. Ibid., p. 452.

38. Ibid., p. 414.

39. Ibid., p. 422.

40. Ibid., p. 424.

41. Ibid., p. 440.

42. "Nary a Speck of Decency," *Time*, May 27, 1996, http://content.time.com/time/magazine/article/0,9171,984604,00.html; Dirk Johnson, "Killer's Prison Video Sparks Illinois Lawmakers' Outrage," *New York Times*, May 16, 1996, http://www.nytimes.com/1996/05/16/us/killer-s-prison-video-sparks-illinois-lawmakers-outrage.html; OLR Report of Connecticut General Assembly, http://search.cga.state.ct.us/dlps97/rpt/htm/97-R-0242.htm (accessed April 4, 2016); "Speck the Mass Murderer Who Grew Boobs in Prison," http://www.liveleak.com/view?i=550_1270458485 (accessed April 4, 2016).

43. Breo and Martin, *Crime of the Century*, p. 176.

CHAPTER 8.   1970–1980: THE TATE-LaBIANCA MURDERS
AND A MAN NAMED MANSON

1. Bradley Steffens and Craig Staples, *The Trial of Charles Manson: California Cult Murders* (San Diego: Lucent Books, 2002), pp. 9–10.

2. Ibid., p. 95.

3. Vincent Bugliosi with Curt Gentry, *Helter Skelter* (New York: W. W.

Norton, 1974), pp. 190–91. *Helter Skelter*, by the prosecutor of Manson at his trial, is the best-selling true crime book in US history.

4. Bugliosi, *Helter Skelter*, pp. 191–93.

5. Ibid., pp. 193–203.

6. Ibid.

7. Ibid., pp. 224–26.

8. Jeff Guinn, *Manson: The Life and Times of Charles Manson* (New York: Simon & Schuster, 2013), pp. 92–93.

9. Ibid., pp. 95–96.

10. Bugliosi, *Helter Skelter*, pp. 226, 237; Guinn, *Manson*, p. 173.

11. Bugliosi, *Helter Skelter*, p. 238.

12. Ibid., p. 157.

13. Ibid., p. 334.

14. Ibid., pp. 238–39.

15. Guinn, *Manson*, pp. 180–81.

16. Bugliosi, *Helter Skelter*, pp. 317–18.

17. Ibid., p. 319.

18. Ibid., p. 317.

19. Ibid., p. 128.

20. Ibid., p. 315.

21. Steffens and Staples, *Trial of Charles Manson*, pp. 50–51.

22. Bugliosi, *Helter Skelter*, pp. 324–26.

23. Ed Sanders, *The Family* (New York: Thunder's Mouth, 2002), p. 422.

24. Jann Wenner, "The Working Class Hero," *Rolling Stone*, January 21, 1971.

25. Steffens and Staples, *Trial of Charles Manson*, p. 50; Bugliosi, *Helter Skelter*, p. 332.

26. Bob Murphy, *Desert Shadows: A True Story of the Charles Manson Family in Death Valley* (Salt Lake City: Sagebrush, 1993), pp. 40–45.

27. Murphy, *Desert Shadows*, pp. 40–45; Steffens and Staples, *Trial of Charles Manson*, p. 62.

28. Bugliosi, *Helter Skelter*, pp. 24, 55–60.

29. Ibid., pp. 27–61.

30. Murphy, *Desert Shadows*, p. 43.

31. Bugliosi, *Helter Skelter*, p. 186.

32. Ibid., p. 356.

33. Ibid., p. 50.

34. Ibid., pp. 358.

35. Ibid., pp. 68–70.

36. Ibid., pp. 13–14.

37. Ibid., pp. 32–34.

38. Ibid., p. 62.

39. Ibid., pp. 90.

40. Ibid., pp. 113–17.

41. Ibid., pp. 117–27.

42. Ibid., p. 139.

43. Bugliosi, *Helter Skelter*, pp. 35–36.

44. Ibid., pp. 130–34, 154.

45. Ibid., pp. 144–50.

46. Ibid., p. 166.

47. Ibid., pp. 453–54.

48. Ibid., p. 217.

49. Ibid., p. 220.

50. Ibid., p. 229.

51. Ibid., pp. 240–43.

52. Ibid., pp. 235–55.

53. Ibid., p. 216.

54. Steffens and Staples, *Trial of Charles Manson*, pp. 40–45.

55. Bugliosi, *Helter Skelter*, pp. 352–54.

56. Ibid.

57. Ibid., p. 258; Steffens and Staples, *Trial of Charles Manson*, pp. 53–57.

58. Bugliosi, *Helter Skelter*, pp. 370–71, 515.

59. Ibid., p. 386.

60. Steffens and Staples, *Trial of Charles Manson*, pp. 57–59; Bugliosi, *Helter Skelter*, pp. 371–72.

61. Bugliosi, *Helter Skelter*, pp. 353–55.

62. Ibid., p. 355.

63. Ibid., pp. 304–305.

64. Linda Deutsch, "Tate Case Defenders in Accord," *The Day*, November 18, 1970, p. 18.

65. Bugliosi, *Helter Skelter*, pp. 271, 290–91, 408–10.

66. Ibid., pp. 338, 352; Steffens and Staples, *Trial of Charles Manson*, pp. 45–47.

67. Bugliosi, *Helter Skelter*, pp. 410–14.

68. Ibid., pp. 420–39.

69. Ibid., pp. 412–503.

70. Steffens and Staples, *Trial of Charles Manson*, p. 64; Bugliosi, *Helter Skelter*, p. 424.

71. Steffens and Staples, *Trial of Charles Manson*, pp. 7–82.

72. Ibid., p. 87.

73. Ibid., pp. 89–90.

74. Bugliosi, *Helter Skelter*, p. 448.

75. Ibid., p. 412.

76. Ibid., pp. 485, 521; Steffens and Staples, *Trial of Charles Manson*, pp. 84–85.

77. Bugliosi, *Helter Skelter*, pp. 473–74.

78. Ibid., pp. 404, 487.

79. Ibid., p. 474.

80. Bugliosi, *Helter Skelter*, pp. 82–84.

81. Ibid., p. 624.

82. Ibid., p. 73.

83. Ibid., p. 80.

84. Ibid., p. 262.

85. Ibid., p. 258.

86. Ibid., p. 413.

87. Ibid., p. 625.

88. Ibid., pp. 297–98.

89. Steffens and Staples, *Trial of Charles Manson*, p. 12.

90. Ann O'Neill, "Manson's Lasting Legacy: 'Live Freaky, Die Freaky,'" *CNN.com*, August 10, 2009, http://www.cnn.com/2009/CRIME/08/10/california.manson.murders/ (accessed April 8, 2016).

91. Bugliosi, *Helter Skelter*, p. 129.

92. Steffens and Staples, *Trial of Charles Manson*, p. 62.

93. Bugliosi, *Helter Skelter*, p. 585.

94. O'Neill, "Manson's Lasting Legacy."

95. Bugliosi, *Helter Skelter*, pp. 73–74.

96. Ibid., p. 540.

97. Ibid., p. 45.

98. Ibid., pp. 34–37.

99. "Actress, Heiress, Three Others Slain," *Washington Post*, August 10, 1969, p. 1.

100. Steven Roberts, "Actress is Among 5 Slain at Home in Beverly Hills," *New York Times*, August 10, 1969, p. 1.

101. Bugliosi, *Helter Skelter*, p. 46.

102. Dial Torgerson, "'Ritualistic Slayings': Sharon Tate, Four Others Murdered," *Los Angeles Times*, August 10, 1969, p. 1.

103. Bugliosi, *Helter Skelter*, p. 54.

104. Ibid., p. 92.

105. Torgerson, "'Ritualistic Slayings,'" p. 1.

106. Bugliosi, *Helter Skelter*, pp. 92–100.

107. Ibid., p. 109.

108. Ibid., p. 220.

109. Ibid., p. 215.

110. Ibid., pp. 223, 389.

111. Roberts, "Actress," p. 1.

112. Bugliosi, *Helter Skelter*, pp. 240–57.

113. Ibid., p. 352.

114. Ibid., pp. 49, 266–68.

115. Ibid., p. 258.

116. Ibid., p. 299.

117. Ibid., pp. 403, 594.

118. Ibid., p. 430.

119. Steffens and Staples, *Trial of Charles Manson*, p. 87.

120. Bugliosi, *Helter Skelter*, p. 607.

121. Steffens and Staples, *Trial of Charles Manson*, p. 91.

122. Bugliosi, *Helter Skelter*, pp. 646–48.

123. Hilary Hanson, "Charles Manson Getting Married to 25-Year-Old Named 'Star,' According to Her," *Huffington Post*, November 22, 2013, http://www.huffingtonpost.com/2013/11/21/charles-manson-married-star-25-_n_4317253.html (accessed December 29, 2013).

124. Steffens and Staples, *Trial of Charles Manson*, p. 92.

125. Elaine Woo, "Susan Atkins Dies at 61; Imprisoned Charles Manson Follower," *Los Angeles Times*, September 26, 2009, http://www.latimes.com/local/obituaries/la-me-susan-atkins26-2009sep26-story.html.

126. Robin McKie, "Charles Manson Follower Ends Her Silence 40 Years After Night of Slaughter," *The Observer*, August 1, 2009, http://www.theguardian.com/world/2009/aug/02/charles-manson-linda-kasabian-polanski.

127. Bugliosi, *Helter Skelter*, p. 604.

128. David Lohr, "Charles 'Tex' Watson: No Parole 42 Years After Manson 'Family' Killings," *Huffington Post*, November 17, 2011, http://www.huffingtonpost.com/2011/11/17/charles-tex-watson-parole-manson-killings_n_1097760.html (accessed January 3, 2014).

129. Patt Morrison, "Vincent Bugliosi: Taking on Charles Manson," *Los Angeles Times*, August 8, 2009, http://www.latimes.com/local/la-oe-morrison8-2009aug08-column.html.

130. Dana Parsons, "Barred From World He Loved, Just Getting By Is a Trial," *Los Angeles Times*, October 25, 1998, http://articles.latimes.com/1998/oct/25/local/me-36102/2.

131. Woo, "Susan Atkins Dies at 61."

132. Bugliosi, *Helter Skelter*, p. 669.

133. Morrison, "Vincent Bugliosi"; "Helter Skelter" (1976), *IMDB*, http://www.imdb.com/title/tt0074621/; "Helter Skelter" (2004), *IMDB*, http://www.imdb.com/title/tt0383393/ (accessed April 8, 2016).

134. Bugliosi, *Helter Skelter*, p. 638.

135. Steffens and Staples, *Trial of Charles Manson*, p. 94.

136. Bugliosi, *Helter Skelter*, p. 637.

137. "Merry Christmas, Charlie Manson!" *Wikipedia*, https://en.wikipedia.org/wiki/Merry_Christmas,_Charlie_Manson! (last modified August 19, 2015)

138. Sarah Netter, "Charles Manson Reign of Terror: 40 Years Later," *ABC News*, August 7, 2009, http://abcnews.go.com/Blotter/MansonMurders/charles-manson-murders-shock-40-years/story?id=8266725&singlePage=true (accessed January 9, 2014).

139. Erik Hedegaard, "Charles Manson Today: The Final Confessions of a Psychopath," *Rolling Stone*, November 21, 2013, http://www.rollingstone.com/culture/news/charles-manson-today-the-final-confessions-of-a-psychopath-20131121.

140. O'Neill, "Manson's Lasting Legacy."

CHAPTER 9. 1980–1990: JEAN HARRIS AND THE DIET DOCTOR

1. Stacey Olster, "'Two People Who Didn't Argue, Even, except over the Use of the Subjunctive': Jean Harris, the Scarsdale Diet Doctor Murder, and Diana Trilling," *Critical Inquiry* 25 (1998): 77–94.

2. Jean Harris, *Stranger in Two Worlds* (New York: Zebra Books, 1986), p. 71.

3. Anthony Haden-Guest, "The Headmistress and the Diet Doctor," *New York Magazine*, March 31, 1980, http://nymag.com/news/features/50454/.

4. Ibid.

5. Harris, *Stranger in Two Worlds*, p. 78.

6. Haden-Guest, "Headmistress and the Diet Doctor."

7. Harris, *Stranger in Two Worlds*, pp. 79–81.

8. Shana Alexander, *Very Much a Lady: The Untold Story of Jean Harris and Dr. Herman Tarnower* (Boston: Little, Brown, 1983), p. 121.

9. Ibid., p. 106.

10. Ibid., pp. 106–107.

11. Ibid., pp. 113–14.

12. Ibid., p. 181.

13. Ibid., pp. 112–16.

14. Ibid., pp. 114–15.

15. Ibid., p. 170.

16. Ibid.

17. Ibid., p. 156.

18. Ibid., p. 161.

19. Harris, *Stranger in Two Worlds*, p. 183.

20. Ibid., pp. 192–93.

21. Alexander, *Very Much a Lady*, pp. 190–200.

22. Ibid., p. 200.

23. Diana Trilling, *Mrs. Harris: The Death of the Scarsdale Diet Doctor* (New York: Harcourt Brace Jovanovich, 1981), pp. 73–74.

24. Trilling, *Mrs. Harris*, pp. 74–75.

25. Alexander, *Very Much a Lady*, pp. 208–14.

26. Ibid., pp. 214, 233.

27. Ibid., pp. 216–22; "Harris Told Police She'd 'Been Through Hell' Over Tarnower," *Washington Post*, March 29, 1980, p. A9.

28. Alexander, *Very Much a Lady*, p. 222.

29. James Feron, "Scarsdale Diet Doctor Slain; Headmistress Charged," *Special to New York Times*, March 12, 1980, p. A1.

30. "Scarsdale Diet Author Slain; Headmistress Held," *Los Angeles Times*, March 11, 1980, p. A1.

31. Lee Lescaze and Blaine Harden, "Madeira School Headmistress Held," *Washington Post*, March 12, 1980, p. A1.

32. Alexander, *Very Much a Lady*, pp. 214–31.

33. Trilling, *Mrs. Harris*, p. 54.

34. Blaine Harden and Lee Lescaze, "Romance Cited in Diet Author's Death," *Washington Post*, March 13, 1980, p. A1.

35. "Harris Told Police," p. A9.

36. Carol Oppenheim, "'Scarsdale' Trial: Passion and Mystery," *Chicago Tribune*, November 2, 1980, p. B14.

37. James Feron, "Officer in Tarnower Case Tells of Arrival on Scene," *Special to New York Times*, March 15, 1980, p. 21.

38. Alexander, *Very Much a Lady*, p. 222.

39. Trilling, *Mrs. Harris*, p. 4; Alexander, *Very Much a Lady*, author's note.

40. Alexander, *Very Much a Lady*, p. 229.

41. Trilling, *Mrs. Harris*, p. 15.

42. Walter Isaacson, "Jean Harris: Murder with Intent to Love," *Time*, March 9, 1981, http://content.time.com/time/magazine/article/0,9171,921003,00.html.

43. "Nation: Death of the Diet Doctor," *Time*, March 24, 1980, http://content.time.com/time/magazine/article/0,9171,921862,00.html.

44. Oppenheim, "'Scarsdale' Trial," p. B14.

45. Alexander, *Very Much a Lady*, p. 234.

46. Trilling, *Mrs. Harris*, pp. 53–54.

47. Ibid., pp. 72–77.

48. Alexander, *Very Much a Lady*, p. 238.

49. Ibid., pp. 219–27.

50. Ibid., pp. 101, 191.

51. Ibid., pp. 171–72.

52. Ibid., p. 188.

53. Trilling, *Mrs. Harris*, pp. 79–81.

54. Ibid., pp. 84–89.

55. Ibid., pp. 120–28.

56. Ibid., p. 129.

57. Ibid., pp. 130–33.

58. Alexander, *Very Much a Lady*, p. 246.

59. Trilling, *Mrs. Harris*, pp. 154–56.

60. Alexander, *Very Much a Lady*, p. 250.

61. Ibid., pp. 250–53.

62. Trilling, *Mrs. Harris*, pp. 208–22.

63. Ibid., pp. 222–26.

64. Ibid., pp. 226–32.

65. Alexander, *Very Much a Lady*, pp. 261–64.

66. Trilling, *Mrs. Harris*, pp. 256–61.

67. Alexander, *Very Much a Lady*, p. 265.

68. Ibid., pp. 266–70.

69. Ibid., pp. 267–70.

70. Isaacson, "Jean Harris."

71. Alexander, *Very Much a Lady*, p. 270.

72. Trilling, *Mrs. Harris*, p. 70.

73. Ibid., p. 106.

74. Alexander, *Very Much a Lady*, p. 237.

75. Trilling, *Mrs. Harris*, p. 141.

76. Lesley Dormen, "No Longer a Cautionary Tale," *New York Times*, January 4, 2013, http://www.nytimes.com/2013/01/06/fashion/jean-harriss-cautionary-tale.html?_r=0.

77. Ann Jones, "Why Are We So Fascinated by the Harris Case?" *New York Times*, November 8, 1981, http://www.nytimes.com/1981/11/08/nyregion/why-are-we-so-fascinated-by-the-harris-case.html?pagewanted=all.

78. Trilling, *Mrs. Harris*, p. 119.

79. Ibid., p. 251.

80. Dormen, "No Longer a Cautionary Tale."

81. "Jean Harris Files Appeal," *New York Times*, November 28, 1991, http://www.nytimes.com/1991/11/28/nyregion/jean-harris-files-appeal.html.

82. "Jean Harris," *Bio.com*, 2013, http://www.thebiographychannel.co.uk/biographies/jean-harris.html (accessed August 5, 2013); Michael Melia, "Jean Harris Dead: 'Scarsdale Diet' Doctor Killer Dies at 89," *Huffington Post*, December 28, 2012.

83. "Jean Harris," *Bio.com*.

84. "The Summer of George," *Wikipedia*, March 16, 2013, https://en.wikipedia.org/wiki/The_Summer_of_George (accessed August 5, 2013).

CHAPTER 10. 1990–2000: O. J. SIMPSON AND THE BLOODY GLOVE

1. For facts about Simpson's past in this and subsequent paragraphs see "A timeline of O. J. Simpson's Life," *CNN.com*, http://www.cnn.com/US/OJ/suspect/bio/ (accessed April 4, 2016).

2. Darnell M. Hunt, *O. J. Simpson Facts and Fictions* (Cambridge: University Press, 1999), p. 52.

3. "Nicole Brown Simpson," *Bio.com*, http://www.biography.com/people/nicole-brown-simpson-21254807 (accessed April 4, 2016).

4. Shelley Levitt, "Facing the Rage," *People*, February 20, 1995, http://www.people.com/people/archive/article/0,,20105126,00.html.

5. Hunt, *O. J. Simpson*, pp. 61–66.

6. Alan M. Dershowitz, *Reasonable Doubts* (New York: Simon & Schuster, 1996), p. 104.

7. Vincent Bugliosi, *Outrage* (New York: Norton, 1996), p. 18.

8. "A timeline of O. J. Simpson's Life," *CNN.com*.

9. Bugliosi, *Outrage*, p. 20.

10. Ibid., p. 169.

11. Clifford L. Linedecker, *OJ A to Z* (New York: St. Martin's Griffin, 1995), p.19.

12. Ibid., p. 63.

13. Dershowitz, *Reasonable Doubts*, p. 81.

14. For this and subsequent paragraphs see Phillip Vannatter, Grand Jury Testimony, June 23, 1994.

15. Mark Fuhrman, Preliminary Hearing Testimony, July 5–6, 1994.

16. Simpson police interview, June 13, 1994, reprinted in Bugliosi, *Outrage*, pp. 291–305.

17. Hunt, *O. J. Simpson*, p. 17; Dershowitz, *Reasonable Doubts*, p. 23.

18. Bugliosi, *Outrage*, p. 98.

19. The entire letter is reprinted in Bugliosi, *Outrage*, pp. 307–308.

20. Hunt, *O. J. Simpson*, pp. 136–39.

21. Ibid., p. 133.

22. Ibid., p. 17.

23. Dershowitz, *Reasonable Doubts*, p. 22.

24. Ibid., p. 140.

25. B. Drummond Aryes Jr. "Absolutely Not Guilty, a Confident Simpson Says," *New York Times*, July 23, 1994, http://www.nytimes.com/1994/07/23/us/absolutely-not-guilty-a-confident-simpson-says.html.

26. Bugliosi, *Outrage*, p. 64.

27. "The O. J. Simpson Trial: The Jury," http://law2.umkc.edu/faculty/projects/ftrials/Simpson/Jurypage.html (accessed April 4, 2016).

28. Bugliosi, *Outrage*, p. 37; Eric Malnic, "The Simpson Verdicts," *Los Angeles Times*, October 4, 1995, http://articles.latimes.com/1995-10-04/news/mn-53182_1_f-lee-bailey.

29. Bugliosi, *Outrage*, pp. 37–40; David Margolick, "O. J. Simpson's 'Dream Team' of Lawyers," *New York Times*, February 5, 1995, http://www.nytimes.com/1995/02/05/us/o-j-simpson-s-dream-team-of-lawyers-are-they-running-out-of-gas.html; Joel Achenbach, "O. J. Simpson's Defensive Linemen," *Washington Post*, January 21, 1995, p. D01.

30. Bugliosi, *Outrage*, p. 116.

31. Hunt, *O. J. Simpson*, p. 87.

32. Ibid., pp. 17–18; Dershowitz, *Reasonable Doubts*, p. 141.

33. Bugliosi, *Outrage*, pp. 79–82.

34. Dershowitz, *Reasonable Doubts*, p. 100; Roger M. Grace, "Trying the O. J. Simpson Case in Terrain Hostile to Prosecution," *Metropolitan News-Enterprise*, May 3, 2010, p. 7; Joel Achenbach, "Jury Selection Could be Key for Simpson," *Washington Post*, September 26, 1994.

35. Andrea Ford and Jim Newton, "Victim's Sister Ends Emotional Testimony," *Los Angeles Times*, February 7, 1995, http://articles.latimes.com/1995-02-07/news/mn-29092_1_nicole-simpson.

36. For the testimony of Park and Williams see "The O. J. Simpson Trial," http://law2.umkc.edu/faculty/projects/ftrials/Simpson/transcript.html (accessed April 4, 2016).

37. For the testimony of Kaelin see "The O. J. Simpson Trial," http://law2.umkc.edu/faculty/projects/ftrials/Simpson/Kaelintest.html (accessed April 4, 2016); "Kato Kaelin, Simpson Houseguest, Now Treated as Hostile Witness," *Chicago Tribune*, March 27, 1995, http://articles.chicagotribune.com/1995-03-27/news/9503280021_1_kato-kaelin-hostile-witness-simpson-houseguest.

38. polymerase chain reaction.

39. restrictive fragment length polymorphism.

40. Bugliosi, *Outrage*, pp. 111–12.

41. Ibid., pp. 114–15.

42. Dershowitz, *Reasonable Doubts*, p. 197.

43. Bugliosi, *Outrage*, pp. 138–39, 200–201.

44. Matthew Kaufman, "Lee: 'Something's Wrong' in Simpson Trial Evidence," *Hartford Courant*, August 26, 1995.

45. Bugliosi, *Outrage*, p. 125; Dershowitz, *Reasonable Doubts*, pp. 74–75.

46. Dershowitz, *Reasonable Doubts*, pp. 75–77.

47. Interview by Laura Hart McKinney, tape no. 4, p. 9, McKinney transcript no. 4, p. 12.

48. Stephanie Simon, Henry Weinstein, Andrea Ford, "Fuhrman Invokes 5th Amendment, Refuses to Testify," *Los Angeles Times*, September 7, 1995, http://articles.latimes.com/1995-09-07/news/mn-43219_1 _detective-mark-fuhrman.

49. Bugliosi, *Outrage*, pp. 133, 154–61.

50. Dershowitz, *Reasonable Doubts*, p. 98; Michelle Caruso, "A Flood of Fury Fills the Court," *New York Daily News*, September 29, 1995 (reference to Hitler); "If it Doesn't Fit, You Must Acquit," *CNN.com*, http://edition.cnn.com/US/OJ/daily/9-27/8pm/ ("Doesn't Fit," Nation of Islam, and Rosa Parks) (accessed April 4, 2016).

51. Hunt, *O. J. Simpson*, p. 41.

52. Bugliosi, *Outrage*, p. 273.

53. Ibid., p. 147.

54. Ibid., p. 91.

55. Ibid., p. 24.

56. Joseph Wambaugh, "Perspective on the Simpson Case," *Los Angeles Times*, August 24, 1995, http://articles.latimes.com/1995-08-24/local/me-38324_1_black-racism.

57. Malnic, "Simpson Verdicts."

58. "I Won't Work to Pay the Goldmans," *CNN.com*, http://www.cnn.com/US/9707/11/simpson/ (accessed April 4, 2016).

59. Mike Downey, "Some Certain Signs of a Sick Society," *Los Angeles Times*, February 19, 1999, http://articles.latimes.com/1999/feb/19/news/mn-9642.

60. "Simpson to Serve at Least Nine Years in Prison," *CNN.com*, December 5, 2008, http://www.cnn.com/2008/CRIME/12/05/oj.simpson.sentencing/index.html?eref=rss_us (accessed April 4, 2016).

61. Garcetti v. Ceballos, 547 U.S. 410 (2006).

62. William Nottingham, "Eric Garcetti is Sworn in as 42nd Mayor of Los Angeles," *Los Angeles Times*, June 30, 2013, http://articles.latimes.com/2013/jun/30/local/la-me-la-eric-garcetti-is-sworn-in-20130630.

63. "Jackie Chiles," *IMDB*, http://www.imdb.com/character/ch0010 183/?ref_=fn_al_ch_1 (accessed April 4, 2016).

64. Associated Press, "Famous Clients Mourn Johnnie Cochran," *USA Today*, April 6, 2005.

65. "F. Lee Bailey Loses His Quest to Practice Law," *ABA Journal*, December 1, 2014, http://www.abajournal.com/magazine/article/f_lee _bailey_loses_his_quest_to_practice_law_again_after_past_misdeeds.

66. "Phil Spector, Attorney Robert Shapiro Settle Dispute," *LATimes .com*, March 4, 2011, http://latimesblogs.latimes.com/lanow/2011/03/ phil-spector-and-attorney-robert-shapiro-settle-dispute.html (accessed April 4, 2016).

67. "Robert Kardashian, a Lawyer for O. J. Simpson, Dies at 59," *New York Times*, October 3, 2003, http://www.nytimes.com/2003/10/03/us/ robert-kardashian-a-lawyer-for-o-j-simpson-dies-at-59.html.

68. V. Dion Haynes, "Fuhrman Bargains Out of Jail Time," *Chicago Tribune*, October 3, 1996, http://articles.chicagotribune.com/1996-10-03/ news/9610030184_1_detective-mark-fuhrman-mr-fuhrman-simpson-civil-trial.

69. Dershowitz, *Reasonable Doubts*, p. 98.

70. Ibid., p. 206.

EPILOGUE: CASEY ANTHONY AND THE TRIALS FOR A NEW CENTURY

1. Christopher Beam, "800,000 Missing Kids? Really? Making sense of child abduction statistics," http://www.slate.com/articles/news_and _politics/explainer/2007/01/800000_missing_kids_really.html (accessed April 8, 2016); "800,000 Children are Reported Missing Each Year," YouTube video, 0:52, from a recording of News Channel, KRON-4 on April 8, 2009, posted by "peinay," April 8, 2009, https://www.youtube.com/ watch?v=hlDj0mFtIQg.

2. Jose Baez and Peter Golenbock, *Presumed Guilty, Casey Anthony: The Inside Story* (Dallas: BenBella Books, 2012), p. 4.

3. John Cloud, "How the Casey Anthony Murder Case Became the Social-Media Trial of the Century," *Time*, June 16, 2011, http://content .time.com/time/nation/article/0,8599,2077969-1,00.html.

4. Keith Ablow, *Inside the Mind of Casey Anthony: A Psychological Portrait* (New York: St. Martin's, 2011), p. 122.

5. Cloud, "Casey Anthony Murder Case."

6. Baez and Golenbock, *Presumed Guilty*, p. 52.

7. Ibid., p. 13; Jeff Ashton and Lisa Pulitzer, *Imperfect Justice; Prosecuting Casey Anthony* (New York: William Morrow, 2011), pp. 35–36.

8. Baez and Golenbock, *Presumed Guilty*, p. 16.

9. Ibid., p. 17; Ashton and Pulitzer, *Imperfect Justice*, p. 41.

10. Baez and Golenbock, *Presumed Guilty*, p. 35.

11. Ibid., p. 55.

12. Ashton and Pulitzer, *Imperfect Justice*, pp. 146–49; Lee Ferran, "Exclusive: Meter Reader Roy Kronk Denies Tip to Caylee's Body," January 13, 2009, *ABC News*, abcnews.go.com/GMA/story?id=6635354&page=1 (accessed April 9, 2016).

13. Ashton and Pulitzer, *Imperfect Justice*, p. 280; Baez and Golenbock, *Presumed Guilty*, pp. 197, 222, 351 (for heart-shaped sticker); Ashley Hayes, "Prosecution to Rest Wednesday in Casey Anthony Trial," June 14, 2011, *CNN.com*, www.cnn.com/2011/crime/06/14/florida.casey.anthony.trial/index.html (for Winnie-the-Pooh blanket) (accessed April 9, 2016).

14. Ashton and Pulitzer, *Imperfect Justice*, pp. 188–89.

15. Ibid., p. 192.

16. Brian Stelter, "Casey Anthony Coverage Gives HLN an Identity," *New York Times*, June 12, 2011, http://www.nytimes.com/2011/06/13/business/media/13hln.html?_r=0; Brian Stelter and Jenna Wortham, "Watching a Trial on TV, Discussing it on Twitter," *New York Times*, July 5, 2011, http://www.nytimes.com/2011/07/06/business/media/06coverage.html?_r=0.

17. Baez and Golenbock, *Presumed Guilty*, p. 304.

18. Anthony Colarossi, "Casey Anthony Trial: A Day of Bombshells," *Orlando Sentinel*, May 24, 2011, http://articles.orlandosentinel.com/2011-05-24/news/os-casey-anthony-trial-opening-20110523_1_defense-attorney-jose-baez-casey-anthony-duct-tape.

19. Associated Press, "Prosecutors Focus on Duct Tape in Anthony Trial," *USA Today*, June 10, 2011, http://usatoday30.usatoday.com/news/nation/2011-06-10-casey-anthony-murder-trial_n.htm.

20. Ashton and Pulitzer, *Imperfect Justice*, p. 277.

21. Stelter and Wortham, "Watching a Trial on TV."

22. Ibid.

23. Baez and Golenbock, *Presumed Guilty*, p. 409.

24. Ibid., p. 414.

25. Ibid., pp. 414–19.

26. Doug Gross, "Survey: More Americans Get News From Internet Than Newspapers or Radio," *CNN.com*, March 1, 2010, http://www.cnn .com/2010/TECH/03/01/social.network.news/ (accessed April 9, 2016).

27. Stelter and Wortham, "Watching a Trial on TV."

28. "The Online Reaction to the Casey Anthony Verdict [STATS]," *Mashable*, July 6, 2011, http://mashable.com/2011/07/06/casey-anthony -sentiment/ (accessed April 9, 2016).

29. Cloud, "Casey Anthony Murder Case."

30. "Online Reaction," *Mashable*.

31. "Kim Kardashian's Response to Casey Anthony Verdict," *Huffington Post*, July 5, 2011, www.huffingtonpost.com/2011/07/05/kim-kardashian -casey-anthony-verdict_n_890616.html (accessed April 9, 2016).

32. Cloud, "Casey Anthony Murder Case."

33. Stelter and Wortham, "Watching a Trial on TV."

34. "State of the News Media 2015," *Pew Research Center*, April 29, 2015, http://www.journalism.org/2015/04/29/state-of-the-news-media-2015/ (accessed April 9, 2016).

INDEX

327